Y0-BWG-393

The Battle
for
Bastogne

GUY FRANZ AREND

THE BATTLE FOR BASTOGNE

"IF YOU DON'T KNOW WHAT NUTS MEANS"

A Chronology of the Battle for Bastogne
with Comments

Acknowledgements

For the part that they played either in the setting up of Bastogne Historical Center or in the writing of this book, I wish to extend special thanks to the following:

General and Mrs. Omar N. Bradley for their trust, their moral support and their help in obtaining the European première of the film *Patton* for the benefit of the Nuts Museum, and especially for the invaluable personal archives given to me by the General which contains all the material written about him, as well as his own works.

General and Mrs. Anthony McAuliffe for their constant affection and moral support. In particular, I wish to thank the General for his help in creating the scenario for the audio-visual program on the Battle of Bastogne which is shown in the Historical Center.

General of Armoured Troops, Baron Hasso Eccard von Manteuffel, for his friendship, his valuable and most constructive help in the organisation of the museum, and for his collaboration on the film scenario and the audio-visual program, as well as for his advice and corrections in the first edition of this book.

The American Ambassador, Mr. Firestone, for having obtained my access to the American National Archives and for having helped in the obtaining of many documents.

The Third American Army Historical Service, for their interest at the opening of the Nuts Museum and for the secret documents that they entrusted to me.

Lieutenant General Harry W.O. Kinnard, Lieutenant General Julian J. Ewell and Major General Joseph Harper for their friendship, their opinions on the book and on the details of the battle.

Monsignor Francis L. Sampson, Major General, padre to the 101st Airborne Division in 1944, for his affection and for his permission to make use of certain material from his book *Look Out Below.*

And finally all the veteran officers and soldiers from the different divisions who took part in the Battle of the Bulge for having honoured me as a life-member of their divisions and veterans' associations, and for their contribution to the enrichment of the collections of the Bastogne Historical Center, and for their help in its documentation.

His Majesty King Baudouin and author.

All the photographic material used in this book was taken during the Battle of the Ardennes. It comes from a very wide variety of sources: news and propaganda films, photographs taken either by war correspondents, combatants, civilians or others.

The varied origins, the limited techniques of the period, the nature of the subject material and the circumstances in which the photographs were taken, means that their quality is often inferior to the usual illustrations found in books.

We have not chosen to enhance the aesthetic quality of this book by eliminating photographs of bad quality, but have instead preferred to illustrate the text as faithfully as possible and to present further important evidence to illustrate this terrible battle.

It should be added that the photographs chosen to illustrate specific texts do not always correspond exactly to the place nor to the time in the battle which they represent.

- Translated by Tim Hayward and Lise Arend.
- American edition revised by Virginia Rohde Anderson.

His Royal Highness Albert de Liège (now King Albert II) with author. Inauguration of the Bastogne Historical Center on May 31, 1976.

Guy Franz Arend 1944

The photos taken during the Battle and all the documents illustrated in this book are part of the Guy Franz Arend Collection.

Guy Franz Arend is

- Honorary Life Member of the 101st Airborne Division
- Honorary Life Member of the following Veterans' Associations:

  United States Army

  101st Airborne Division
  82nd Airborne Division
  17th Airborne Division
  4th Armored Division
  704th Tank Destroyer Battalion
  6th Armored Division
  7th Armored Division
  9th Armored Division
  27th Armored Infantry Battalion
  10th Armored Division
  28th Infantry Division
  30th Infantry Division
  78th Infantry Division
  80th Infantry Division
  99th Infantry Division
- Freeman of the town of Carentan, Channel Province, France.
- Founder of the "NUTS" Museum in 1950. (closed)
- Founder of the Ardenne Offensive Museum in Spa in 1956 (closed).
- Founder of the Carentan War Museum in 1969 (closed).
- Founder of the Bastogne Historical Center in 1976.
- Founder of the Victory Memorial Museum in 1990.

Lieutenant-General Harry W.O. Kinnard.

FOREWORD

by Lt. General Harry W.O. Kinnard

This is an unusual book by an unusual man. Guy Arend did not **fight** on either side, but nevertheless had a first hand view of the fighting when, as a young student in Bastogne, he was an involuntary witness to the epic battle. Slowly at first, then with gathering strength the idea of memorializing the battle took hold of Guy and ever since has been a dominant theme in his life.

As a young man, soon after the battle, he proposed setting aside the entire (then largely ruined) town of Bastogne as a memorial to the fight. When that idea was indignantly rejected by the people of Bastogne, he began to gather the disabled tanks, trucks, guns, etc., which still littered the battlefield and began to dream of a museum to commemorate the battle. Many hard years later, his visions had become reality. He had planned, built and was running a splendid museum next to the Bastogne Memorial. In addition to the highly authentic military equipage in that museum, he had collected, catalogued and totally repaired a veritable arsenal of military vehicles and other equipment which today is one of the most complete private collections in the world.*

While creating the museum and gathering his world famous collection of military equipment, Guy had acquired a deep understanding of how and why the Battle of Bastogne took place. He quite naturally decided to write a book on the battle.

The resulting book reflects the author and his background. His great depth of detailed knowledge is apparent, as are his passion for authenticity and attention to detail.

Also typical of Guy, he chose not to use the normal sequential style of describing the battle; instead he chose the more difficult, but more realistic, format of simultaneous treatment of the unfolding fight. Bearing in mind that "a picture is worth ten thousand words", Guy drew on his extraordinary collection of photographs taken by both sides during the battle to provide a visceral feeling for the great battle.

Guy's passion for authenticity and attention to detail led him to seek out and interview many who fought at Bastogne on both sides. Thus he writes from an understanding not only of what happened but the reason the battle developed as it did. Further, by knowing the battle from both sides, his account is more objective and more complete.

The French version of this book is probably better than the English simply because French is Guy's native tongue. The syntax is definitely French, but the resulting English (in the translation I read) is more charming than objectionable.

All in all, Guy has done a fine job of documenting the historic fight at Bastogne in probably the most balanced and complete account yet written.

* Now presented in the Victory Memorial Museum.

Lieutenant-General Julian J. Ewell.

PREFACE

by Lt. General Julian J. Ewell

14 March 1986

Dear Guy —

Congratulations on your new book - Bastogne. It brings back vividly many memories of the bitter fighting during the battles around Bastogne.

I trust that stark example will help convince the coming generations that the readiness and willingness to defend our hard earned freedoms is the best road to peace in the days to come.

With warm regards

Julian J Ewell

Lt. Gen., U.S. Army, Retired

Brigadier-General Anthony C. McAuliffe
during the battle for Bastogne.

PREFACE
by General Anthony C. McAuliffe

I first met Mr. Guy Arend in June 1950.

This young man had been born in Bastogne.

It was also in June 1950 that I returned to the town and assisted in the inauguration of the American Memorial and the brand new "Nuts Museum".

Without any help, Guy Arend has organized this museum, which keeps alive the memories of the Battle of the Bulge. From the beginning Guy had one idea: realize a unique museum on the Mardasson site near the Memorial. After years of effort, I am very happy to know that he has succeeded.

1974 is the 30th anniversary of the Battle and the year of the opening of the brand new Bastogne Historical Center.

I never tire of reading about the Battle of the Bulge. Guy has presented an excellent chronology of the events of the Battle. I particularly enjoyed the quality and the quantity of photographs in the book.

Thirty years ago, surrounded by German divisions, we celebrated a sad Christmas. It was an occasion we shall always remember. Our finest present arrived when the 4th Armored Division from General Patton's Third Army broke through the encirclement and joined us.

30th April 1974

Anthony C. McAuliffe
General U.S. Army (Ret.)

Text that the General wrote as an introduction to the first English edition.
(The General died in 1975).

HASSO VON MANTEUFFEL

May 1st 1978.

My dear friend Guy,

m a n y ,m a n y thanks for your book "Bastogne"DasLoch Im Krapfen"- and for your friendly dedication!A very good report numerous and excellent photos -

Thankyou once more- and my very best wishes

affectionatelyin friendship

Yours

PREFACE
by General Hasso Eccard von Manteuffel

Hitler's view of the war on the Western Front of the Reich in the autumn of 1944 was that he could repeat the success that the Wehrmacht had achieved in May 1940 – namely, breaking through the enemy lines which had, up till then, limited military action in the West. This break-through was to be followed by a fast surprise push to the desired objectives. If this did not succeed in the Ardennes' offensive, which started on 16th December 1944, it is the result of entirely different initial circumstances – from the political, strategic and economic point of view – as well as the state of the army whose effective fighting material was exhausted. Among other things the enemy had undisputed superiority in the air which, despite its initial successes, did not allow an expansion of the German offensive. That the Fifth Panzer Army broke through was achieved thanks to the dedication of the soldiers of all ranks and all functions, who gave themselves body and soul with, for the most part, exemplary devotion. If later on in the course of things, especially after the beginning of the enemy offensive from 3rd January 1945, the strength and, in part, the morale declined, I attribute this to the fact that on the German side the expectations held out by Göbbel's propaganda machine were too great. For this reason, I was not surprised by the breakdown in the physical and mental state of men.

We owe to the German soldiers all our thanks for their devotion to the freedom of our people. The value of their sacrifices can be measured only by the spirit which motivated them and not in terms of success or failure.

Hasso Eccard von Manteuffel
General of Armored Troops
General Commanding the Fifth Panzer Army

Diessen / A June 1977

Translation from the text written by the General as an introduction for the German edition.
The General died in 1978.

General Dwight D. Eisenhower,
Supreme Commander of the Allied Expeditionary Forces.

INTRODUCTION

THE MONTHS BEFORE THE ARDENNES OFFENSIVE*

Before looking at the Battle of Bastogne itself, it is necessary to consider the military events of the second half of 1944, just before the Ardennes offensive, of which the Battle is a part.

On the Allied side, things were not going very well.

The misunderstandings between the British and Americans were increasing, and both the Air Force and the Army were showing signs of discouragement and lassitude. Some pilots were deserting and landing in Switzerland or Sweden; the foot-soldiers were worn out, while more and more of the injuries were from self-inflicted wounds. In addition, many cases of combat fatigue were being reported.

Up to the beginning of November, the Americans, unlike the British, had been able to replace their losses in the ranks with fresh troops, but subsequently this had become impossible, with the result that the morale fell as the ranks thinned.

The equipment left much to be desired, and the decision of General Bradley on the 19th October, not to authorize the supply of winter clothes, in order to keep all transport available for carrying fuel, ammunition and food, did not improve matters. A larger and larger gap was appearing between the fighting men and the staff officers behind the lines, who were getting maximum benefits from the comfortable life, while those on the front slithered around in the mud or huddled together, soaked to the skin and suffering from the daily increasing cold, in trucks that nobody even thought to cover, despite the pouring rain.

The weather was indeed awful, which furthermore hindered the transport of supplies, resulting in shortages. These had halted Patton's victorious break-through and had enabled the Germans to recover for the first time since the invasion.

And Hitler had not been idle.

* Also known as the Battle of the Bulge or the Battle of the Ardennes or von Rundstedt's Offensive.

Barely recovered from his injuries and the shock of the July assassination attempt, he had devised a plan for a new offensive, spending September with his military and industrial advisers studying the means of gathering sufficient forces to launch a major offensive.

He had not forgotten his triumphal break-through in the Ardennes in 1940, and it was there that he planned to strike again, throwing in his armour to destroy the Allied forces in the West.

Obliged to stay in bed ten days at the end of September because of jaundice, he spent the time poring over maps and putting together the final details of his plan. He had found the weak point in the Allied lines, the front held by the Americans in the Ardennes which consisted of three very thinly stretched divisions. Two of these, the 99th and the 106th Infantry Divisions, had no battle experience, and the third, the 28th Infantry Division, an excellent fighting unit, had been totally exhausted by the recent fighting in the Hurtgen Forest. It was licking its wounds and waiting for replacements to fill the large gaps in its ranks.

These three divisions were part of the VIIIth Corps of Major-General Troy H. Middleton, and the area they held was known to be particularly quiet. The G.I.s called it "The Kindergarten" and "Old Folks' Home". The green divisions, those which had never seen action, were trained there, and the veterans used it as a rest area. In fact, this part of the front was held by only a third of full troop strength...

The force which Hitler intended to throw against the Americans in total surprise was supposed to thrust them aside without difficulty. No means were spared: two armoured Armies, the 6th SS Panzer and the 5th Panzer, would make the victorious break-through, protected in the south by the 7th Army.

These Armies were to have the necessary materials, and resupply was to be assured. But above all, strict security measures were to be taken to maintain secrecy which was the major condition for success.

Then, having pushed aside the three American divisions, the German forces would push on across Belgium to Antwerp, splitting the British and American forces. Cut off from supplies, the British would be decimated and the Americans forced to negotiate.

Of course, this plan presupposed certain basic conditions for its success – the total air-supremacy of the Allies could no longer be defeated, and only the weather conditions could resolve this key problem. What was needed was a long period of bad weather which would force the Allied aircraft to remain on the ground. It was also necessary that the Red Army should not

BASTOGNE

STEAK
AMERICANA???

advance, while the German forces were occupied with the destruction of the Allies in the West.

Was Hitler just lucky or a genius? It so happened that both conditions were fulfilled: for a whole week the sky remained totally overcast, and the Russians did not move at all.

But even more extraordinary, the Allies were totally surprised. Not that they had not been informed as to Hitler's plans, on the contrary, they simply failed to take any notice.

From November onwards numerous intercepted messages revealed information as to what was being prepared. One example among many occurred on 9th December, when Colonel Dikson, the G-2, intelligence officer, of the 1st Army, informed his commanding officer, General Hodges, that the 6th SS Panzer Army had taken up position opposite the 1st Army.

The SHAEF generals ignored this information, probably more interested in shopping for Christmas presents for their families back home and enjoying the good life offered by the excellent hotels, restaurants and clubs of Paris, Brussels and Luxembourg.

No precautionary measures were taken – and it is necessary to reject later attempts at justification, based on assertions of calculated risks or deliberate strategy. This can be proved by a number of facts: for instance, on the American side, Eisenhower had bet five pounds with Montgomery that the war would be over by Christmas; and the day before the German attack, on 15th December 1944, a few hours before the first German grenadiers took a front line village, an American general, Leroy Lutes, was walking round there. Brigadier-General Edward Timberlake's 49th AAA Brigade left the Hotel du Moulin in Ligneuville few minutes before the arrival of one of Jocken Peiper's panzer groups !

But the English did even better!

Field-Marshal Montgomery wrote to Eisenhower on 15th December to inform him that unless otherwise instructed, he intended to leave for England on 23rd December to spend Christmas with his son. On the day before the attack, he signed a report from the 21st Army Group which read "The enemy is at present fighting a defensive campaign on all fronts; his situation is such that he cannot stage major offensive operations. Furthermore, he has to prevent the war from entering on a mobile phase at all costs; he has not the transport or the petrol that would be necessary for mobile operations. The enemy is in a bad way".

We shall see that the enemy had by no means run out of steam.

GENERAL VON MANTEUFFEL'S PLAN OF ATTACK

Hasso von Manteuffel, General of Armoured Troops, first bravely and openly criticized the plans drawn up by Hitler and then, backed by his superior, Generalfeldmarchall Walter Model, presented an alternative plan which was much less ambitious in its objectives. But he was finally obliged to go along with Hitler's ideas.

How did he foresee the attack of the troops under his command?

How did he prepare it?

He was given less than eight weeks to assemble several divisions with all the necessary material in the forests near Prüm, a remarkable feat when we take into account the draconian restrictions imposed on him:

- Total radio silence, communications were to be carried by messengers
- Strict control over noise so as not to warn the enemy
- Movement only allowed at night and without lights
- No wood to be burnt, with food only being cooked during the day on coal fires
- Soldiers could neither leave the forest nor were any visits allowed
- The plans of the attack were only to be communicated to the lower ranks at the last minute.

Even the General himself took a number of precautions. He went about dressed in the uniform of a colonel, trying to gain maximum information on the habits of the Americans and on their patrols, and trying to find the junctions between the different regiments and battalions which opposed him. He considered these to be the enemy's weak points.

The tactics he had chosen for the attack were as follows:

No "softening up" by the artillery an hour and a half before the attack as planned, because, as the General said, "I don't want to disturb the Americans' sleep".

Attack the junction points of the American units with shock troops – no attack in line.

Destruction of the American telephone lines by an intense artillery barrage which should begin at the same time as the attack.

Maximum infiltration of the area by troops prior to the attack,.

After the shock troops had penetrated two or three miles, the American front line units should be encircled and either made prisoner or eliminated. Then the attack could develop.

BASTOGNE

The attack against Bastogne was led by the 5th Armoured Army commanded by General von Manteuffel.

It is worth noting that the General considered the taking of St Vith on the first day of the attack as vital whereas Bastogne was not very important.

The German High Command thought that the two armoured divisions, the 2nd Panzer and the Panzer Lehr, could quickly get beyond Bastogne before any resistance could be organized. The 2nd Panzer was to race towards the "Barrière Hinck" cross-roads near Sprimont, going round the north of the town, while the Panzer Lehr was to take the town with an attack from the south.

This initial plan was in fact only changed in one detail.

On 12th December, General Baron Heinrich von Lüttwitz, commander of the XXXXVIIth Armoured Corps, addressing his divisional commanders and especially Generalleutnant Fritz Hermann Bayerlin, commander of the Panzer Lehr, said:

"Bastogne must be taken. If not, it will remain an abscess in our lines of communication. We must clear out the Bastogne area and then advance."

The detail which was changed was that, in case there was some unexpected resistance from the town, it would be taken by the 26th Volksgrenadier Division of Generalmajor Heintz Kokott.

So it would seem that before the offensive, the fall of Bastogne was taken for granted.

We shall see what happened.

* Manteuffel Ethint 46.

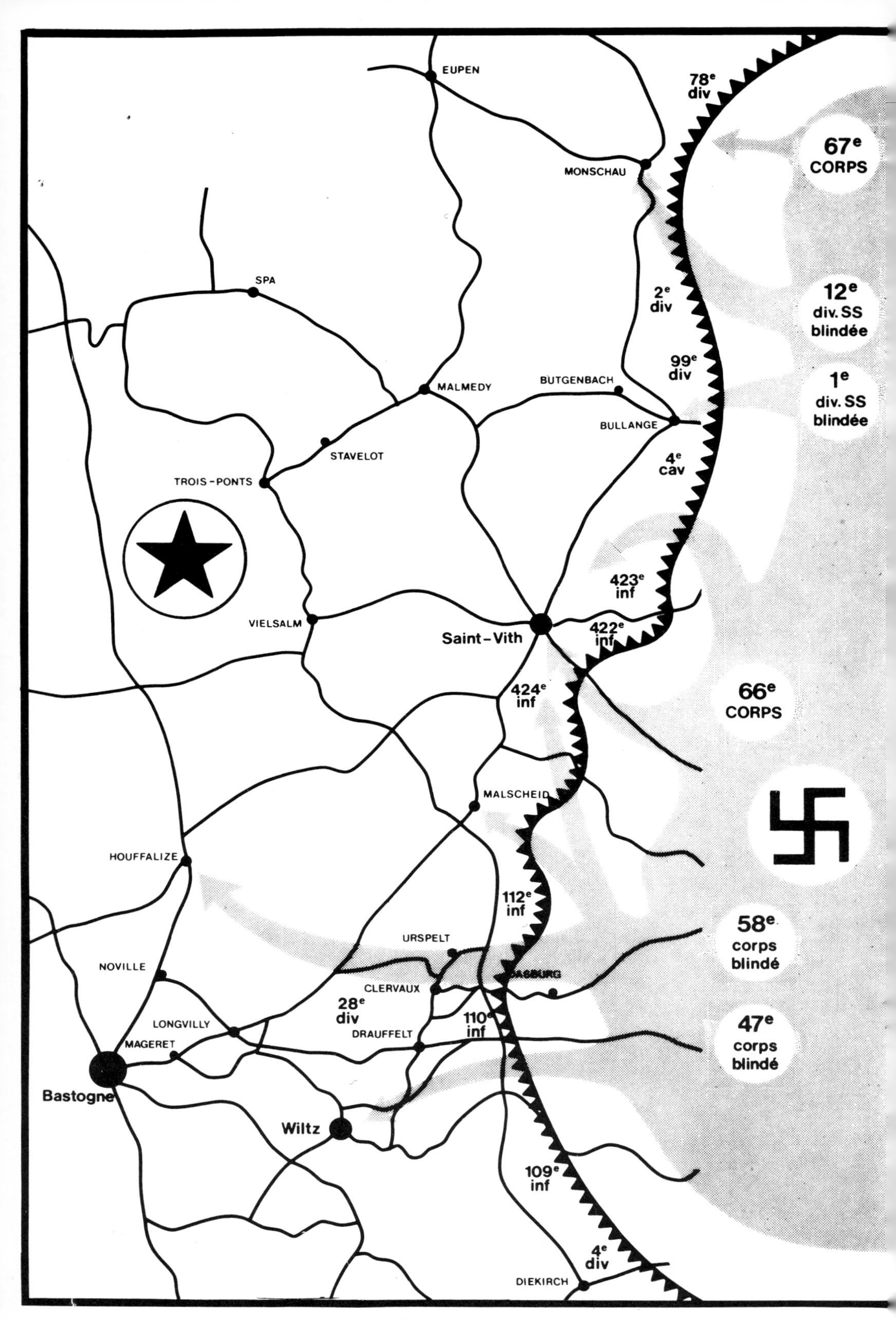

16th december.

SATURDAY 16th DECEMBER 1944

The night of 15th-16th December was pitch black and freezing cold.

Generalmajor Heintz Kokott, commander of the 26th Volksgrenadier Division (VGD) received the order from his superior, Panzergeneral Hasso von Manteuffel, commander of the Fifth Panzer Army, to cross the Our River with part of his command, before the beginning of the major attack.

Kokott seized the opportunity of infiltrating two of his regiments into the American forward lines. His grenadiers were so close to the Americans that they could have had breakfast together.

These 2000 Americans, under the command of Colonel Hurley Fuller, were part of the 110th Regiment of the 28th Infantry Division led by Major-General Norman D. Cota.

The 28th Division held a discontinuous line 24 miles long, 10 miles of which were defended by only two battalions of the 110th Regiment. The third battalion was held in reserve, 3 or 4 miles from the River Clerf and could be brought into action only on the orders of the Divisional Commander.

The two front line battalions were in defensive positions by companies around the villages bordering the road running along the hilltops (known to the Americans as the Skyline Drive), an important line of communications for the Americans going North to South along the river Our.

By day American infantrymen held the outposts between the Skyline Drive and the river, but at night they retreated into the villages. These were the vantage points which the men of the 26th VGD were to occupy at the beginning of the offensive.

4 a.m. At about 4 in the morning, General von Manteuffel was at his advanced command post at Waxweiler. Stylishly dressed in a long leather coat, he told his officers, "We are going to start the attack. Our Fatherland is completely encircled by the enemy, and our comrades fighting at the front are expecting each one of us to perform his duty".

Note: on page 329 the reader will find the order of battle of the 5th Panzer Army on 16th December 1944.

General von Manteuffel,
stylishly dressed in a long leather coat...

To your posts! Let's get underway!

"To your posts! Let's get underway!"

General Hasso Eccard Baron von Manteuffel was younger than his Corps and Divisional commanders. Aged 47 and commander of an armoured army, he was a small man, slim, elegant and aristocratic, belonging to one of the oldest noble families of Prussia. He was highly esteemed throughout the German Army and considered a great leader of armoured forces, a master of the art of rapid attack and surprise. Hitler himself had great regard for him.

5.30 a.m. The assault started at precisely half past five. The clouds were low, and the fog covered the ground.

Along the attacking front of the Sixth Panzer Army, hundreds of artillery batteries, from mortars to heavy guns, plus Nebelwerfers (rocket launchers), had opened fire at 4 o'clock.

In the Fifth Army sector, on the other hand, the attack continued the infiltration which had begun during the night, and the artillery barrage started at the same time as the first fighting, cutting most of the American telephone lines.

Surprised, deprived of communications in many cases, Colonel Fuller's 2000 men found themselves face to face with the first of the 31,000 men of the 26th VGD and the 2nd Panzer Divisions, who attacked them along a 6 mile front. These first attackers had crossed the river Our on bridges constructed of rubber boats or on rafts.

The 26th attacked on the left flank and the 2nd Panzer on the right. The Panzer Lehr (Training) Division was due to follow as soon as the heavy bridge at Gemünd had been built. But the inexperience of the sappers slowed down the work considerably.

6 a.m. At 6 a.m., the 26th attacked en masse at Holzthum, but the Americans threw them back as soon as the enemy was identified. Then the grenadiers attempted to get past on the northern side, but already warned by radio, the American artillery based at Bockholz turned their guns in that direction and pinned them to the ground. Later on, trying to get through via a secondary road, the Germans were met by an American half-track and were mown down by the fire of a "meat chopper", the famous quadruple. 50 calibre machine-gun.

They were thus immobilised between Holzthum and Consthum, wearing themselves out, contrary to orders, trying

Colonel Hurley Fuller,
Commander of the 110th Infantry Regiment.

General Omar N. Bradley, Commanding General of the 12th Army Group, and Major-General Troy H. Middleton, Commander of the VIIIth Corps.

to take the villages. Thwarted in their attempt to capture the narrow but vital bridge on the Our, 2 miles away, the 26th VGD lost the time gained during the night.

Major-General Troy H. Middleton, commander of the American VIIIth Corps, of which the 28th Division formed a part, was asleep in his comfortable campaign caravan, situated next to his headquarters in Bastogne, when he was awakened by the German shelling. He was soon informed from all sides that several German divisions had attacked his sector.

9.15 a.m. At 9.15 a.m. Middleton ordered, "Troops may only retreat from their positions, repeat only, if their positions can no longer be held".

Colonel S.L.A. Marshall, military historian, U.S. Army, was later to declare that, "Middleton's decision was the first tactical step that led, eventually, to the salvation of Bastogne".

10 a.m. At 10 a.m. Middleton informed Omar N. Bradley, commander of the 12th Army Group, that he thought a real attack had started and not a divisionary manoeuvre.

Meanwhile, General Cota issued the order, "Hold at all costs", to his men who were being overwhelmed by the weight of the attack of the German divisions.

1 p.m. The bridge at Dasburg was finally completed by the sappers under Major Loos. The first heavy tanks of the 2nd Panzer began to roll forward on the approach road which was so narrow as to make access to the bridge difficult and to have ruled out the use of prefabricated building materials, forcing the sappers to construct the bridge by hand and to transport all material themselves. Only about a dozen tanks got across before a driver's error caused an accident and blocked the access road.

At Weiler, an infantry company repulsed two grenadier battalions with mortars and anti-tank-guns. Twice the Germans asked for and were allowed a truce to collect their wounded.

1.30 p.m. At half past one, the Germans offered the Americans an honourable surrender. The Americans refused and continued heavy fighting.

4 p.m. The access road at Dasburg was reopened, and the 2nd Panzer began to cross in earnest.

These trees had been cut down by the Germans themselves when retreating in September.

The Panzer Lehr, slowed down by heavy traffic congestion...

Shortly after that, the tanks of the 2nd Panzer were stopped by tree trunks lying across the Clervaux road. These had been cut down by the Germans themselves when retreating in September and now resulted in a massive traffic-jam on both sides of the bridge.

The Panzer Lehr was finally able to begin its river crossing at Gemünd on a bridge built by the sappers, again in difficult conditions. But they made slow progress on roads crowded by the horse-drawn vehicles of the 26th VGD and blocked by trees cut by American sappers. The vehicles wasted much precious time manoeuvering between the trunks, destroying the road surface and the shoulders, making later passage much more difficult.

The Germans had been able to cross the "Skyline Drive" between Hosingen and Marnach, to reach a further bridge on the Clerf River at Dauffelt. Once again, though, the artillerymen from Bockholz pinned them down.

The light elements of the 2nd Panzer, the panzergrenadiers, removed the tree trunks, reaching and occupying Marnach during the evening.

The Fifth Parachute Division was to cross the Our, to the left of the 26th VGD, with ten 75mm self-propelled guns. They moved forwards along a 4 mile front, fighting all day against part of Fuller's 110th Regiment on the northern side and the 109th Regiment of the 28th Infantry Division on the southern side. Wiltz, base of the 28th Division headquarters, had become their target.

9. p.m. At 9 o'clock, Fuller asked General Cota to release the 2nd Battalion. This was done at midnight with the exception of one company left to defend the headquarters. But it was already too late.

The sappers of the 26th VGD had pushed forward their bridgeheads to open the secondary roads by which the Panzer Lehr could cut all communications south of Bastogne and attack the town from that direction.

However, slowed down by heavy traffic congestion, the Panzer Lehr had managed to get only a small part of the reconnaissance battalion across the Our, while the main body of the division had been unable to reach the river.

Only two regiments of panzergrenadiers of the 2nd Panzer had advanced as expected.

Lieutenant-General Omar N. Bradley's car.

What was the situation at the end of the day?

General von Manteuffel was disappointed and was conscious that time lost on their timetable could never be made up. The American defence had been stronger than anticipated so it was not possible to follow the order to avoid all resistance and push forward. Only two regiments of panzer-grenadiers of the 2nd Panzer had advanced as expected.

General von Lüttwitz had not reached his objective for the day which was the crossing of the river Clerf. The slow speed of building bridges, the incredible overcrowding of the roads, the time taken to destroy points of resistance, and the late arrival of the armour as a result of the slow bridge building, were all reasons for his failure.

On the American side, the infantry had borne the brunt of the attack. Awakened with a shock, they had been faced with resolute German troops. When they had tried to warn their command posts, they found that most of the telephone lines had been cut. But the infantrymen stood up well.

The SHAEF generals were incredulous, thinking the attack to be a diversionary one launched to counter their plans for an offensive against Cologne and the Ruhr. In the morning at the Britannique Hotel in Spa, headquarters of the 1st Army, General Bradley, General Quesada, and General Hodges had a cup of coffee which lengthened their breakfast time. What was filling their minds above all was choosing a hunting rifle from among the magnificent weapons presented to them by the Belgian industrialist Mr. Francotte, and having it adjusted to their requirements.

Then Bradley left Spa for Luxembourg, where he found his headquarters as relaxed as he was, and at the end of the day, he made a quiet trip to Paris. Eisenhower later maintained that this journey was justified because of the necessity of discussing the question of replacing losses from fighting units. Bradley stayed the night in Paris where he had a happy dinner with his friend General Everett Hughes, who was well known as Eisenhower's eyes and ears.

But in Spa, Hodges began to fear the worst. He tried in vain to reach Eisenhower and Bradley who, at the end of the day, had decided to attach the 10th Armored Division to Middleton's VIIIth Corps.

A conference quickly brought together Middleton and the representatives from the 10th Armored Division, Colonel Basil G. Thayn, Lieutenant-Colonel John W. Sheffield and Major Roger Rawley.

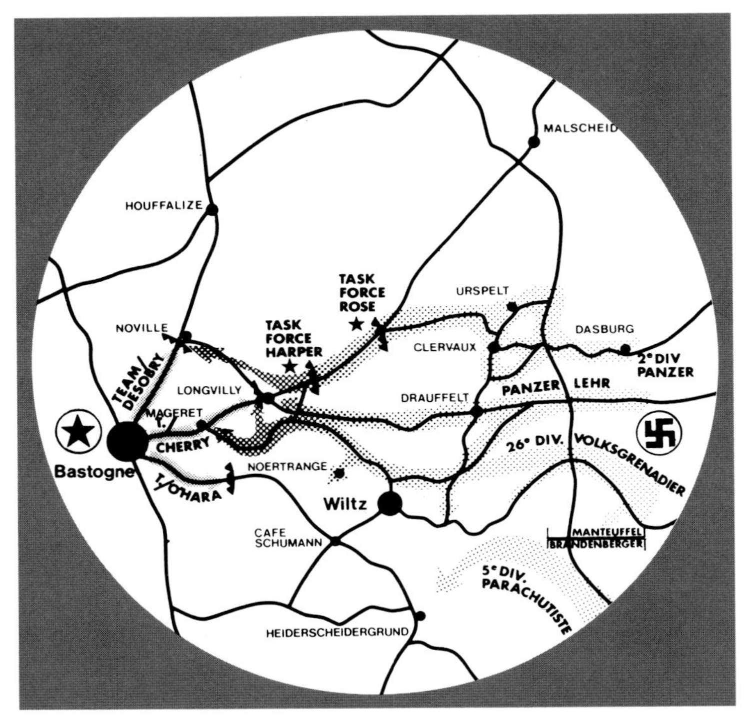

16-17-18-December

But his division was now rushing forward...

SUNDAY 17th DECEMBER 1944

12 p.m. Just after midnight German artillery and rocket-launchers, guided by two observers equipped with radios who were hidden in a house in Clervaux, began to bombard the area. This enabled German patrols to infiltrate the town and to begin to harrass the defences of the 110th Infantry Regiment.

As a precaution, Battery B of the 109th Field Artillery Batallion displaced to the rear so as to be less threatened and to support a counter-attack.

4 a.m. Battery A was captured with all its guns intact, and three half-tracks of the 447th Anti-Aircraft Battalion also fell into the hands of the enemy, who immediately turned the guns on the Americans.

Battery C remained in action near Bockholz but was seriously threatened by German troops.

Fuller had managed to obtain the 2nd Batallion, which was understrength. On arrival, and well before dawn, they were sent towards Reuler with orders to reach Marnach. At the moment that they were setting out on the road that climbs up to Reuler, the half-tracks and tanks of the 2nd Panzer were already coming down towards Clervaux.

The road was so narrow that Colonel von Lauchert, commander of the 2nd Panzer, decided to make use of another route as well, a road which led from the hill in the north by a series of tight difficult bends for tanks towards Clervaux station. Nearby was the Hotel Claravallis where Fuller's headquarters were installed.

Impatient, Lauchert was to knock at both the front and back doors.

This fiery officer had only recently taken command of the 2nd Panzer and had not even had time to get to know most of the officers in his command. But his division was now rushing forwards, a formidable force to clear away the weak forces that opposed it, which were simply brushed aside. American tanks which tried to attack on different sides to try to stem its advance were violently thrust aside with heavy losses.

Colonel Meinhard von Lauchert,
Commander of the 2nd Panzer Division

The German tanks were on the Marnach road...

The 110th Regiment of the 28th Infantry Division found itself in a difficult position, but conducted an outstandingly courageous defence to the point of launching counter-attacks, entailing heavy losses.

9 a.m. The order was simple, "Nobody retreats – hold at all costs".

The German tanks were on the Marnach road moving towards the larger of the two bridges in Clervaux.

9.30 a.m. The second platoon of Company A of the 707th Tank Batallion crossed the Clerf River to engage the 2nd Panzer. Fighting started quickly with four Mark IV tanks being destroyed and the Americans, in their turn, losing three tankdestroyers. The 1st platoon came up in support, using a small road which followed the river. A well placed shot from the leading tank-destroyer immobilised the first Mark IV, and the road from Marnach towards Clervaux was blocked.

10.30 a.m. Seventeen American tanks of Combat Command R (CCR) of the 9th Armored Division arrived under the orders of Captain Robert L. Lybarger.

Fuller immediately sent them to the hot-spots, one platoon to hold the left flank and the other to reinforce the defence on the northern side of the town. He kept the rest of the tanks to defend the town centre.

11.30 a.m. About thirty German tanks reached Clervaux, destroyed the two American tanks on the left flank, and started to cross the Clerf.

Notified of the gravity of the situation in Clervaux, General Middleton had already taken steps to defend the approach roads to Bastogne.

Reinforced by all the available able-bodied men, including administrative and service troops, three combat batallions of the 1128th Engineer Group had been positioned in a semi-circle around Foy, 4 miles to the north of Bastogne on the Liège road, and around Neffe, 2,5 miles from Bastogne on the Clervaux road.

11.40 a.m. On confirmation of the inevitable fall of Clervaux, General Middleton decided to order CCR of the 9th Armored Division at Trois-Vierges to block the road to Bastogne. Led by Colonel Joseph H. Gilbreth, this command consisted of the 52nd

General of Panzer Troops Baron Heinrich von Lüttwitz,
Commander of the XXXXVIIth Armoured Corps.

Three combat battalions of the 1128th Engineer Group had been positioned in a semi-circle around Foy.

Armored Infantry Batallion, the 2nd Tank Batallion, and the 73rd Armored Field Artillery Batallion.

Two blocks were set up:

The first was at Anthoniushaff, at the junction of the roads from Clervaux and Trois-Vierges, under the orders of Captain L.K. Rose, commander of Company A of the 2nd Tank Batallion. Task Force Rose consisted of a company of Sherman tanks, an armoured infantry company, and a platoon of armoured engineers.

The second was at Fetsch (Allerborn), at the junction of the roads from Clervaux and Wiltz, under the command of Lieutenant-Colonel Ralph S. Harper. Task Force Harper comprised the rest of the 2nd Tank Battallion and two companies of the 52nd Armored Infantry Battalion.

12 a.m. German General von Lüttwitz visited the front lines where his tanks were pushing westwards from the bridgeheads.

General of Armoured Troops, Baron Heinrich von Lüttwitz, commander of the XXXXVIIth Armoured Corps, was a man of 58 years old. He had the full trust of his superior, General von Manteuffel, and was the perfect example of the Prussian cavalry officer in the old German military tradition.

Tall, fat and potbellied, he wore a monocle in a well fed and satisfied face. He was a courageous and ambitious soldier, and the severity which existed in his command was apparently contradicted by the care that he had for the men under his orders.

1.30 p.m. Combat Command B (CCB), a third of the 10th US Armored Division, left Remeling in France for the Grand-Duchy of Luxembourg.

General George S. Patton, commander of the Third US Army, was furious that the 10th Armored Division had been withdrawn from it and put at the disposal of the VIIIth Corps, "Hell", he growled, "it's probably nothing more than a spoiling attack to throw us off balance down here and make the Third Army call off its offensive".

At the start of the afternoon, as the German advance continued in the sector defended by the 28th Division, the tension was increasing in Bastogne.

...as the German advance continued...

3 p.m. Clervaux was almost completely encircled.

3.30 p.m. The Command Post of the 110th Infantry Regiment in the Claravallis Hotel was now defended by only half a platoon of infantrymen and a single anti-tank gun.

5 p.m. The 26th VGD captured a bridge, still intact, south of Clervaux and carved a way into the town. The rest of the Division was to cross the river after nightfall without any opposition. The situation was desperate for the defenders when the final assault took place. Grenadiers, tanks, and self-propelled tank-destroyers advanced, knocking out the 57mm anti-tank guns which were defending the northern bridge.

6.30 p.m. Clervaux was now in the hands of the Germans. Only the château fort was still holding out, threatening the grenadiers' movements all round but unable to stop the advance of the tanks.

7 p.m. Bradley arrived from Paris at the headquarters of the 12th Army Group in Luxembourg, located in the building of the Caisse d'Epargne (Savings Bank). He finally managed to get into contact with Hodges who, worried by the latest news from the front, urged him to send reinforcements from the SHAEF strategic reserve.

Bradley informed him that Eisenhower had just made the difficult decision to send the 82nd and 101st Airborne Divisions to the Ardennes.

8.30 p.m. The 101st Airborne received their order to leave for the Belgian Ardennes from the XVIIIth Airborne Corps, commanded by Major-General Matthew B. Ridgway*.

* According to Major General James M. Gavin, commanding the 82nd Airborne Division and in temporary command of the XVIII Airborne Corps, in the absence of Major General Matthew B. Ridgway, the initial orders were to prepare both the 82nd and the 101st for movement "toward Bastogne" at dawn on December 19. At 9.30 p.m. on December 18, a new SHAEF order arrived directing that both divisions move "without delay in direction of Bastogne" (Gavin's afteraction report, 1945). Arriving next morning at 9 a.m. to Hodges' 1st Army headquarters, Gavin was informed that his 82nd Division and the independant units would be attached to Gerow's Vth Corps and take position on the north front near Werbomont, while the 101st was attached to Middleton's VIIIth Corps in Bastogne.
The version of the 101st, which is reproduced in this book, is somewhat different.
As far as General Ridgway is concerned, he landed in France in the early afternoon of the 18th December. When arriving in Bastogne to spend the night at Middleton's Corps Command Post on his way to Werbomont, he learned for the first time that the 101st was to remain in Bastogne under VIIIth Corps control.

Major-General Maxwell D. Taylor,
Commander of the 101st Airborne Division.

Lieutenant-Colonel Paul Danahy,
G.2, 101st Airborne Division.

The 101st had arrived at Mourmelon three weeks earlier after the fighting in Holland and was supposed to rest and train for a minimum of three months, to prepare for an operation in the spring.

Most of the officers and men were on leave, and the military police had a big job to find them in Paris, Reims or in the other French towns where they were relaxing.

9 p.m. About a dozen of the regimental and camp headquarters' officers and division staff officers were present for the briefing at the headquarters of the 101st Airborne Division. Brigadier-General Anthony C. McAuliffe, officer in charge of the divisional artillery, assumed the command in the absence of the commander of the Division, Major-General Maxwell D. Taylor, who was in Washington, probably trying to obtain, among other things, the departure of his division to the Pacific, as the chances of achieving fame in Europe were becoming slim. As a result, the brilliant general was going to miss the opportunity of a lifetime.

McAuliffe was somewhat different from most of his fellow officers. At first sight he seemed out of place among the paratroopers, and in fact this career officer had been serving in the Pentagon, where he was in charge of the Army's weapons development. At the age of 46, three years older than Taylor, he volunteered for combat duty when the war came, leaving his comfortable place in Washington. He had two exceptionally staunch supporters in the young officers Danahy and Kinnard, who appreciated this considerate, affable, and hard-working man.

The contrast between his impassive face which did not show his feelings and his expressive voice was surprising. It increased his direct style as he lacked any oratorical skills. Those who heard him speak knew they were dealing with a man without artifice. In the presence of his younger companions, he referred to himself as "Old Crock".

McAuliffe, pointing to the map of the Ardennes on which Danahy had marked what was known of the situation, said, "All I know of the situation is that there has been a break-through and we have got to get up there".

From the end of the room, an officer approached silently, looked at the map of the Ardennes and said, "That is where the goddam Krauts always come bursting out of Germany lookin' for trouble".

Without waiting for a reply, Lieutenant-Colonel Julian J. Ewell went out to give orders for the departure of his 501st Parachute Regiment.

On the German side, at the end of this second day of fighting, the fears of General von Manteuffel were being realized. The Panzer Lehr, on which such a lot depended, should have progressed more rapidly.

A weakness had appeared in the American lines at the junction of the Fifth and the Seventh Armies. This eased the task of the south wing of the Fifth Army, but it appeared that, due to lack of sapper units, the Seventh Army was unable to exploit its advantage.

At the crucial moment, this caused the Army to lose its best chance of advancing. Additionally, it was becoming apparent that the Seventh Army would not be able to accomplish its mission of protecting the Fifth Army. Although weak, the American defences had put up a considerable and, in some cases, an obstinate resistance.

Suddenly, the taking of Bastogne became of major importance.

It did so not only because its road network would facilitate the German breakthrough, but because the interception of the American message ordering the 82nd and 101st Airborne Divisions to move to Bastogne, made the taking of the town necessary. If not, it would hinder the development of the offensive and would constitute a dangerous menace as it would serve as a base for an American counter-offensive.

Manteuffel noted: "Bastogne could seriously endanger our attack".

Bayerlein consoled himself by throwing responsibility for the Panzer Lehr's delay on von Lüttwitz. The commander of the XXXXVIIth Armoured Corps had taken a regiment of panzergrenadiers from him to attack Consthum. Bayerlein had organized a rapid attack force, made up of an armoured reconnaissance company, two companies of motorized armoured grenadiers and a company of Panther tanks. This vanguard force, destined to open the route and push forwards, had been worn down outside Hosingen, slowing down the momentum of the division.

On the American side, at least in Paris, the atmosphere remained calm.

But at Spa, on the other hand, tension was mounting, and the headquarters of the 1st Army was at sixes and sevens. The news from the front became still more frequent and worrying.

On the English side, there was no reaction. Montgomery distributed medals to the 2nd Canadian Division, and Brigadier-General Elliot Rodger hunted pheasant.

When Bradley was informed that at least 14 divisions were attacking, he asked "where did that bastard get such a force?". To the suggestion that he should move his headquarters to the rear, he replied that he would do nothing "because there is too much prestige at stake".

General Middleton began to feel a little better after having had the most disagreeable feeling that the situation was getting out of hand, like sand flowing through his fingers. At one moment he asked himself whether it was he or the Germans who would meet the reinforcements in Bastogne. But the announcement of the sending of the reserve divisions and the visit of the commander of the 10th Armored Division, Major-General H.H. Morris Jr., to his headquarters, increased his confidence. Realizing that the race for Bastogne was on, he ordered Morris to get Combat Command B under way towards Bastogne from Luxembourg where they had arrived and were now under canvas near the town.

The Panzer Lehr made very slow progress...

A patrol from Task Force Rose discovered its first Germans...

MONDAY 18th DECEMBER 1944

12 p.m. A little after midnight, Task Force Harper and Rose were in position.

Task Force Harper was reinforced by a hundred men and ten officers from the 110th Regiment of the 28th Division. These men came from Clervaux under the orders of Colonel Theodore A. Seely, who had commanded the regiment before being wounded in earlier fighting and who had returned to duty as soon as the German attack had been announced, although still convalescent.

The two road-blocks were also reinforced with artillery support.

A battery of the 73rd Field Artillery Battalion dug in a short distance away was ready to intervene if the roadblocks were attacked.

1 a.m. At Mourmelon near Reims the 101st was on alert, and preparations for departure were underway. Military police had been sent in every direction to "recover" the men on leave.

5.28 a.m. The final message from the last resistance in the Château at Clervaux was received.

The consequences of this battle of Clervaux were important:

For the Germans, a loss of 36 hours from their planned timetable.

For the Americans, the almost complete destruction of the 110th Regiment, the Commander, Colonel Fuller, being taken prisoner.

9 a.m. The Panzer Lehr crossed the Clerf and made very slow progress between Clervaux and Bastogne, impeded more by road obstructions than by American resistance.

The 2nd Panzer reached a wide plateau, a favourable area for the deployment of its armour but split betweeen the two resistance points of Rose and Harper, whose defenders began to distinguish the sinister outline of panzers in the distance.

Lieutenant-Colonel Ned D. Moore,
G.1, 101st Airborne.

...pushed into enormous, uncovered 10-ton trailers...

10 a.m. A patrol from Task Force Rose discovered its first Germans, the scouts of a reconnaissance group, asleep in a wood, having arrived there during the night.

10.30 a.m. Fighting started between the scouts of the 2nd Battalion of the 3rd Armoured Regiment of the 2nd Panzer and the first defenders of the Rose road-block. While combat with small arms continued, the first tanks arrived between 11 o'clock and midday. The road-block was quickly surrounded. The tank battle began.

12 a.m. Shortly before midday, General McAuliffe, his aide-de-camp, Lieutenant Frederic D. Starret, 23 years old, and Lieutenant-Colonel Harry W.O. Kinnard left Mourmelon in a command car. "Step on it", said McAuliffe to the driver.

Lieutenant-Colonel Ned D. Moore in charge of divisional personnel was responsible for supervising the Division's departure. This was led by Lieutenant-Colonel Julian J. Ewell at the head of his 501st Parachute Infantry Regiment. The Division was short of mortars, rifle bullets, spades for digging trenches, arctic clothes and shoes, gas masks, and blankets, etc.

As the men arrived, they were pushed into 2 1/2 ton GMC trucks or into huge, uncovered 10 ton trailers, pulled by Autocar tractors. All these vehicles, jeeps and weapon carriers were lined up in front of the barracks. It had not been easy to assemble so many vehicles, and it had sometimes been necessary to dump their loads by the roadside to make space. The Division was, of course, designed to be transported by air rather than by road. The men had hastily grabbed together anything useful: bazookas, machine-guns and rifles, as well as blankets and thick army overcoats. Not everyone had these, and the soldiers who did not were to shiver in their new olive-green field jackets or in their lightweight beige windbreakers. They were, however, able to carry with them as many K rations as they wanted from the pile that had been dumped near the trucks, and the men helped themselves.

The divisional band which had not been allowed to take part in the fighting in Normandy or Holland, ignored orders and took the opportunity of slipping into the convoy. They had thus the chance of fighting valorously and of quieting the gibes of the combat veterans.

"Started again have they! We'll show those goddamned Krauts".

...had swept away the barriers put up by Rose.

(Photo taken after the battle showing the tanks from Rose's road block)

Hundreds of raw recruits, who had arrived a week before to replace casualties in the ranks, suddenly found themselves thrown into the war without divisional training and without any combat experience. A week later, they were veterans too, and the division was no longer a collection of individuals but a tightly knit fighting unit.

For the time being Colonel Kinnard, stuck in his corner of the elephantine rear leatherette seat of the Dodge, was worried. While the command car bounced across the frozen roads, trying to overtake the endless vehicle column of the 82nd Airborne, a rival but friendly division which was already en route for the Ardennes, he thought of the state of the Division and especially of how it was going to be used. Before leaving he had dropped to his friend Danahy, the divisional intelligence officer: "This looks like a lousy use of airborne troops".

Sitting on the wooden benches of the GMC trucks or squashed one against the other standing in the trailers, the men were in a very bad mood. They were moaning about the unexpected departure, their lack of sleep, hangovers, and the freezing fog that surrounded them. However, as he grabbed a friend's hand to get into the truck without dropping his roll of blankets, one of them said, "Started again have they! We'll show them goddamned Krauts".

The trucks lumbered into movement.

2 p.m. At Anthoniushaff, a complete tank battalion was fighting against the Task Force Rose of which a third had already been destroyed.

2.05 p.m. Colonel Gilbreth, informed by radio of the hopeless situation that Rose was in, asked for his subordinate to be given permission to retreat. Middleton refused.

2.30 p.m. The left wing of General von Lüttwitz's XXXXVIIth Panzer Corps had swept away the barriers put up by Rose, who was now retreating with his suviving men. This enabled the 3rd Regiment of the 2nd Panzer Division to forge on towards Bastogne.

3 p.m. After driving three hours, following the Libramont-Houffalize road, General McAuliffe noticed how close he was to Bastogne. He decided to pay a visit to the VIIIth Corps head-

Colonel William L. Roberts,
Commander of the CCB of the 10th Armored Division.

A general view of Bastogne.

quarters and ordered his driver to turn off at Sprimont and follow the National 4 Road to Bastogne not far away.

"Harry, I think I'll check up on the situation before we go on up there. There's a road junction ahead. We'll turn and go to the VIIIth Corps headquarters at Bastogne and see what we can find out".

"That sounds like a very good idea, General", Kinnard answered.

A rendez-vous with destiny was being prepared*.

4 p.m. Colonel William L. Roberts, commander of CCB (Combat Command B) of the 10th Armored Division, arrived at VIIIth Corps headquarters in Bastogne, from Merl. The CCB column followed shortly after.

The immediate decision made by Middleton, whose headquarters were in the process of being moved to Neufchâteau, was that the CCB would be divided into three forces:

1. Team Desobry, named after its commander, Major William Desobry, consisting of 500 men and 15 tanks, would block the road at Noville on the Bastogne-Liège road.
2. Team Cherry, commanded by Lieutenant-Colonel Henry T. Cherry, consisting of 500 men, 17 medium and 10 light tanks, was to set up a road-block at Longvilly on the Bastogne-Clervaux road.
3. Team O'Hara, commanded by Lieutenant-Colonel James O'Hara, consisting of 500 men and 20 tanks, was to set up a road-block at Wardin on the Bastogne-Wiltz road.

All the retreating men were to be drafted into the CCB. General Middleton also decided to abandon Houffalize.

4. p.m. At the end of a long straight piece of road, Bastogne suddenly appeared before the parachutists' eyes as their command car reached the top of a hill. They knew nothing of this area, with

* "Rendez-vous with Destiny", title of the book telling the story of the 101st Airborne.

Lieutenant-General Courtney H. Hodges,
Commander of the 1st American Army.

its old town situated on the high Ardennes plateau at the junction of all the main roads in the area. Throughout the ages, its military role had been of great importance, and this had increased with motorization.

There had been little traffic on the road from Marche by which they had arrived, so that they were struck by the contrast with the town which was congested with vehicles and soldiers moving in all directions.

The civilian population was anxiously watching this activity from their doorsteps or hanging out of windows, their faces bearing the anxious question "What is happening?".

But the soldiers carrying duffel bags, bedrolls, footlockers and kit bags did not take notice of the civilians. The atmosphere was quite tense and seemed unusual to the officers as their vehicle tried with difficulty to cross the town through the traffic and the military police who were trying to keep it moving.

They had the impression that all these men were getting ready to leave. Kinnard said, "Sir, unless these people are having a premature case of jitters, I'd say the Germans must be barreling this way fast".

"So am I thinking", replied McAuliffe. "We'll soon find out".

4.15 p.m. The command car approached the barracks where Middleton's headquarters were installed. While the sentries checked the vehicle, Kinnard noticed to his left a curious neighbour: above a stone wall showed a forest of wood and stone crosses with small constructions looking like chapels – it was a cemetery. He decided it was better to keep his sense of humour, and he made a mental note that he would tell his fellow officers that they had a cemetery handy in which to bury the general staffs of divisions under the Corps command.

General McAuliffe presented himself to Middleton who briefed him on the latest situation as far as he was able. Middleton stood out among his officers of the VIIIth Corps for his calm, while they seemed to be nervous, their conversation loud and their faces haggard.

Middleton informed McAuliffe that his superior, Lieutenant-General Courtney H. Hodges, commander of the 1st American Army, had decided that the 101st were to defend Bastogne.

Lieutenant-Colonel Harry W.O. Kinnard,
G.3, 101st Airborne.

...the Germans' thrust was coming towards Bastogne...

McAuliffe and Kinnard left immediately, because night was falling, to go and pick out an assembly point for the Division. They chose the outskirts of Mande-St-Etienne beside the road along which they had come, while on the other side of the town, the first elements of the Panzer Lehr were approaching Mageret.

Kinnard's choice was particularly appropriate.

Harry W.O. Kinnard was the G-3 officer in charge of Division plans and operations, a task he had fulfilled in the 501st Parachute Infantry Regiment before he had been given this post of heavy responsibility at divisional level after the campaign in Holland. Although he was flattered, Kinnard was concerned, and he was becoming increasingly worried by the present circumstances. A Lieutenant-Colonel at 29, this elegant man of Scottish origin was outstanding for his sharp intelligence. Of medium height, he had had a superb military training, but looked more like a boy-scout than a staff officer. His delicate elegance and his soft cheeks hid a cold military machine, great inherent leadership qualities and an unquestioning devotion to duty. Faced with serious problems, he maintained an impressive calm.

On their return to Bastogne, the two officers went to a meeting with General Middleton at his headquarters. He wanted personally to explain the situation in detail, which was far from encouraging. None knew how far the Germans were from Bastogne, but they had certainly broken through the first lines of defence. The map displayed a large number of red symbols, representing the Germans, and very few blue ones, representing the Allied forces.

The map also showed that the Germans' thrust was coming towards Bastogne, and both McAuliffe and Kinnard realized immediately that the situation was very serious and that they would be attacked very shortly. They had to act quickly if they were not to be surprised and so left the meeting to rejoin and organize their troops without any delay.

5.30 p.m. Scouts from the 3rd Armoured Regiment of the 2nd Panzer reached Allerborn and stopped at Harper's roadblock, waiting for reinforcements.

6 p.m. Lieutenant-Colonel Templeton, commander of the 705th Tank Destroyer Battalion, received the order to move to Bastogne immediately with his battalion, which was based in Germany at Kohlscheid some 60 miles away.

Task Force Rose slipped across the fields with five tanks and one assault-gun platoon, all that remained from the recent fighting, but just before reaching Houffalize they fell on a reconnaissance battalion of the 116th Panzer which destroyed all the group's vehicles. Very few of the men managed to escape to Bastogne.

6.30 p.m. Heavy tanks arrived at the Allerborn defences. Fighting started. Two American tank-platoons were annihilated.

Incendiaries setting fire to the light vehicles gave the Germans enough light to massacre the Americans with systematic machine-gun fire. Colonel Harper was killed, and the second road-block was destroyed.

7 p.m. The spearhead of the 2nd Panzer reached a point half a mile from the Longvilly road-block and turned right, off the main road, obeying their orders to avoid Bastogne and push on towards the river Meuse. The men of Colonel Gilbreth's 9th Armored CCR, who were holding this road-block, continued to wait for a frontal attack from the main road, unaware of the turn taken by the Germans.

By changing directions, the 2nd Panzer now exposed its left flank to the American Force. Thinking that the Americans were moving against them, the Germans took the precaution of protecting this exposed flank.

It became inevitable that the two forces would have to fight, but only within the bounds of their respective missions. This would reduce the impact.

8 p.m. Cherry arrived with his S-3 at the command post of the CCR, where he learnt that the situation was "confused". The CCR was sticking to the order to "Hold at all costs", but had no precise plan of defence. Cherry told them that his orders were not to advance to the east of Longvilly, which disappointed the members of the 9th Armored Division. He then decided to return to Bastogne and report to Roberts, leaving orders with First Lieutenant Edward P. Hyduke to send out patrols and to establish defence points to the west of Longvilly.

The survivors from Forces Rose and Harper, some riflemen from one company of the 110th Regiment (Clervaux) together with other stragglers from previous battles were organized with four tank destroyers* of the 630th Tank Destroyer Battalion to protect the 58th Armored Field Artillery Battalion positioned south of Longvilly where, a while later, the advance party from Team Cherry, commanded by Lieutenant Edward P. Hyduke, arrived, followed by a larger force under the command of Captain William F. Ryerson, which was between Mageret and Longvilly.

General Bayerlein himself commanded the vanguard of the Panzer Lehr when it left Niederwampach for Mageret. The unit was composed of 15 Mark IV tanks, an artillery battery and four companies of the 902nd Panzergrenadier Regiment.

Unlike von Lauchert, Bayerlein had not been formally ordered to avoid all combat at Bastogne, and he wanted to take the town himself. The best way to do it was to get there as quickly as possible, and to do so, he chose the shortest route which had been recommended by local farmers who assured him that, although the road was bad at the beginning, it improved later. In fact this was untrue, and the forward elements of the Armoured Division spent most of their night skidding around the road, covering only a short distance. After the passage of the first tanks, the earth road became impassable to wheeled vehicles which had to be towed by those with tracks – as also

* The Americans used two types of tank-destroyers, the M10, named the "Wolverine", with which the infantry divisions were equipped, and the M18, called the "Hellcat", which had been issued to the armoured divisions. One M18 can be seen in the Victory Memorial Museum.

Colonel Thomas L. Sherburne,
Commander of the Artillery of the 101st Airborne.

The roads were crowded with vehicles fleeing from the front.

happened to some of the half-tracks. The crews wore out their nerves and expended their energy attaching towing-cables, manoeuvering, and directing vehicles in the dark.

8 p.m. Colonel Thomas L. Sherburne, acting artillery commander of the 101st Airborne (temporary replacement for General McAuliffe), was on his way to Werbomont with his men when they met the tail of the 82nd Airborne's column, also on their way to Werbomont. As the road was clogged, they decided to make a detour via Bastogne where the road was clear. When he was told by a military policeman that General McAuliffe and his party had done the same, Sherburne ordered the M.P. to direct all the 101st Division units towards Bastogne.

But certain units were already on the Werbomont road, and there was no news of Danahy. Information was so vague that the officers were beginning to fear that his group had been captured by the Germans.

The atmosphere around Bastogne remained very confused.

The roads were now crowded with vehicles fleeing from the front, many of them being those involved in removing the headquarters of the VIIIth Corps. The Neufchâteau road was insufficient so the vehicles used the Marche road by which the 101st Airborne was arriving. The result was a steadily increasing level of chaos, and the traffic became totally paralysed when a column of trucks from the 28th Infantry Division insisted on parking on the road in the assembly zone of the Airborne Division.

The darkness of the night did not help either.

The captain commanding the 28th Infantry column absolutely refused to move without a written order from VIIIth Corps, maintaining that the zone had been assigned to him.

Colonel Kinnard, who was already heavily involved in the organization and positioning of the division units, returned to the headquarters of VIIIth Corps, where he found Brigadier-General Higgins who had just arrived in Bastogne.

They learnt that the 101st had been attached to the VIIIth Corps, and Higgins then enquired about what was worrying Harry Kinnard who explained the problem to him. Gerry Higgins' face, naturally a ruddy colour, became even redder during the explanation.

Brigadier-General Gerald J. Higgins,
second in command of the 101st Airborne.

A column of trucks of the 28th Infantry Division.

Brigadier-General Higgins was probably the youngest general in the American army. Born at Buhl in Idaho, this 185-pound, six-foot man of 35 seemed a complete contrast to the frail Kinnard. He jumped into his jeep saying, "Come on, we'll fix that fellow".

Arriving at Mande-St-Etienne, they had great difficulty in getting to the captain of the 28th Infantry, because his vehicles were blocking the road.

"Our division is coming up here to fight, Captain", Higgins insisted, "and we must use this road to bring them in".

The captain replied petulantly that he could not move because he had his orders and had blocked the road to stop deserters getting away.

"Get the goddam things out of the road!" shouted Higgins fingering the holster of his pistol. "That's an order!".

The captain stared stupefied, and then seeing the General's steely stare did not hesitate to pull the column into a single file at the side of the highway and begin moving.

Kinnard had ordered Lieutenant Starrett to set up the command post in a farm, but the Lieutenant chose the village school as being more appropriate. Kinnard congratulated him for his initiative, a virtue soon to be much needed.

The two groundfloor classrooms, heated by a big wood stove and lit by oil lamps, had the windows blacked out with blankets, and the telephones were already installed and working.

That is how Lieutenant-Colonel Ewell arrived there having found his way by following the telephone wires as advised by the members of the Signal Corps, who suggested that this was the best way of finding one's way. At once, General Higgins sent him off to Bastogne Corps Headquarters for a conference with General McAuliffe.

General McAuliffe, faced with so many tactical unkowns, decided to adopt a "good old Leavenworth solution" (from the name of the American Staff College): the 501st Regiment, led by Ewell, was to go and see what was happening around Longvilly, at 6 a.m. the following morning.

McAuliffe and the other officers stood in front of a map attached to the wall, one of the 15 precious maps of the region

Lieutenant-Colonel Julian J. Ewell,
Commander of the 501st Parachute Infantry Regiment
of the 101st Airborne.

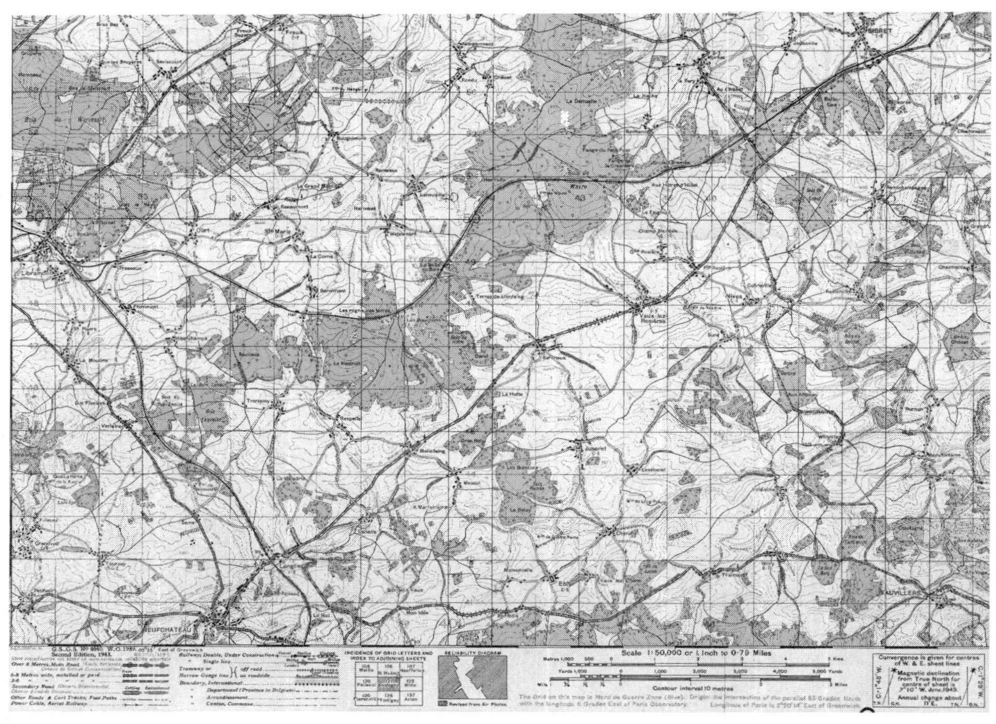

Part of a map of the type used by the Americans at Bastogne.

that they possessed for the whole division, a problem that was giving Kinnard white hair. On the map, the German forces were marked in red and the American in blue. All the eastern part was red.

With his usual phlegm Ewell thought that they might be about to live a few rough moments and said in his drawling voice, "It looks like it's got the measles".

The eyes of McAuliffe and Higgins met. No doubt about it, Julian was in shape.

When he received his orders "Move out along this road at six o'clock, make contact, attack and clear up the situation", not a muscle on his face moved. He replied laconically, "Yes, Sir".

Ewell, like his class mate Kinnard, was 29 years old.

Kinnard said of him: "Julian acts like he was born on a battlefield", which was almost true because, like Kinnard, Ewell was an army child, born in an army camp, the son of a professional soldier. He affected a certain nonchalance in his dress which was reinforced by his mountaineers twang. He was tall, almost gaunt, the rigorous life of the airborne had cut his weight down to a bare 135 pounds. He moved like a cat. His face showed his intelligence, and he emanated a calm dignity. One could feel great strength in him.

After leaving the command post, he rejoined his men who were starting to assemble in zone number one, the nearest to Bastogne. He brought together his own staff officers and explained what he knew of the situation.

"Any questions?".

Silent, his officers looked at each other open-mouthed. Their ignorance of the situation left them speechless.

Ewell burst out laughing. "Cripes, what a mess, huh?".

The atmosphere became more relaxed, and Ewell took the opportunity to add:

"Well, nuts! The situation is bound to clarify in the morning. In the meantime, the enemy are sure to be just about as confused as we are".

The officers were reassured. They had great trust in their leader.

Major-General Troy H. Middleton,
Commander of the VIIIth Corps.

Lieutenant Hyduke set up his defensive position in the hills to the west of the village.

Ewell had an advantage over the other officers of the 101st Airborne – he had been in Bastogne before. When the 101st was relieved in Holland and went to France for a rest, he had taken a detour through the Ardennes and stopped overnight in Bastogne. As a result he had a general idea of the road net and terrain.

8.30 p.m. General Ridgway arrived at Middleton's command post in Bastogne. He was told that the 101st was to operate under VIIIth Corps and defend the town. General Middleton phoned General Omar N. Bradley, commanding the 12th Army Group, to inform him that the 101st was going to stay in Bastogne and would probably be surrounded.

At Longvilly the situation was extremely confused.

While Lieutenant Hyduke was setting up his defensive position in the hills to the west of the village with a platoon of cavalry, four Shermans and seven light tanks, the major part of Team Cherry was with Captain Ryerson. Hyduke had not been able to mine the area leading to their position because men were retreating all the time and would have been the first victims.

While two artillery batteries of the 9th Armored Division fired to protect the village – the only firing at that moment – Colonel Gilbreth gave orders to his staff to get ready to pull back to Bastogne.

His order caused a veritable panic, and Gilbreth's entire force set out without hesitating before the astonished eyes of the men of Team Cherry, who tried to force a passage to take over their positions.

The congestion was indescribable: on one hand were the vehicles of Captain Ryerson, which were moving towards Longvilly or were trying to dig in; and on the other hand were the men and vehicles of Colonel Gilbreth who were literally running away. Gilbreth managed to cut the fleeing column into two and ordered those who were still in the village to stay where they were until daybreak, hoping that dawn would permit him to clarify the situation. But he had not been able to stop the first part of his force, and they congested the Mageret road and all the country lanes which became cul-de-sacs for the

The first tanks of the Panzer Lehr were approaching Mageret.

Throughout the night, the 101st continued to arrive in the assembly zone.

vehicles as they became bogged down one after another, creating a giant jam impossible to untangle.

During this time, Bayerlein had crossed the Luxembourg frontier with the first tanks of the Panzer Lehr, and his forward units were approaching Mageret where they arrived at 11.30 p.m. opposite a road-block established by the 158th Engineer Battalion and some men of the CCR of the 9th Armored Division. Sporadic fighting broke out in the night between the 12 Panzers, the artillery battalion and the armoured infantry battalion which made up Bayerlein's group, and the Americans.

11.30 p.m.

After two hours of fighting, the village was in the hands of the Germans.

At Mande-St-Etienne, 1200 men from the 501st Regiment of the 101st Airborne had set up camp in thick fog.

Throughout the night, the 101st continued to arrive in the assembly zone.

At that moment, the two divisions that were to clash head on, the 101st and the Panzer Lehr, were equidistant from Bastogne!

Only the 2nd Panzer was to continue its advance to the Meuse.

The American generals had finally become aware of the seriousness and the size of the German attack. General Bradley had telephoned General George Patton, charging him to come immediately to Luxembourg with his staff officers for a conference. Patton made the journey from Nancy to Luxembourg by car.

Visibly under the effect of the shock, Bradley showed him on the map the situation as he knew it. The American defences had been pierced. Before Bradley could say anything to him, Patton knew what Bradley wanted from him. He had to cease his current offensive and pivot his army so as to counter the German offensive.

In fact, he had already thought out a plan, though he would have preferred to let the Germans advance more deeply and then take and destroy them from the rear. But nobody asked his advice, just his power to intervene and his dazzling speed of action.

Without a moment's hesitation he undertook to send his famous 4th Armored Division towards Longwy at midnight, to send the 80th Infantry Division towards Luxembourg the next morning and, if it became necessary, to prepare the 26th Infantry Division to get under way in 24 hours.

When he arrived at Nancy after dark, he was informed that Bradley had telephoned several times.

At 8 p.m. Patton got through to him.

Things were getting worse and worse, and he was to send the divisions immediately and get ready for a conference at Verdun the next morning at 11 a.m.

The commander of the XXXXVIIth Panzer Corps, General von Lüttwitz, did not know that reinforcements had already reached Bastogne, but thought that it would not take long before they did. So, he ordered an attack by all available forces the next day so as to ensure control of the town.

Only the 2nd Panzer was to continue its advance to the Meuse.

Von Lüttwitz had inadequate intelligence as to the real situation. He did not know that Longvilly was still in the hands of the Americans, and that his forces were not in a favourable position to launch the attack that he wanted.

See page 329 for details of enemy forces around Bastogne.

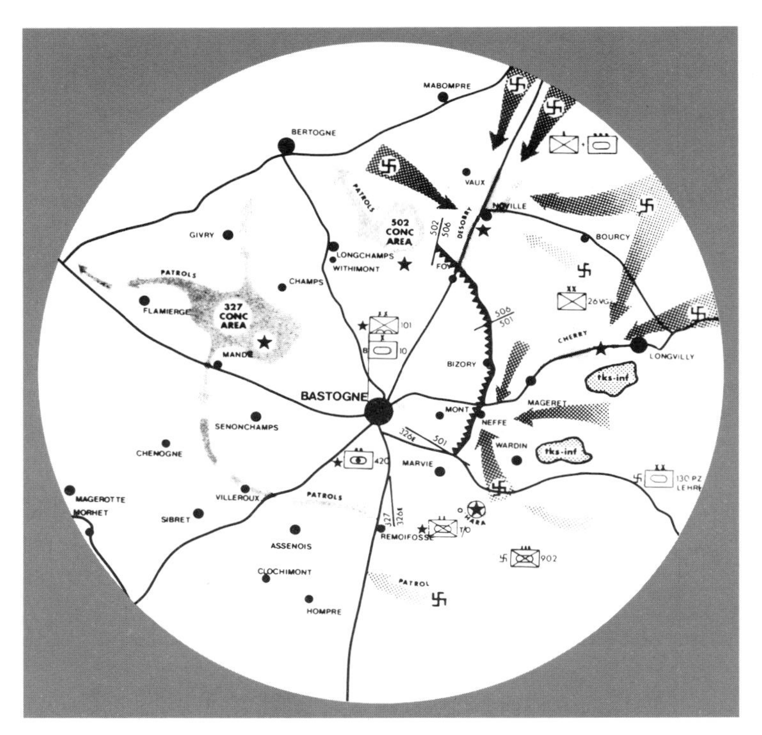

19th December

The most advanced elements of the Panzer Lehr...

TUESDAY 19th DECEMBER 1944

"There is a battle now going on for Bastogne" (General Middleton).

1 a.m. General Bayerlein and his combat group, the most advanced elements of the Panzer Lehr, had taken up position in Mageret.

Now the fate of Bastogne was being decided.

If Bayerlein, reinforced by the tanks and armoured half-tracks that were arriving slowly, had continued towards Bastogne which was at the same distance from him as from the 101st, he would have entered the town without any problems because no adequate defence had yet been organized between his troops and the town. But Bayerlein did not know this. On the contrary, he was very worried because all day he had heard extensive and heavy artillery fire all round him, largely accounted for by the attack of the 2nd Panzer on the positions held by Rose and Harper. He had heard the sound of engines – those of the Americans trying to get away from Longvilly or to get clear of the roads where they had become bogged down. Added to this were the noise of the guns defending Longvilly and the sound of his own vehicles coming to join him. But he had no reliable information permitting him to obtain an accurate analysis of the situation. He was in the dark, literally and metaphorically, with the thick fog further restricting any useful reconnaissance.

To try to get a better picture of the situation, Bayerlein had questioned a villager, Emile Frère, who revealed that a strong American force had passed through the village a few hours previously in the direction of Longvilly under the command of a general. The civilian had of course grossly exagerated the strength of the combined force of Ryerson and Hyduke, but Bayerlein did not know this. He adopted a good old principle: "When in doubt, dig in".

And a first road-block was established on the Neffe-Longvilly road with three tanks, infantry support and a minefield preventing the approach.

The Neffe Château.
(The château was destroyed during the fighting and never rebuilt.)

Ryerson sent a half-track full of infantrymen...

This road-block split Team Cherry in two, forcing the CCR survivors of the 9th Armored Division to stop their retreat to Bastogne by the main road and caught Teams Ryerson and Hyduke in a crossfire.

Cherry and his superior Colonel Roberts agreed that Longvilly had to be abandoned. However, Roberts decided to wait until daylight before ordering the retreat.

What was Team Cherry's situation?

Around Longvilly, the most advanced group had been in position for a few hours under Hyduke's orders. He had placed his tanks in a good position to control the main road. Located on a hill, they were protected from an attack by the soggy or steep fields which were impossible terrain even for the best of tanks.

Captain William F. Ryerson was at the head of the second group, the main part of the force, in position between Mageret and Longvilly.

The third group defended the command post set up in the Neffe Château.

2 a.m. Desobry arrived at Noville with the major part of his force made up of a company of Sherman tanks of the 3rd Tank Battalion, a company of the 20th Armored Infantry Battalion, with engineers, medics and scouts, in all about 400 men.

2.30 a.m. Road-blocks were established on all access roads to Noville except the Bastogne road.

The road-block on the Bourcy road had barely been put into place when a platoon of the CCR of the 9th Armored Division arrived, having managed to extricate themselves from the traffic jam. The men were incorporated into the village defence, with any other survivors.

3 a.m. Ryerson sent a half-track full of infantrymen towards Mageret to investigate the situation. On the other side, at about the same time, a tank destroyer of the 811th Tank Battalion of the 9th Division tried to do the same thing. Very quickly the men of the half-track and the tank destroyer realized that it was impossible to get through except by fighting. The Germans were blocking the road.

But the Germans continued their advance with the troops clustered around the tanks.

Private Bernard Michin adjusted his bazooka.

All night German patrols prowled round the American positions, some even managing to steal weapons or trying to capture the stuck vehicles, taking advantage of the confusion.

4 a.m. The 73rd Field Artillery Battalion started to pull out under the protective fire of the 58th. On their side, the Germans who had consolidated their positions in Mageret also opened fire.

4.30 a.m. Suddenly, at Noville, the stream of retreating Americans stopped.

5.30 a.m. The first German half-tracks could be heard. There was a short 20 minutes' fighting between a reconnaissance group of the 2nd Panzer and the defenders of the road-block on the Noville-Bourcy road commanded by Sergent Leon Gantt.

The German scouts, impressed by the American defence, retired and reported to Colonel Meinhart von Lauchert, commander of the 2nd Panzer. Overestimating the adversary, he obtained permission from General von Lüttwitz to start a sweeping move from the north in order to attack Noville from several directions. Fighting started in dense fog and two hills were taken by the Germans, one south-east of Noville and the other about 800 yards north-east of the village.

The twelve leading tanks of the Panzer Lehr with two companies of panzergrenadiers began their advance from Mageret towards Neffe and Bastogne. As they moved forward cautiously in the dark, they came under small arms fire probably from some retreating soldiers of the CCR of the 9th Armored Division who were positioned on the hill top waiting for the arrival of the remainder of the column or of daylight...

But the Germans continued their advance with the troops clustered around the tanks. They approached a road-block established by the 35th Combat Engineers Battalion. This was part of the defence line that Middleton had ordered to be set up between Foy and Neffe under the command of Lieutenant-Colonel Sam Tabets of the 158th. The Panzer Lehr had already run up against this line at Mageret the night before.

One of the road-block's defenders, Private Bernard Michin suddenly saw the shape of an enemy tank looking out of the fog. He adjusted his bazooka and fired at the monster at a distance of less than 10 yards. The German tank exploded and seriously burned Michin. But the courageous sapper did

A German infantry company slipped round by the south across the fields.

...the sodden ground prevented the tanks from leaving the roads.

not run away. Burned and blinded, he threw some hand grenades in the direction of the noise of a machine-gun which was spraying the road-block. The firing stopped, indicating that his grenades had reached their target, and he collapsed.

But this heroic action was not enough to silence the German arms, and the road-block continued to suffer a withering fire.

The Germans did not know that the defenders were pulling back, carrying Michin and some thirty other wounded towards Bastogne, while one of the two tanks defending the cross-roads retreated towards the Neffe Château.

Cherry's command post had lost the protection of the road-block which had stopped access to Neffe, but the Germans seemed hesitant to pursue their advantage. The fighting was limited to a small arms duel. While the grenadiers cleared the access by removing the mines, an infantry company slipped round by the south across the fields and advanced towards the château, but without the help of tanks because the sodden ground prevented them from leaving the roads.

At Bastogne, Lieutenant-Colonel Julian Ewell, knowing well his bold men from the 501st Parachute Infantry Regiment, nicknamed the "Geronimos", thought he had better calm them down before the unknown situation instead of letting them rush into a trap, and said, "Take it slow and easy, I don't want you to beat them to death".

In fact, there was no coordination between the parachutists of the 101st and the tank men of the 10th Armored Division – each was unaware of what the other was doing, and Ewell did not know either of the presence of Bayerlein in Mageret and of his advanced guard at Neffe.

6 a.m. Under the command of Major Raymond Bottomly, the first group, consisting of the 1st Infantry Battalion, an anti-aircraft unit and a reconnaissance platoon, a total of about 400 men, moved towards its objective, Longvilly! The remainder of the regiment was waiting in the Main Square, Place du Carré, in Bastogne.

At Noville, Sergeant-Major Jones held a road-block, with two tanks and a combat section, on the Houffalize road. Through the fog he heard the sound of approaching tanks, and although unaware of the nationality of the oncoming troops,

At Neffe, the panzergrenadiers reached the small railway station.

Route taken by Ewell's paratroops to leave Bastogne. On the right the Seminary, on the left the Hospice and in the distance, the church.

he opened fire, without scoring a hit. The return was rapid, and his two tanks were destroyed by three German panzers which pushed the section back toward Noville, leaving the route open for the 2nd Panzer to reach the Houffalize-Bertogne-Sprimont road. This latter village was on the route taken by the 101st Airborne to get to Bastogne.

A German 88mm gun, firing from the Houffalize road, destroyed six vehicles in the centre of Noville.

7 a.m. At dawn, with 300 men, First-Lieutenant Richard B. Miller, leader of the Scouts Section of the 705th Tañk Destroyer Battalion, advanced slowly along the Liège road north of Houffalize. His progress was made difficult by the number of American troops on the road. They told him that Houffalize was occupied by the Germans, so he diverted to La Roche where he set up a road-block, while the battalion commander, Lieutenant-Colonel Clifford D. Templeton, carried on to Bastogne where he hoped to get a clear picture of the situation at VIIIth Corps headquarters.

Shortly after daybreak, General Middleton's Packard was ready to set off for Neufchâteau, where VIIIth Corps headquarters were beeing set up in a school. Just as he was leaving, Middleton said to McAuliffe, "Now, Tony, you will soon be surrounded but don't worry. Hold tight! Patton is coming to help. You have first-class troops. There is plenty of artillery that can saturate any area near Bastogne. I would have liked to stay, but Hodges told me to go. I will keep in touch".

The panzergrenadiers and General Bayerlein's eleven panzers reached the small railway station at Neffe, where they remained for nearly an hour which lost them their last chance of entering Bastogne while it was still undefended.

In fact, it was during this hour that the first 400 American parachutists left Bastogne. Passing the church, Ewell's men pushed out into the fog and semi-darkness, mistaking their route and heading towards Marvie instead of Neffe. They marched for a short time when a rumour from the rear of the column reached the scouts. They had got lost. Ewell, who had waited with the remainder of the regiment on the Place du Carré, arrived in his jeep, realized the error and joined the

All those who did not have correct equipment had to return to the town.

This unpublished photgraph, taken by Luther E. Barrick of the 907th Glider Field Artillery Battalion, shows the first German prisoners captured by Ewell's men between Bastogne and Neffe. They are driven to Bastogne under the control of a Sherman and two jeeps with .30 machine guns.

head of the column the moment they turned back. There were plenty of ripe comments among the Geronimos:

"Whatsamatter, you guys gotta have a pathfinder plane?"

"Whatsamatter, you guys miss the drop zone?"

"Whatsamatter, you guys got shit up your necks?"

"Hey, you guys get on the ball. Us Geronimos got a date with the Krauts."

7.45 a.m. They marched finally on the right road, but without any protection of their flanks, because Ewell had ordered Major Raymond Bottomly, commander of the 1st Battalion, not to slow down the march by placing guards on their flanks before getting to Mageret. They were followed by Battery B of the 81st Anti-Aircraft Defence Battalion, consisting of seven 57mm guns.

It is important to remember that the parachutists had no idea that Bayerlein had got between them and Team Cherry. Some of them had no helmets, others no ammunition, and Ewell ordered all those who did not have correct equipment to return to the town.

The unfortunates who went back up the column were not spared sarcastic comments: "Running away then ? You gonna join them goddam stragglers".

To which the badly equipped retorted, "Yeah, why not ? This ain't my war no more son. Yeah you'll wind up in one of them rapple-depples and get reassigned where the pay ain't so good, son. What'll you do with no Gerominos taking care of you, son ? Yeah, I'll get me reassigned to the States, buddy. Yeah.".

Darkness and fog continued to limit visibility and the same did the bends in the road. They passed a group of gunners from the 9th Armored Division who offered to support their attack.

8 a.m. Suddenly, after another bend, when they were about 600 yards from Neffe, they heard the hammering of a machine-gun. The rounds whistled everywhere, and the first soldiers threw themselves to the ground while others jumped into the roadside ditches.

The machine-gun was hidden to the west of Neffe but had claimed no victims. Bottomly placed his men on the road

This battery of the 907th Glider Field Artillery Battalion was positioned in a field under the Hill of the Mardasson where the American Memorial and the Bastogne Historical Center are now standing. The guns, as it can be seen on the photographs, were firing in all directions.
Above, from left: Strand, Phillips, Baumgardner, Grevatt, Coladnato.
Below, from left: Deangles, Udy, Grevatt, Strand, Barrick.
Unpublished photographs: Bud Lauer.

banks and near-by hills. Panzers began to open fire sweeping the road which the Geronimos had just abandoned.

Obviously, the Americans could do nothing against tanks in open country.

A hundred or so yards to the rear of their positions, a farm house, hidden by the curve of the road and a small hill, was found suitable for an advanced command post. Ewell established himself there and, using liaison officers, called up artillery support.

Meanwhile the parachutists had discovered that the Germans were also attacking elsewhere as well. They were firing at a large building – the Neffe Château, and they concluded that it contained friendly troops under attack by tanks and grenadiers coming from the direction of Mageret. On the Bastogne road, the panzergrenadiers did not continue their attack in the face of the determined American opposition.

8 a.m. At Longvilly, the 58th Artillery Battalion, who was still defending the road-block, was heavily attacked with mortar fire, when suddenly through the fog they saw two huge panzers. Quickly loading and firing their guns, they destroyed both tanks.

8.30 a.m. The outposts at Noville had been evacuated, and while the defenders were being incorporated into the village defences, the Germans moved into the abandoned positions. The village was showered with tank and armoured artillery shells. Two panzers approached along the Houffalize road to within 20 yards of the American fox-holes. Behind them was a medium tank equipped with a 75mm gun and a 57mm cannon. Bazooka and cannon fire broke the enemy advance and machine-gun fire drove off the grenadiers who were following the tanks.

10 a.m. With his 1st Battalion bogged down outside Neffe, Ewell sent out the 2nd with orders to assemble outside the town beyond the bridge which crossed the railway line, sheltered by the positions held by the 1st Battalion.

Severe losses were inflicted to the Panzer Lehr by Battery B of the 907th Glider Field Artillery Battalion, commanded by Captain Gerald J. McGlone, when, from its position 500 yards behind the Geronimos, it started to shell the Germans round Neffe. The powerful 105mm howitzers killed or seriously

The panzergrenadiers hesitated to follow the tanks across open country.

Desobry lost a tank-destroyer.

injured nearly 80 grenadiers, and General Bayerlein, listening to the sound of firing through the fog, thought that he was under fire from an armoured force, so he took cover in the basement of a house near Neffe station.

Meanwhile in Bastogne, the 755th Armored Field Artillery Battalion arrived, under the command of Lieutenant-Colonel William F. Hartman, having left Germany the previous evening. The 155mm howitzers had to stay outside the town because of the traffic congestion.

At Noville, the fog was lifting in places by 10 o'clock, and the visibility was improving. Suddenly Desobry's men were confronted with the impressive sight of a large number of panzers moving in a semi-circle towards the village. In the swirling fog, a ridge was momentarily visible some 200 yards to the left – overhung with panzers. In another brief break in the fog, they saw 14 panzers on a long hill 800 yards to the north-east. Just from the window in his command post in the village school, Captain Omar R. Billet could count 30 panzers.

Major Desobry realized that his team was facing a whole division.

10.30 a.m. The panzergrenadiers hesitated to follow the tanks across open country, and the combat became a duel between armoured vehicles. As the battle was beginning, a platoon of self-propelled guns of the 609th Tank Destroyers arrived at Noville just in time to join the forces already in place. On the other side, the 2nd Panzer was assisted by a regiment of the 16th Panzer Division which was also bypassing Bastogne.

By making use of shelter provided by village houses, the Americans gained an advantage which enabled them to hit 9 out of the 14 German tanks on the hill. Three panzers were burning, but one Panther tank was still continuing to advance by a small earth road towards Noville. But it was stopped short by a lucky shot from a small calibre scout car gun.

The result of this engagement was very favourable to Team Desobry, which only lost four light vehicles, a tank destroyer and about 30 wounded. The 2nd Panzer had paid dearly for its attack, with 19 tanks put out of action. But sheltering under the protection of the hills, the 2nd Panzer remained danger-

Previously unpublished photograph taken on the 19th december 1944 from a slope looking east towards Bizory. The Saint Jacques Wood is on the left.
From left to right: Lieutenant Joseph Harman, who was to be killed on the 22nd December by a stone from a house blown up by a shell, and Walter A. Lengieza from Chicopee, Massachusetts.
Company F, 3rd Platoon, 501st Regiment.
Photograph: M. Bando.

ous and began to destroy the village with systematic shell-fire.

As his superior and friend had warned him, Desobry began to think it might be preferable to abandon the village.

In Bastogne, Ewell now ordered his last Battalion forward with the sole idea of driving the Germans from the area round Neffe.

The defence of Bastogne was far from secure. However, the decision had been taken to move the divisional headquarters from Mande-St-Etienne to the barracks in Bastogne left vacant by the departure of the VIIIth Corps.

11 a.m. At Verdun, Eisenhower had arrived by road from Paris and opened the meeting by a direct question to Patton: "When will you be able to attack?"

"The morning of December 22nd", Patton said, "with three divisions: the 4th Armored, the 25th and 80th Infantry divisions".

This reply created a shock among the other officers. Some were relieved while others were openly sceptical. Eisenhower lost his temper: "Don't be fatuous, George", he said, sternly.

But Patton was radiant. This was the greatest moment in his career.

12.30 a.m. The 2nd Battalion of the Geronimos took two hours to reach their destination, Bizory, where they were to join forces with the engineers, sent the previous day by Middleton.

Ewells' 3rd Battalion had difficulty in clearing a way through Bastogne, hindered by the number of vehicles and men who were accelerating the evacuation of the VIIIth Corps General Headquarters, thus congesting the traffic. The parachutists of the 3rd Battalion were not idle, howerer; they took the opportunity of increasing their supply of equipment by taking anything useful left by Middleton's men.

On the other hand, the quartermaster service of the CCB of the 10th Division had gathered all the arms and ammunition available, in order to increase the Geronimos' fire power.

Ewell ordered his 2nd Battalion to advance and seize Mageret, thus hoping to trap the Germans in Neffe.

Major Sammie N. Homan, commander of the 2nd Battalion, set off at the head of one of his companies to capture a small

Lieutenant-General Fritz Hermann Bayerlein,
Commander of the Panzer Lehr.

They decided to send the 1st Battalion of the 506th to reinforce Noville.

wood directly north of Mageret. He followed the Bizory-Mageret road.

Climbing a hill towards Mageret, he ran into a reconnaissance platoon from the 77th Regiment of the 26th VGD, well dug in on the crest. The Americans won the first round and the Germans retreated, suffering heavy losses from the mortar fire of the Geronimos and the artillery fire which had been called in. Homan, however, decided that he could do no more and radioed Ewell to say that he would not be able to take Mageret for the time being.

General Bayerlein was pessimistic. He was unable to move forward, and he heard firing on both sides of him – on the right from Homan's men and on the left from the Neffe Château defenders. He concluded that several infantry battalions were marching towards him on three sides, so he decided to retreat to Mageret. He passed through the village just a while before the main body of Ryerson's force ran into his road-block.

Lieutenant-General Fritz Bayerlein, commander of the Panzer Lehr, was aged 49, thick, strong, and an aggressive energetic leader. The sharpness of his look was striking. He had been Rommel's chief of staff in North Africa. But although he was an excellent soldier, he did not seem to be at his best form.

The 3rd Battalion, under the orders of Lieutenant-Colonel George M. Griswold, had reached Mont, a village on the route towards the objective fixed by Ewell which was to reach Neffe by the south passing via the château. To ensure his protection, Griswold had to send a company to the village of Wardin which Ewell thought was held by Team O'Hara.

Events were moving fast!

An impromptu conference took place between Roberts, Brigadier-General Gerald J. Higgins, assistant to the 101st Airborne Commander, and Colonel Robert F. Sink, who commanded the 506th Parachute Infantry Regiment. They decided to reinforce Noville with the 1st Battalion of the 506th, while the 2nd and 3rd would be sent to Foy, halfway between Bastogne and Noville.

Desobry asked for permission to withdraw from Noville. Roberts told him that reinforcements were on their way and

"Smiling Jim", Lieutenant-Colonel James O'Hara, Commander of Team O'Hara.

left him free to make his own decision. Desobry answered, "In that case, I am going to launch a counter-attack".

Near Wardin, Lieutenant-Colonel James O'Hara and his team had very cleverly set up a road-block which controlled all the approaches on the Wiltz-Bastogne road. Well situated in a bend, they swept the straight road towards the Grand-Duchy, also permitting the defenders to be sheltered from direct fire by retiring a few paces to the protection of an embankment bordering the right of the road.

O'Hara was a very tall man, 32 years old, and always smiling no matter what the situation was, which gave him the nick-name of "Smiling Jim". He had installed his command post in a small house well back from the road-block.

The night had been calm and the defenders had spent their time gathering retreating men in the fog, mainly survivors of the 28th Division.

By about 10;30 a.m., when the trickle of stragglers had stopped altogether, O'Hara figured that it must mean that the Germans were coming next. He sent out a scouting party towards Bras, in the direction of the nearby Luxembourg frontier.

As they made their way along the ditches, the scouts saw a Kübelwagen* filled with grenadiers which was coming towards them. At the moment they opened fire on it, killing the occupants, they saw two Mark IV tanks and an amoured half-track a few hundred yards away. They were part of the Panzer Lehr reinforced by the 39th Riflemen of the 26th VGD. Lacking anti-tank weapons, the American platoon returned to the road-block.

* Volkswagen military model, two wheel drive light cross-country vehicle that the Americans called the "German jeep".

O'Hara asked the 420th Armored Field Artillery Battalion to concentrate their fire on Bras. He was convinced that the village was full of Germans.

He sent Captain Edward A. Carrigo, the S-2 (intelligence officer) of the Team, and one of his company commanders, First Lieutenant John D. Devereaux, to see what was happening at Wardin. As their jeep entered the village, they came across the local inhabitants who were streaming out of their cellars and running everywhere in great panic.

A professional actor and member of Barrymore family, Lieutenant Devereaux jumped into the bonnet of his jeep and spoke to the people in an unexpected French: "Don't be afraid. We Americans are here to stay. Keep to your cellars and don't be afraid any more".

Having pacified the villagers, they continued on their way across the village, but as they were leaving it, a projectile hit the shock absorber of their jeep. It did not explode, but a gap in the fog enabled the two officers to see a half-track and another German light armoured vehicle which were arriving from Benonchamps.

They skidded on all four wheels and turned around fleeing at top speed. The villagers, who had been watching, saw them racing past like a whirlwind, shouting, "The Germans are coming. Get back to your cellars". The flabbergasted look on the villagers' faces was equalled only by the grieved look on Devereaux's face.

12 a.m. O'Hara had the disagreeable feeling that the enemy was getting near. At noon, he sent Lieutenant Theodore R. Hamer in a light reconnaissance tank, followed by five medium tanks, to the top of a small hill to have a look around. The moment the first tank reached the top, and before the men could even scan the country-side, the vehicle was hit by an 88mm shell. The tank caught fire, the driver was burnt alive, and the rest of the crew wounded. Another tank was hit by a shell that killed the driver, and the remaining four tanks retreated behind the hill as rapidly as they could.

Things were starting badly for O'Hara.

1 p.m. Now German artillery fire began to hit the Team's position.

Taking advantage of the fog a Kübelwagen arrived close to the road-block, and some grenadiers were trying to clear the mines off the road; but a slight break in the fog revealed this to the American observers, and from only 200 yards away, five half-tracks and five medium tanks opened fire on the German party. However, the Germans jumped into the car and drove off unscathed. The fog was not helping the Americans.

A while later, another group of Jerrys was reported to be in the wood north-east of Wardin. A light American tank went to machine-gun them. Team O'Hara saw men coming towards them from the woods at the rear. If they were Germans, the road-block was surrounded, but their uniforms seemed strange with their trousers held tight in their short ankle-length boots. The tanks were about to fire when someone in the approaching company yelled – they were the men of Company I of the 3rd Battalion of the 501st Parachute Infantry Regiment. The main body of the Company was right behind them in the wood. This was good news for Team O'Hara.

However, the Germans were infiltrating everywhere, and the situation was "obscure" for the Americans.

1.30 p.m. The 1st Battalion of the 506th Parachute Infantry Regiment under Lieutenant-Colonel James L. Laprade arrived at Noville under a terrible barrage from German tanks and artillery. The 506th had left Mourmelon in such a hurry that, as with other parachutists, many of the men did not have helmets, and others were short of weapons and ammunition. The problem had been resolved by loading a jeep with cases of hand grenades and M1 ammunition. As the men marched towards Noville, the jeep was feeding them with ammunition. Further along, a truck had unloaded helmets, field jackets, shovels, etc., alongside the road in separate piles, and the men from the "Five-O-Sink" (the nickname of their 506th Regiment commanded by Colonel Robert F. Sink) could pick up the things they needed as they passed. Although it incurred delays, the Regiment was far more useful than before.

The American forces at Noville now counted a thousand men, 30 medium tanks and 6 tank destroyers. They faced 7000 men and 80 panzers, many of which were fitted with the famous 88mm gun, reinforced by many self-propelled guns and the divisional artillery.

Major-General Heintz Kokott,
Commander of the 26th Volksgrenadier Division.

The 506th Regiment left Bastogne.

2 p.m. At Longvilly things were getting very difficult. The order to retreat at any cost was received, but when the first tank set off for Mageret, a Pak 40 gun put it out of action, blocking the road in front of the column before it could get under way. Two half-tracks immediately behind were also destroyed.

General Bayerlein was still convinced that his Panzer Lehr Division might be attacked on all sides. He thought that the enemy forces on both his flanks had to be destroyed before he could get his full freedom of action and launch an offensive. He was still shaken by the American opposition which had stopped his progress and was further impressed by the concentration of fire of the US artillery, which he mistook for tank gun fire. He told Lüttwitz that, in his own opinion, the whole of the XXXXVIIth Corps should attack.

During the afternoon he allowed himself a short distraction. He had asked the nurses from the American hospital captured near Mageret to take care of his wounded. While he was walking among them, he noticed a very attractive young lady, shapely in her nurses' uniform with a small white cap balanced on her blond hair. He began flirting with the girl, but she did not reciprocate at all. Realizing that he was not getting anywhere – the circumstances were not really in his favour – he quickly returned to the reason he was there: the capture of Bastogne.

General Kokott agreed with Bayerlein. He thought that the initial plan was not valid anymore and that the three divisions positioned round Bastogne should assault this recalcitrant town together.

Major-General Heintz Kokott, aged 52, commander of the 26th Volksgrenadier Division, was a shy man who seldom raised his voice when speaking. Erudite and dignified, he had the respect of Manteuffel and the other commanders, who saw him as a solid, intelligent and naturally optimistic officer.

Because of accidental circumstances Longvilly had become an ideal target for three German divisions:

Furious at the delay caused to the 2nd Panzer at Noville, von Lüttwitz ordered the 77th Regiment of the 26th VGD to attack Longvilly.

Bayerlein who was determined to remove the threat on the side, sent 2 companies of armoured grenadiers, an artillery battalion and 20 self-propelled anti-tank guns through the woods.

Von Lauchert, annoyed by the continous shelling along his flank by a battery from CCR of the 9th Armored Division, sent six 88mm self-propelled guns and fifteen tank-destroyers to silence it.

Against this, stuck in their traffic jam, the Americans were able to oppose merely a handful of Shermans which could not manoeuvre adequately and the few guns positioned there.

Bayerlein attacked from the south-west, the 26th VGD from the south-east and the 2nd Panzer from the north-east.

Attacked on three sides and completely hemmed in, the Americans were literally paralysed. More by luck than design, the result was quickly achieved.

Dug in a short distance from the tangle of vehicles, Lieutenant Hyduke and his men resisted for an hour near a grotto dedicated to St-Michael and managed to put eight tanks of the 2nd Panzer out of action. When further resistance became impossible, Colonel Cherry gave them permission to retreat, which was feasible for the men but not for the equipment because the roads were already blocked by other vehicles. Hyduke ordered the destruction of their material, and all vehicles which could not be saved were blown up one after the other.

When General von Lüttwitz came to examine the results of this massive destruction of equipment, he noticed that it was a most unusual place: along the road defended by Hyduke was a grotto decorated with statues of saints and crucifixes, and partly burnt candles were strewn on the ground among the broken pieces of plaster statues. He noticed that most of the damage had been caused by the 2nd Panzer. But, even though the CCR of the 9th Armored Division had been practically wiped out, and although in this one attack, Team Cherry had lost 175 officers and men, 17 half-tracks and an unimaginable number of jeeps, trucks and light vehicles, the Germans, too, had paid a high price, leaving 15 panzers immobilized in the fields round Longvilly.

2.30 p.m. The Americans launched a counter-attack at Noville. The objective was to take the hills which surrounded the village to make their position more tenable. The attack was stopped in its tracks, however. Four Shermans were put out of action only 300 yards from their starting point, and a platoon and a half of armoured infantry was mown down by machine-gun fire. One company of the 1st Battalion of the 506th reached the bottom of the hill, but the Germans held tightly to the crests.

To the north, three-quarters of an American armoured infantry company and three Shermans supported by two parachutist companies were stopped 250 yards from their starting points.

On the left, the G.I.'s hung on at the bottom of the hill facing the village of Vaux, but on the right the men were retreating.

3 p.m. The Germans counter-attacked with sixteen tanks leading a panzer-grenadier battalion in two columns. The panzers hesitated under the bazooka fire, then retreated. Noville was on fire, and the combination of smoke and fog – which had returned – brought the visibility down to zero. The Americans made use of this to fall back and entrench themselves in Noville. The attack had been a total failure.

In Bastogne, a retreating column of 155mm guns, the famous "Long Tom", was requisitioned by Sherburne acting on McAuliffe's orders. They arrived at the right moment and were sent to give reinforcement to the artillery installed south-east of the town, but they were to be captured by the Germans the following night.

The positioning of the available artillery continued: one battery of the 907th Field Artillery Battalion equipped with 105mm guns was situated 1500 yards to the north-east of Bastogne, and another at 1000 yards to the east of the town.

The Americans in Bastogne were commanded by an artillery specialist – McAuliffe had been the officer commanding the artillery of the 101st Airborne before taking over command from the absent General Taylor – and the strong point of the Bastogne defences was to be the artillery. Eleven artillery battalions were assembled at this moment, about 130 guns, which was a considerable force when used well. And it was!

Captain James E. Parker in conversation with officers of the 101st Airborne
(In the centre with a microphone in his left hand).

A platoon worked its way forwards under cover of the trees.

Until then, the air force had been unable to play any role in the battle, but they sent Captain James E. Parker of the 9th Air Force to Bastogne. He was the air controller and needed a high frequency transmitter in order to communicate with aircraft. There was none but a similar set was found in a 10th Armored Division jeep, and his deputy was able to make it work.

4 p.m. A platoon of Ewell's 3rd Battalion of the 501st worked its way carefully forwards from Mont towards Neffe, taking advantage of the cover afforded by the trees. They reached the Château which Cherry and his men were occupying – a welcome reinforcement but unfortunately too late in coming because the Germans had managed to get close to the château walls in spite of the intense fire of the defenders who had been running from window to window to make the attackers believe there were more of them. The grenadiers slipped along the walls, threw incendiary grenades into the windows, and set fire to the château. Breathing smoke and surrounded by fire, the defenders continued to fight until nightfall when they escaped towards the nearest American lines at Mont.

Before leaving, Cherry, remembering Middleton's order of "no retreat", sent the following message to Combat Command B: "We are not driven out... we're burned out. We're not withdrawing... we're moving".

At Wardin, the course of events had not gone so well either. At 2.15 p.m., Company I of the 3rd Battalion of Lieutenant-Colonel M. Griswold had surprised a patrol of 25 panzergrenadiers. But General Bayerlein, who felt threatened, had sent part of his reconnaissance battalion towards the village and the parachutists had a rough time. They fought courageously in close house fighting, as Bayerlein's self-propelled long-range artillery knocked out their defensive points one after the other.

One parachutist rushed out to meet one of the guns, fired his bazooka and put the tracked vehicle out of action, but collapsed, cut down by enemy fire.

5.15 p.m. Finally the parachutists received the order to retreat. The survivors of the Company fell back to a ridge north of Marvie,

Finally the parachutists received the order to retreat.

Lieutenant-Colonel Robert A. Ballard had established a regimental command post in the Petit Seminaire.

under the cover of a huge artillery barrage by the 420th Artillery Battalion. The fire was not returned, but the fight had cost the Company dear: the commander, 5 officers and 85 men had been killed, wounded or were missing.

Wardin was in the hands of the Germans, and Devereaux's promise to the villagers had not been kept – their terror had been justified.

5-6 p.m. After the resistance encountered at Neffe, Bizory and Wardin, Colonel Ewell was convinced that he did not have sufficient strength to attack. He went to McAuliffe's headquarters and suggested that he should establish a line of defence on the hills which ran from Bizory to the south. McAuliffe agreed, though certain members of his staff thought that Ewell was being somewhat cautious, despite the fact that his flank facing Wardin had become very vulnerable and that he had had to organize an all-round defense.

O'Hara received the order to retire to a line located to the north of the village of Marvie to link up with Ewell's men, who had received the reinforcement of a battalion of the 327th Glider Infantry Regiment.

The new front line was to be situated less than one mile from Bastogne, which increased its density by decreasing its length. But the Germans were getting closer to Bastogne, and the officer in charge of operational planning for the 501st Regiment, Captain Elvy Roberts, could not help thinking, "I'll probably lose my job tonight". But this did not happen, and those who doubted the wisdom of Ewell's proposal were soon to learn its strength.

While this was happening and in the absence of Ewell, Lieutenant-Colonel Robert A. Ballard, second in command of the 501st, had established a regimental command post in the Petit Seminaire, a large group of buildings on the edge of Bastogne on the Neffe Road.

Shortly after nightfall, Captain Ryerson and his men, Company C of the 20th Armored Infantry Battalion of Team Cherry, having waited all day to be reinforced by the infantry, still held the three houses situated north-east of Mageret.

General Bayerlein's men attacked and destroyed three vehicles with their anti-tank guns. The grenadiers followed them

An artillery barrage by the 420th Battalion.

The village of Foy. (Photograph taken in January 1945).

but were halted by an artillery barrage by the 420th Battalion, which had been very active and useful all day long.

7.30 p.m. General Higgins arrived at Noville to find it quiet. He promised his G.I.'s assault guns and tank destroyers for the following day.

After Higgins' departure, Colonel Robert F. Sink, commanding the 506th, discussed plans for that night with LaPrade and Desobry.

They were joined by Major Robert F. Harwick, executive officer of the 1st Battalion of the 506th, who arrived unexpectedly in Noville.

During the conference, an 88mm shell shot through a large cupboard which had been placed in front of the window for protection. LaPrade was killed and Desobry was badly wounded in the head by splinters which entered the back of his head and removed an eye. Harwick, newly arrived, found himself in charge of the Noville defences, and Major Charles L. Hustead replaced Desobry, who was evacuated by jeep to a first-aid post of the 506th Infantry Regiment. There, transferred to an ambulance, Desobry was en route to a hospital when he was captured by a German patrol.

Noville was bombarded all night by German artillery. Two panzers tried to enter the village but were destroyed.

The Americans held on tight. However, when they realized that their hours were numbered and that they would be unable to hold Noville for another day, Sink and Higgins asked McAuliffe to get authorization to retreat towards Foy.

Middleton refused. "No, if we are to hold on to Bastogne, you cannot keep falling back".

During the night, the 3rd Battalion of the 506th positioned itself at Foy, while the 2nd Battalion took up position at Luzery. They formed an east-west line of resistance, between Noville and Bastogne. On the right they rubbed shoulders with Ewell's 501st, along the railway line which led from Bourcy in the north-east to Bastogne. On the left was Chappuis' 502nd.

Lieutenant-Colonel Clifford Templeton, an officer who loved to discuss any subject, visited General Middleton at Neufchâteau. From there he went on to Bastogne where he

The 705th Tank Destroyer Battalion.

The 101st Airborne hospital.

left McAuliffe's headquarters in the afternoon to meet his armoured column, the 705th Tank Destroyer Battalion, which had left La Roche for Bastogne on his orders. At Bertogne, Templeton was ambushed. Three of his companions were wounded and his jeep destroyed, but he managed to escape on foot and reach Bastogne. His Battalion continued its way to Bastogne under the command of Lieutenant Victor L. Miller. They were obliged to make a detour via the bridge at Ortheuville, because the bridge to the north of Bertogne had been destroyed. Miller left two platoons and eight tank-destroyers to protect the bridge, reinforced by the survivors of the 158th Combat Engineers of Lieutenant-Colonel Sam Tabets.

8.30 p.m. The remainder of the 705th arrived in Bastogne, a precious reinforcement of 36 tank-destroyers armed with the powerful 76 mm guns.

The 101st Airborne hospital had been set up to the west of the assembly zone at the crossroads close to the "Barrière Hinck", near Sprimont, where McAuliffe had chanced to turn toward Bastogne on the 17th, to be followed later by most of his division.

10.15 p.m. An armoured group from the 116th Panzer – six armoured vehicles, tanks and half-tracks – together with about 100 infantrymen, some curiously dressed in civilian clothes, reached there along the Houffalize road, under the orders of Captain Kroll. The moment they reached the crossroads, a dozen American GMC trucks arrived from Bastogne, and these were immediately destroyed, despite the resistance of the truck drivers and their mates using. 50 calibre machine-guns firing from turrets in the cabs of some of the trucks.

Lit up by the flames from the burning vehicles and the building at the crossroads, the red-crosses on the American tents making up the hospital were clearly visible. But the Germans took no notice and attacked, destroying many vehicles. The tents were cut to pieces by machine-gun fire, and tracer shells set some alight.

After fifteen minutes of hopeless resistance, the senior officer and divisional surgeon, Lieutenant-Colonel David Gold, surrendered to Captain Kroll. He was given half an hour in which

Captain Kroll simply ensured German control of the crossroads.

A thirty-strong German patrol infiltrated...

to move the wounded, his personnel and all the equipment in the remaining ambulances behind the German lines.

Thus the Division lost its hospital, 11 doctors and 119 corpsmen, all from the 326th Airborne Medical Company, and the 501st Regiment lost its supply trucks which were stationed near the hospital.

But though he had the road to the Meuse wide open before him, Captain Kroll simply ensured German control of the crossroads and then ordered his men to retreat and take up positions in the village of Salle, a mile back from the crossroads, obeying the orders of the Commander of the LVIIIth Armored Corps, General Walter Krüger.

This was similar to General Bayerlein's earlier halt before an undefended Bastogne.

On the American side, an artillery barrage began to protect Team O'Hara's withdrawal, which was carried out without any losses. The engineers set up road-blocks with tree-trunks and mines, under the protection of patrols. Wardin was bombarded by fire from the available artillery.

11 p.m. A thirty-strong German patrol infiltrated between the sectors occupied by the 501st ande 506th, by way of the railway line running from Bourcy to Bastogne. A large gap already existed at that point where the two American regiments had not yet linked their defences.

In the woods, alongside the railway line, a company of the 501st was in a forward assembly area before being ordered into the line. The U.S. 907th Glider Field Artillery Battalion was a few hundred yards behind them.

A sentry from A Company spotted the German column and raised the alarm. As the Germans went past the woods, the Americans, with the aid of artillery, opened fire. The Germans scattered and the majority escaped in the woods. However, one German was made prisoner, and he revealed plans to infiltrate between the two regiments and to cut off the Bastogne-Neffe road near Bastogne, in order to isolate the 501st.

Thus the Germans had lost their second chance of getting into Bastogne.

The longest day of the Battle of Bastogne had ended.

It was decisive. The Germans could have triumphed that day, the town being taken without much trouble by the Panzer Lehr and occupied by the 26th VGD, whose primary mission would have been to protect the enormous movement of divisions which could have converged on the Meuse by all available routes. Had this happened, Bastogne, most probably, would have shared the fate of St-Vith, Houffalize, La Roche and other towns captured by the Germans: when the sky cleared up, it would have been levelled by the Allied Air Force, causing enormous losses among the civilian population hidden in its cellars.

What might have happened later? It is difficult to say. But one can imagine that things could have happened totally differently from their actual evolution.

Now Lieutenant-General Baron von Lüttwitz, commander of the German XXXXVIIth Armoured Corps, and his divisional commanders were convinced that the whole of the Corps had to attack Bastogne if they were to take the town.

General Baron von Manteuffel was not pleased. He raged against Bayerlein whom he reproached for getting lost on a mud track like a raw officer cadet unable to read a map properly. He also blamed him for a lack of fighting spirit and an undue caution.

Manteuffel knew that the Germans had just missed the chance of taking Bastogne and that if the town remained in American hands – and the Americans seemed determined it should do so – then all progress towards the west would be considerably hindered, resupply made much more difficult and important forces, needed later, would be immobilised and used up around Bastogne.

Further, if they failed, Bastogne would remain an abscess in the centre of their advance which would put their whole operation in danger.

If all the XXXXVIIth Armoured Corps was used to take the town, it would suffer, even on the best hypothesis, yet more delay in its move towards the Meuse.

But this was mere speculation, because their orders were clear: they had to advance. Bastogne was not the objective.

General Kokott had done a magnificent job in bringing up his division, the 26th VGD, composed in large part of grenadiers on foot and large wagons, drawn by 5000 horses, as quickly as the two motorized armoured divisions, the 2nd Panzer and the Panzer Lehr. At present the taking of Bastogne was his business.

Having helped his men not to be crushed on the roads by the vehicles of the two armoured divisions, Kokott was going to have to sacrifice them to take this important road junction which was blocking their advance. Manteuffel gave him the order to attack from his current positions and as soon as possible from the north which they thought less well defended. Units of the Panzer Lehr would reinforce the Volksgrenadiers, while the remainder was to continue towards the Meuse.

The town's civilian population, reassured by the American presence, stayed calm taking shelter in their cellars, in family or neighbour groups. The villagers were much worse off, trying to flee from those villages which were not yet in German hands.

The town's civilian population stayed calm taking shelter in their cellars.

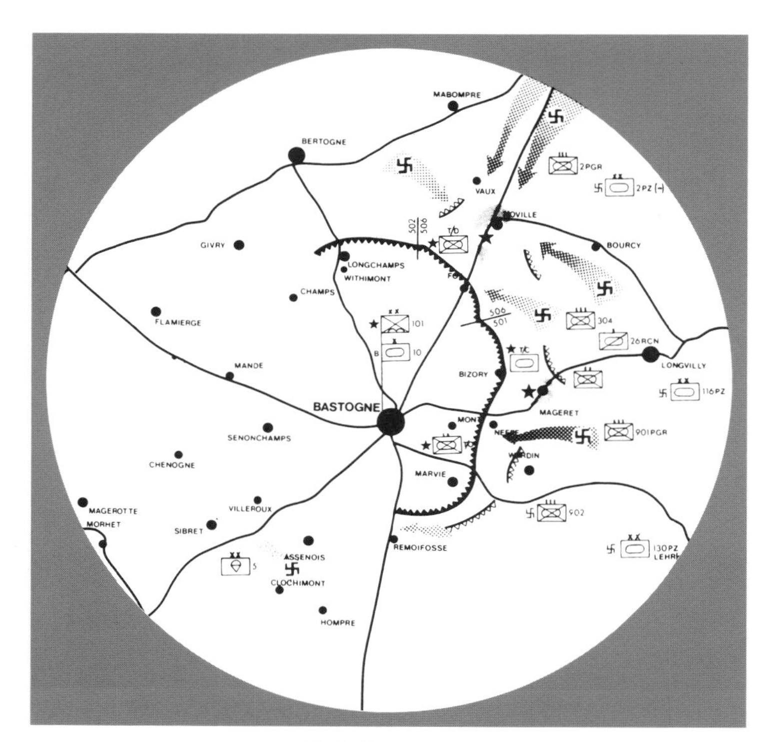

20th December

Many retreating American soldiers...

Wednesday 20th december 1944

Throughout the night, many retreating American soldiers used the cover of darkness to rejoin their lines surrounding Bastogne. They became an important personnel reserve for the organized regiments.

2 a.m. The 2nd Platoon of Company B of the 705th Tank Destroyer Battalion arrived with five 76 mm, self-propelled, long range guns to reinforce the 2nd Battalion of the 501st Regiment, commanded by Major Homan. Their guns were placed south of Bizory.

The 602nd Tank Destroyer Battalion of the Third Army was alerted for night movement. They left for "somewhere" in Belgium.

3 a.m. Colonel Roberts asked Ryerson to disengage and retreat towards Bastogne with the remainder of the 9th Armored Division to reinforce the second Battalion of the 501st Regiment at Bizory. This difficult manoeuvre was accomplished before daybreak.

4 a.m. The command post and the 2nd Battalion of the 327th Glider Infantry Regiment received the order to move from Flamizoulle, their assembly zone, to Bastogne, where they arrived at six o'clock. While the new command post was being set up, the 2nd Battalion continued towards Marvie to reinforce the 326th Engineers. The 3rd Battalion of the 327th was left at Flamizoulle where they set up their command post in a nearby wood.

5.30 a.m. Around Noville, the Germans were ready to attack again. At half past five, the entire artillery of the 2nd Panzer began to shell the village while the grenadiers attacked on three sides supported by tanks.

Team Desobry and the 1st Battalion of the 506th held the farthest position from Bastogne. At Foy, between Noville and Bastogne, the 3rd Battalion of the 506th Parachute Infantry Regiment had strengthened its positions as had done the 2nd Battalion at Luzery, a mile from McAuliffe's command post in Bastogne.

...stopped the Mark IV in its tracks. (Photo taken after the battle).

The communications centre of the 101st Airborne. (Drawing made at the time).

6.45 a.m. The Germans started to shell the road-block which O'Hara had set up on the Wiltz-Bastogne road, 1300 yards beyond Marvie. They could not be seen because of the thick fog, but a while later the Tigers (a self-imposed nickname for members of the U.S. 10th Armored Division) heard panzer movements near the road-block.

At Mageret, Bayerlein moved his panzers into a wood close to the American defences at Bizory, which were manned by the 2nd Battalion of the 501st Regiment and had been positioned at the same place where the Battalion's attack had been stopped the previous day.

Six German panzers approached from the south-west. Sergeant Floyd A. Johnson took his section to a hill situated north of Bizory and positioned two tank-destroyers on each side of the Foy Road, while Lieutenant Frederic Millon led his group to the crests of the hills south-east of the village.

7.30 a.m. The attack started with an assault by the 2nd Battalion of the 76th Regiment of the 26th VGD, followed, 400 yards behind, by a Mark IV, a Mark V and two 75mm self-propelled guns.

The American machine-guns opened fire on the grenadiers and halted their advance. Meanwhile, a duel had begun between the tank-destroyers and the panzers.

During the first salvo, one of the American destroyers was hit but it was able to reverse and take cover. The second tank-destroyer stopped the Mark IV in its tracks, then reversed, aiming into the village of Bizory, damaging its gun against a brick wall during the sudden manoeuvre. The two remaining tank-destroyers opened fire at a range of 600 yards and destroyed the damaged Mark IV as well as one of the self-propelled guns.

The day started with a tremendous noise, the reason for this being that all available American artillery opened fire for twenty minutes and broke the attack. Apart from the two damaged tank-destroyers, the American losses were minimal. The German losses were heavier because of the concentrated artillery barrage from all the guns around Bastogne.

In the divisional headquarters, McAuliffe, Higgins, Moore, Danahy, Kohls and Kinnard were becoming impatient for news. Colonel Sherburne joined them, anxious to know if his

A King Tiger charged right into the heart of Noville...

...crushing a jeep under its tracks.

artillery had been effective. Colonel Kinnard put down the telephone saying: "Julian (Ewell) says you took care of the sonabitches real, real, good, General".

For the first time in a long time, they all burst out laughing. Even McAuliffe's generally impassive face showed his feelings. He knew now that he could stand up to the enemy. Turning to Sherburne, he said: "Let your people know I appreciate it, Tom".

At half past seven, two German panzers, coming from the north, rolled into Noville at full speed, offering each other mutual protection as they crossed the village boundary. Unfortunately for them, they stopped beside a house about 10 yards away from an American team equipped with bazookas. A first shot hit one tank and set it afire, and at the same time Sergeant Michael Lesniak jumped into his Sherman and shooting at point-blank range, destroyed the second one.

A third German tank, left behind, fired a few rounds and managed to hit the turret of Lesniak's Sherman. The German artillery opened a non-stop fire. Six panzers rolled forward but were stopped by the tank-destroyers of the newly arrived 705th Battalion, the Shermans having used up all their anti-tank shells.

Finally a German King Tiger tank charged right into the heart of Noville and stopped in front of the command post of Company B of the 20th Armored Infantry Battalion, commanded by Captain Omar Billet. While the tank swung its gun uncertainly toward the door – so that someone remarked, "Don't look now, but there is an 88 pointing at the end of our noses" – manually rotating his damaged turret, Lesniak managed to fire three rounds. the Tiger backed too quickly and crushing a jeep under its tracks kept on pushing back, the jeep under it. It next collided with a half-track, and the tank tipped dangerously over on its right side. That was enough for the Germans who escaped, protected by the fog.

8. a.m. For the first time, the U.S. staff officers were assembled in their mess in one of the buildings in the barracks, a few yards from the operations room.

The head cook was a Californian of Chinese origin, Chuck Wong. With a certain self-importance he served thick hot pan-

...hot pancakes...

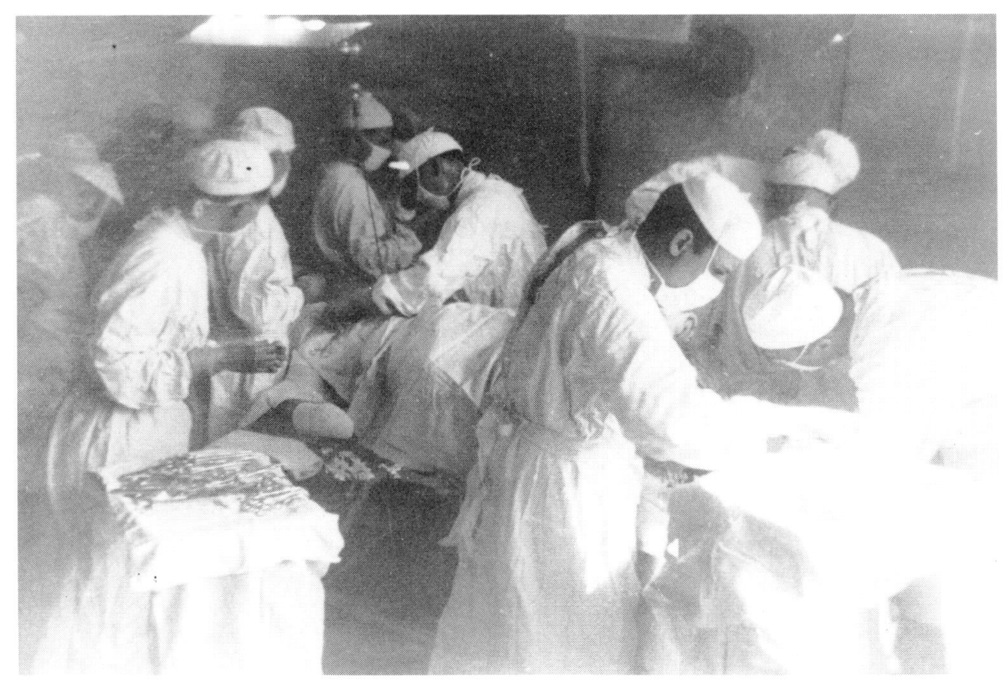

The medical stations were packed to overflowing.

cakes, which the officers spread with maple sirup and wolfed down with great satisfaction. There was no more coffee, but the Americans had adopted the Belgian wartime drink, ersatz coffee, which had the sole advantage of being hot. The walls of their mess were decorated with portraits painted by members of the Hitler Youth during their many stays in Bastogne. It was strange to see the Americans relaxing without paying the least attention to the swastikas and pretentious, idealized figures of the Aryan race.

Every day at 8 a.m. and 4 p.m. they were to meet there for a few minutes, if circumstances allowed.

8 a.m. While General Kokott was in Wardin, his special mobile command post was hit by an American shell, all the passengers being killed except for Kokott who was thrown out and who hit a church wall.

Although shaken up badly, he was still able to give orders to the 39th Regiment and the Reconnaissance Battalion of the 26th VGD regarding their advance towards Sibret. Then he went with them to check that his instructions were being carried out.

While doing this, he had the superficial impression that Bastogne was wide open and that American morale was very low, because a number of their troops were seen scattering in all directions, suggestive of a possible rout.

Meanwhile, at Foy, the 3rd Battalion of the 506th was attacked, at 8 o'clock, by tanks and armoured infantry troops coming in from the north-east and north-west. They held steadfastly until half past ten, when they had to retreat to a hill. Now, the road was cut. Noville was isolated and could not be assisted from Bastogne.

The two medical stations in the village were packed to overflowing, and most of the medical staff were wounded.

Harwick transmitted the following message, "All our reserves are engaged. The situation is critical".

This critical situation worried General McAuliffe, who was weighing the cost of maintaining this post which was difficult to defend, and which could not be covered by 75mm artillery with accuracy because their range was too limited.

And his men could not use 105 mm guns because of ammunition shortages.

What had happened since to the King Tiger which had been abandoned with its radio on and transmitting gutteral messages to the Noville defenders? A tank-destroyer team blew it up with a mine, later on catching hell from Colonel Roberts for not bringing the tank, which was actually still intact, back to Bastogne. But they had good reason. Already the losses among the tank drivers were such that they did not have enough men to handle their own tanks. Two paratroopers had to be recruited to drive the remaining Shermans.

The 2nd Platoon of Company C of the 705th Tank Destroyer Battalion, positioned south of Noville, could see no further than one hundred yards, but they were able to hear, through the fog, the muffled sounds of tracked vehicles. These noises indicated that a panzer formation was moving towards their positions, and when one of their gun crew was killed by a direct hit, the platoon opened fire. They kept firing for two hours in the general direction of the noises but saw no results.

10 a.m. When the fog lifted quite suddenly, at about 10 o'clock, the sky was clear and the artillerymen saw 15 panzers facing them. Four were destroyed – the Americans were convinced that this was the result of their firing – and the remaining eleven retreated to the cover of hills one thousand yards away.

10.30 a.m. As Noville was cut off from Bastogne, following the withdrawal from Foy, Kinnard ordered the 3rd Battalion of the 502nd, positioned near Longchamps, under the command of Lieutenant-Colonel John P. Stopka, to attack Recogne and attempt to reopen a line of communication with Noville.

11.30 a.m. The Battalion advanced without meeting any serious resistance and reached Recogne, where they ran up against the first Germans. At the moment that fighting was about to start, the order to advance was withdrawn.

The reason for this was that General McAuliffe had reached the conclusion that it was pointless to sacrifice any more men for Noville which was bound to be abandoned in the end. The order to retreat was issued with the agreement of Colonel Roberts.

In the meantime, what was happening at Marvie?

A German regiment advancing to the left of the Panzer Lehr, and who had had their share of problems already passing through the narrow roads of the Wiltz valley, came into contact with the Bastogne defences. Their commander decided that they should leave the main road to avoid the roadblock and go cross-country towards Marvie, where he hoped to rejoin the main road. However, a few men were despatched to try to open the road-block. These were the German sappers who appeared suddenly, to the surprise of O'Hara's men, when the fog had lifted for a while at about 9 o'clock. An artillery concentration from the 420th fell amongst these dozen men, and two were killed. The Germans made a smoke-screen around the road-block, but the Tigers kept firing just in front with mortars and assault guns.

When the Panzer Lehr attacked at 11.25 a.m. after a brief bombardment, it seemed to them that the village of Marvie was wide open. A self-propelled gun led four medium panzers and six half-tracks carrying infantrymen. The Germans destroyed a light tank and damaged another, and the remaining American light tanks, useless against the German heavy armour, retreated as soon as permission was received.

The German vehicles drove at full speed towards the village and, without seeing them, they went past two Shermans in ambush 700 yards away. The two American tanks destroyed two panzers and a half-track, using flanking fire. A third panzer entered Marvie without slowing down, only to be hit by bazooka fire from men of the 327th. The fourth retreated to the cover of the woods. The self-propelled gun destroyed three empty American vehicles before being blown up by concentrated fire from the Shermans and bazookas.

1.30 p.m. Four of the German half-tracks had managed to enter Marvie; the panzergrenadiers jumped from their vehicles and put up a stiff fight. By half past one, about 30 were dead and a similar number had surrendered. The sixth half-track had got caught in the mud and did not reach the village. It was abandoned and blown up quite quickly by the Shermans.

General Bayerlein's bad luck increased, and the day was not yet over!

Wrecks of the tanks of Team Cherry and the CCR of the 9th Armored Division at Longvilly.

The Company G of the 327th Glider Infantry Regiment, commanded by Colonel Harper, fought brilliantly. Although they had 15 wounded including Colonel Inman and the Company Commander, Captain Hugh Evans, they had driven out the Germans house by house and had not retreated an inch. Their five dead bore witness to their courage: when Colonel Harper examined their bodies, he realized that they had all died facing the tanks, firing with their rifles at the monsters which crushed them.

Patton asked General Middleton to attend a conference at his headquarters in Arlon. When Middleton arrived he was greeted with Patton's usual bluff manners, "Troy, of all the goddam crazy things I ever heard in my life, leaving the 101st Airborne to be surrounded in Bastogne is the worst".

Middleton made no comment, being used to Patton's abruptness. He did, however, point out the importance of Bastogne's road network.

Later on, Patton was to admit that the decision was "a brilliant one".

Patton asked Middleton what his plan would be: to attack from Arlon or Neufchâteau. Middleton replied that in his opinion the road from Arlon to Bastogne and those to the east would flank the German attack rather than running straight into it. But he added that it was quicker to get to Bastogne from Neufchâteau. And this was the road he would follow if the choice were his.

Although Patton had orders to liberate Bastogne, he liked the idea of dividing the Germans, by pushing towards St. Vith, so that he could massacre them from their rear. So he chose the longer and the more heavily defended route to Bastogne via Martelange for his main attack.

At the beginning of the afternoon, the last survivors of Colonel Cherry's armoured group, commanded by Captain Ryerson, managed to rejoin Colonel Ewell's lines at Bizory, with a few vehicles loaded with their wounded.

Meanwhile, on the Noville front, General McAuliffe had ordered heavy attacks, on both sides, to clear Foy, while the evacuation was under way at Noville. A large quantity of ammunition had to be destroyed, including a considerable

...when the fog conveniently returned, thus hiding the manoeuvre from the Germans.

While the machine-guns from the half-tracks returned the Germans' fire...
(Good example of a "meat-chopper" in action, mounted on a half-track).

number of mortar shells that could not be taken away. Over 50 wounded soldiers were put into the available vehicles, together with the armoured infantry and most of the parachutists.

The order to move out was to be given at the beginning of the fighting at Foy. As soon as the noise indicated that the battle had started, the column was to get under way.

1.15 p.m. The American column was ready to move in open view of the enemy, when, as if by some miracle, the fog conveniently returned, thus hiding the manoeuvre from the Germans.

At the head of the evacuation column was a parachutist company on foot supported by three tanks. There then followed 4 half-tracks and 5 tanks whose job was to protect the trucks carrying their many wounded. The remainder of the group followed in all sorts of vehicles, while the rearguard was made up of another company of parachutists backed by 4 tank-destroyers.

As the column was moving towards Foy, taking advantage of the fog, the first half-track which was filled with wounded ran into trouble, stalled, and was hit violently by the following half-track.

The progress of the column, whose head had reached Foy, was stopped, and the Americans immediately came under fire from automatic weapons.

The Germans were firing from the sides of the road and from a farm. While the machine-guns from the half-tracks returned the Germans' fire, the American soldiers dove into the road side ditches for shelter.

Then the column got under way again, continuing to fire with all available weapons. The half-tracks quickly arrived at Foy, but the first tank hesitated to advance in the fog. Major Hustead had to intervene. He ordered the tank crew to fire on the farm and the driver to move forward. The farm was soon burning, and the tanks set out again. Three panzers hidden in ambush behind the farm building opened fire on the Shermans, burning the first and immobilizing the second.

By nightfall, the American column had reached Bastogne.

Captain William G. Schutz, commander of a tank company, left the fifth Sherman to make the third one in the column move forward again. It quickly reached Foy in its turn, but was hit while it was crossing the village.

Captain Schutz and the crew abandoned the tank and continued on foot towards Bastogne. When the fourth tried to get moving, a well aimed shot removed its turret. The fifth tank had no driver because he had gone to help extricate the second tank. So the column was stuck, and Major Hustead searched in vain for a replacement driver among the tank crews.

Meanwhile, the parachutists had left the road and reached Foy across the fields, followed, without problems, by the tank-destroyers. A parachute officer spotted the panzers which were hidden at a short distance from the farm, jumped into a tank-destroyer and ordered the driver, Thomas E. Gallagher, to take on the panzers. Gallagher pointed out that he had no crew, and two parachutists came to fill this gap. The new crew manoeuvred so well that the first shot fired by the parachutists destroyed one of the German tanks, forcing the two others to retire.

Freed from the menace of the panzers, the remainder of the column was able to continue on its way. Some of the armoured vehicles, among them the fifth tank, were driven by parachutists, who were grinding the gears of those “bloody tanks”.

By nightfall, the American column had reached Bastogne.

The battle for Noville was over. Of the fifteen tanks which had gone into battle on 19th December with Team Desobry, four returned to Bastogne. Two hundred men from the Tigers were out of action, and the parachutists of the 3rd Battalion of the 506th Regiment had lost 13 officers and 199 men.

During the afternoon, patrols had confirmed reports that indicated that the location known as La Halte was in German hands. It was located on the Bastogne-Bourcy railway line at the junction of Ewell’s and Sink’s men. But there had been no link up, and Sink was furious at not having contacted the Geronimos. With his usual manner of brusque speaking, he telephoned Kinnard: “If you want me to make contact with them damned Geronimos, you’d better attach ‘em to me”.

Colonel Robert F. Sink,
Commander of the
506th Parachute Infantry Regiment.

Corporal Frank Lasik, accompanied by one of his men...

Sink was the only surviving commander of the original regiments. His nervousness could be explained by his fear at seeing the Germans slipping round his right flank, which he felt to be undefended, to attack his men from the rear.

Unperturbed, Ewell had carried out a personal reconnaissance and had not found the Five-O-Sink either. The reason was simple: Sink's men were several hundred yards further forward than Ewell's, and the fog was hiding them from discovery.

6 p.m. Corporal Frank Lasik, of Company D of the 2nd Battalion of the 501st, accompanied by one of his men, was sent towards La Halte to discover the strength of the German force. They counted seven panzers, reinforced by infantry, advancing along the railway line towards Bastogne. Lasik and his companion withdrew quickly and alerted Company A which was positioned in the wood, south of the railway line, and which was to assure liaison with Sink's 506th.

They planned an ambush by deploying the 3rd Platoon of Company A along the edge of the wood, north of the railway line. The fog was so thick that the hidden soldiers opened fire when the column was only 10 yards away. The leading Germans retreated rapidly, but the rest of the column, reacting quickly, opened fire on the 1st and 2nd Platoons of Company A with mortars, grenades and automatic weapons. A fight started in the fog which caused confusion. Each soldier could see only his opponent's fire and so, aimed at that. Company A lost 15 men, 3 of whom were killed in this action. The night was so black that only the clatter of the weapons enabled one to locate anyone – friend or foe.

Apart from the continous throwing of hand-grenades by both sides, things quietened down for about an hour and a half. Then the Germans started to withdraw through the wood on their left. The Americans, worried about being encircled, withdrew also.

By 10.30 p.m., the whole of Company A had disengaged.

7. p.m. At Neffe, Bayerlein decided on a new attack using the 902nd Panzergrenadier Regiment. The American positions at Bizory, Mont and the crossroads were subjected to a violent bombardment from tanks and self-propelled guns.

At Neffe, Bayerlein decided on a new attack using the 902nd Panzergrenadier Regiment. (Drawing made at the time).

Two Panthers and a King Tiger were destroyed when they passed the last houses of the village.
(Although taken after the battle, this photo shows exactly the vehicles destroyed on the outskirts of Neffe).

At the same time, the 1st Battalion of the 501st was attacked from the Neffe road. The clatter of tracks was heard by Major Raymond V. Bottomly, but he could see nothing in the darkness, whereas a patrol from Team O'Hara spotted Bayerlein's tanks which were edging their way up the road. The patrol informed the artillery observers, and all the guns of eleven artillery battalions of the Bastogne perimeter concentrated their fire on the area between Neffe and the forward positions of the 1st Battalion of the 501st Regiment.

This was the most violent artillery barrage to take place during the whole battle for Bastogne.

The column of the 902nd was taught a severe lesson. Many vehicles exploded under the American fire. Two Panthers and a King Tiger were destroyed when they passed the last houses of the village.

The German infantry which had advanced along the Bastogne road beyond Neffe, was suddenly caught by the fire from a machine-gun nest, cleverly hidden in an isolated house at the roadside. This concentrated fire alone was sufficient to keep the grenadiers at bay and, eventually, to kill them all. The furthest grenadiers were 300 yards beyond the destroyed panzers.

At the same time, the 3rd Battalion, defending the Mont sector, was attacked as well. At the end of the day, the 1st Platoon of Company B of the 705th Tank Destroyers, led by First-Lieutenant Robert Andrews, had come to reinforce the men of the 3rd Battalion of the 501st Regiment. One of the tank-destroyers was positioned at a bend in the road, so that its gun could cover both the road and the valley. The second was placed against the last house in the village, so that its fire would cross that of the other tank-destroyer. The rest of the platoon reinforced the north side of Mont.

The German tanks, respectful of the American tank-destroyers, remained hidden in the Neffe Wood close to the château. From this position, they fired on Mont. The grenadiers charged bravely across the open fields between Neffe and Mont and along the road joining the two villages; three self-propelled guns supported them and followed along the railway line.

Bundled up in their winter clothing which enlarged their silhouettes, many got caught on these fences.

The famous Panzer Lehr's 901st Regiment had suffered heavy losses.

Using the light created by explosions, they started climbing over the numerous barbed-wire fences which divided the pasture into small paddocks for cattle. Bundled up in their winter clothing which enlarged their silhouettes, many got caught on these fences. Outlined by the light from the burning tanks, they were unable to release themselves, and so they died, still attached to the wire, under the heavy machine-gun fire of the parachutists.

Caught in a vast natural trap, their bodies, frozen and covered with snow, like ghostly phantoms, were left on the barbed-wire until the end of the Bastogne siege.

Their companions who has advanced up the road had not been luckier in open terrain, and they were killed one after the other.

The three self-propelled guns were blown up by the tank-destroyers. The famous Panzer Lehr's 901st Regiment had suffered heavy losses, and they did not risk trying to break through on this side again – the Geronimos were too tough.

A bad day for General Bayerlein.

He had followed the battle from his cellar in Neffe and then, by telephone, contacted General von Lüttwitz who was at his command post on the east bank of the Ourthe, some fifteen miles north-east of Bastogne. But Bayerlein's superior was not able to offer him any comfort as the news was gloomy. And there was no question of acceding to his repeated request to use the whole Corps against Bastogne.

Despite his taking of Noville, Colonel von Lauchert had little to celebrate either. His 2nd Panzer had lost 20 tanks, including 3 Marks IV's, and 25 others were out of action for urgent repairs. He did not know when they would be available again, though at that moment he could not use them. He was short of petrol because he had not been resupplied. His men could march on an empty stomach or plunder farms, but petrol had to be sent to him.

A whole panzergrenadier battalion of his 3rd Regiment was wiped out, and 142 men had been taken prisoner. But above all, time had been lost!

On the American side, the optimism which McAuliffe had begun to feel after the morning's artillery success at Bizory

McAuliffe in his jeep.

...to get back to Bastogne as quickly as possible.

was confirmed throughout the day. After all, the Germans did not seem as tough as all that. Except for the losses at Noville, Longvilly and Wardin, his forces were intact, his defences in place ready to confront the enemy wherever he appeared.

The moment had come for General McAuliffe to decide whether to hold or abandon Bastogne. In the latter case, the retreat would have to be organized immediately along the only route still open, the Neufchâteau road. Having listened to the advice of his staff officers, particularly Danahy's affirmation that the Germans were using American equipment, not to fool the enemy but because of their own shortages, McAuliffe thought for a moment and said, "I'm staying".

That evening, General McAuliffe went to Neufchâteau.

Despite the enormous risks involved in getting there and the uncertainties of the situation, he wanted to confer with Middleton and inform him of his decision to stay in Bastogne. To do this, he needed an assurance that he would be supplied, and it was mainly to discuss this point that he wanted direct contact with the commander of the VIIIth Corps.

The conversation which followed was intense.

Middleton was very worried; he told McAuliffe that he would have to manage alone, if the Neufchâteau road, along which supplies had to pass, was cut. McAuliffe said that he was able to hold for at least 48 hours and perhaps longer. When the VIIIth Corps' commanding general indicated on the map the course followed by the German 116th Panzer Division and added, "You are going to get a fourth division on your back. You have a tough time in front of you", McAuliffe replied, "I think we can take care of them".

As the defender of Bastogne left him, Middleton shook his hand and said, "Now, don't get yourself surrounded, on your way back, Tony". McAuliffe jumped into his jeep and told the driver to get him back to Bastogne as quickly as possible. And he got through.

Half an hour later, the road was cut by Kokott's grenadiers.

The Chaplain of the 501st, Lieutenant-Colonel Francis L. Sampson, had less luck than McAuliffe. "Father Sam", as he was affectionately nicknamed by all the parachutists, had heard the officer in charge of communications, Warrant Officer

They found themselves face to face with a party of grenadiers.

"Father Sam", before his capture by the Germans, preparing an improvised altar to celebrate a mass. (Photo taken in Holland).

Sheen, say that a group of soldiers had been caught in an ambush and machine-gunned on a road leading to the north. Sheen could not tell him the exact location, and the priest set off towards Marche to find them.

After driving around fruitlessly, his driver, Corporal Adams, was getting ready to return, when the priest remembered that the day before the divisional hospital had been captured near where they were. Father Sam persuaded his companion to drive him to the "Hinck Barriere" in the hope of recovering some medicines which were sorely needed in Bastogne. Father Sam probably thought too that some survivors, if not the dead, might have need for his services; but he did not tell this to his unbelieving driver. Having arrived there, they set about loading the jeep with everything useful that remained in the devastated hospital.

As they returned towards Bastogne, they noticed a sentry sitting on the edge of his fox-hole, smoking a cigarette. The priest asked him if he had heard of the ambush. The soldier informed him that there had been a lot of machine-gun fire on the other side of the hill on the previous night. The Chaplain was convinced that the affair had taken place up there.

He managed to convince Adams to turn back, and they took the Salle road where they found themselves face to face with a party of grenadiers. The corporal braked hard, but it was too late, for an armoured vehicle pointed its guns in their direction while enemy soldiers stepped out from behind the trees surrounding the jeep, sub-machine-guns in their hands.

These were the men of the Armoured Group of the 116th Panzer who had captured and abandoned the crossroads the night before.

Adams stopped the jeep and sheepishly the two men raised their hands, "I'm sorry I got you into this mess", said the priest. "That's O.K., Father", Adams mumbled. They were prisoners of the Germans.

During this day, the problem of command in Bastogne was again raised.

Roberts had his Tigers, McAuliffe his Eagles (nickname of the 101st Airborne because of the eagle's head that they wore on their left arm), while Cota wanted to get his men back from SNAFU and to regroup what remained of his 28th Division. An officer of the 10th Regiment of the 28th Infantry Division, Captain Charles Brown, was in charge of recovering the many retreating soldiers, inevitable in a big battle. Brown sorted out the men, obtained clothes for them, got them a hot meal and a rest period before regrouping them in a force called SNAFU, so-named by a young retreating officer, standing for "Situation Normal All Fouled Up".

Most of the retreating men came from the CCR of the 9th Armored Division and the 28th Infantry Division. General George A. Davis, second-in-command of the 28th Division, had obtained Middleton's permission to recover 300 infantrymen to reinforce the division which was still in combat. But Cota, nicknamed Dutch, was not satisfied. Having one star of rank more than McAuliffe, Cota ordered him to come to his command post at Sibret, but McAuliffe replied that he had too much to do, adding that Cota could come and see him if he wished.

So Cota came to Bastogne and was amazed at the intensity of the movements of troops and artillery there. Without seeing the commander of the 101st Airborne, he returned to his command post where he called Middleton to inform him of what he had seen and to advise him to remove from the town all the reinforcements which might get through, because they risked jamming up the area completely. He also recommended that the defence of the town should be in the hands of one man.

It does not seem that McAuliffe had asked for this command when he went to Neufchâteau, but after his departure, Middleton informed Roberts by radio that McAuliffe had overall command of the town.

Colonel Roberts placed himself willingly under McAuliffe's orders. But his efforts were spent particularly on one point which was most important to him: to keep his armoured forces mobile rather than to have them tied down defending the parachutists' defence points. He organized for this, keeping one part of his tanks in a mobile defence force, with one group stationed at the centre of the locality, ready to go at any moment, to any point on the perimeter. He was very pleased to have requisitioned 8 new tanks with their crews who had been blocked in Bastogne after trying to get through the town to their destination. They were of inestimable value in replacing a part of the heavy losses of his Combat Command.

Despite the removal of the 300 men from the 28th Division, Team SNAFU still had a strength of 600 men. They were to be very useful in guarding road-blocks and replacing a part of the losses in the front line.

What were the officers of the 101st Airborne thinking about the decision to let themselves be encircled?

Danahy, officer in charge of intelligence, and the only non-careerist among the staff officers, felt that he was enjoying a rare privilege. He was to be thrown into a fraternal collaboration and was to be able to show to McAuliffe his profound loyalty and devotion.

Kinnard had influenced the General's decision by remarking that, as soon as the sky cleared, the problem of their resupplies would be resolved by parachute drops. When McAuliffe told him of his decision with a certain solemnity, he made the eloquent gesture of shaking his hand, expressive of problems still to come, but he was undoubtedly pleased by the decision.

Informed shortly afterwards when he visited headquarters, Ewell commented, "Well, I just wanted to know whether to begin digging startin' holes for the race out of here, or graves". On returning to his command post, he telephoned the officers commanding his battalions, "Batten down the hatches".

Harper, whose sector was calm, with the exception of Marvie, was in radio contact with his friend Sink. The two regimental commanders were older than the headquarters' staff, whom they considered juveniles. "Those goddam kids have really cooked up one for us this time".

Steve Chappuis in the Rollé Château, command post of the 502nd Regiment, said nothing as usual. This was a good sign, because as Kinnard had said to Danahy a short time before, "If Chappuis says he's in trouble, you'd better believe it and do something about it fast, because silent Steve will be in real big trouble and he won't call back to tell you again".

The Americans were going to have to live on their own resources.

The 101st Airborne was suffering seriously from the loss of their hospital and had very few medical personnel. They had also lost a lot of trucks, and a number of those which had been sent to fetch supplies had been unable to return. Further, airborne divisions carry much less ammunition than other divisions and have fewer transport facilities.

In contrast, the CCB of the 10th Armored Division was abundantly supplied in material, equipment and ammunition and was able to make up the shortages of the parachutists. Numerous depots had been discovered including the stocks of wine and liqueurs carefully hidden by the officers of the VIIIth Corps for Christmas, which was to give great pleasure to the besieged forces and cause frustration to the others. Thanks to a large stock of Red-Cross flour, the town's defenders were sure of having pancakes which became the main food of the defenders. Everything that could be found in the houses was carefully used, blankets for the wounded, and sheets to make bandages and camouflage.

This requisitioning was not always achieved without the running up against the civilian population.

There is a nice story that after the war people spoke of villagers who freely gave their sheets to cover and camouflage the soldiers and vehicles. This did indeed happen but not in all cases. Many tried to preserve and keep the few belongings that the horror had left them, and the civilian population was as cold as the soldiers. While there was no problem in the abandoned houses, this was not always so in the houses that were still occupied. The inhabitants took turns to guard what they had left.

In Bastogne, the Mayor, Léon Jacquemin, also did something about the problem. He started a passive defence, one of whose aims was to protect the inhabitants' property. Some of the soldiers did not restrict their searches to food and blankets or sheets.

The system of communications was well taken care of thanks to the different specialist services who were part of the besieged troops. Communications with VIIIth Corps were kept going thanks to the telephones, teleprinters and radios. The civilian telephone too was a great help, as curiously, many of its lines continued functioning.

Manteuffel's doubts were confirmed. As he had foreseen, the plan of the offensive was too ambitious, and he knew then that the objectives would not be achieved.

Von Lüttwitz was very dissatisfied with the delays of the Corps. Despite the Americans' retreat from Noville, the apparently successful encirclement of Bastogne, and the appearance of a favourable though slow evolution of events, he had so far failed in his object. He had not been able to find the weak point in the lines of defence of the town.

Fritz Bayerlein was disillusioned. The Panzer Lehr had suffered more serious damage than it had inflicted, and on that day it had been very seriously damaged indeed.

Colonel von Lauchert was furious that he had not been able to settle matters with Bastogne. His courageous division, the 2nd Austrian Armoured Division, whose strength Patton had come to know as "The best damned armored division in the German Army", considered their lack of success as an affront. Late in the day, while his men were finally taking up position in the ruins of Noville, he contacted his superior von Lüttwitz by radio asking him for permission to take Bastogne. The reply was clear, "Ignore Bastogne and head for the Meuse".

Kokott still maintained that, without the assistance of two armoured divisions, the taking of the town was uncertain. The honour which he had been given of taking Bastogne with his courageous grenadiers, reinforced by part of the Panzer Lehr, was a dubious one. He had been very impressed by the strength and the determination of the American forces defending Bastogne.

At the Führer's headquarters, there was a mixture of surprise and self-assurance. Hitler had learnt, just by chance, that Bastogne continued to resist when SS Gruppenführer Fegelein remarked, "We shall take Bastogne tonight".

At McAuliffe's headquarters, there was a degree of perplexity because the noises surrounding the town indicated constant movement. The defenders did not know that the divisions were by-passing the town with the Meuse as their objective, and they thought their sole aim was to encircle the town.

In fact, the encirclement was taking place, but only by the infantrymen of the 26th VGD.

During the night, an American Corps enquired by radio of the situation in Bastogne. Kinnard suspecting that the Germans might be listening and not wishing to let know anything, answered, "Visualize a hole in the doughnut. That's us !".

The ring was closing on Bastogne.

An exceptional yet little known event of the Bastogne Battle deserves to be described separately.

It seemed unrealistic to expect help to come so early from the 4th Armored Division of Patton's 3rd Army. Nevertheless, just before 12 a.m. on the 20th December, an advanced force of the Combat Command B of the 4th Armored Division was actually on the outskirts of Bastogne.

How was this possible?

On the 8th December, the 4th Armored Division had been pulled back from the Maginot Line for rest and fitting. The men and vehicles of the Division were exhausted after incessant fighting during heavy November rains. The CCB, commanded by Brigadier General Holmes E. Dager, had taken a short rest in Domnon-les-Dieuze, a village about 40 miles northeast of Nancy. It was from there that, at 12.30 p.m. on the 19th December, it left for renewed fights. The CCA was to follow nine hours later.

At the head of the CCB was the 8th Tank Battalion, under the command of Major Albin F. Irzyk, reinforced with the half-tracks of the 10th Armored Infantry. From his jeep, General Dager directed Irzyk in his leading tank through the darkness, relying on the only map of the whole Combat Command.

Having passed the Belgian border they rolled on through the towns of Arlon and Neufchâteau without slackening the pace. At 11 p.m. on the 19th December the column reached the village of Vaux-les-Rosières, after having covered 161 miles in 22 hours, partly in total black-out and constantly expecting enemy fire. Once again, Patton's men had proved their discipline and perfect organization.

On the morning of the 20th December, General Middleton ordered General Dager to send the CCB to Bastogne. Dager protested because of the terribly confused situation and the risk of losing part of his troops. The order was maintained, but only a task force was to be sent.

Dager transmitted the order to Major Irzyk who also protested vehemently. Irzyk formed a task force consisting of Company A of the 8th Tank Battalion, Company C of the 10th Armored Infantry Battalion and Battery C of the 22nd Armored Field Artillery Battalion, placing Captain Bert P. Ezell in command. His mission was to report to General McAuliffe, to learn the situation, receive instructions and render support, if so ordered.

The Task Force Ezell moved north-east on the Neufchâteau-Bastogne road and reached Bastogne without encountering any resistance from enemy troops. Upon entering the town, Captain Ezell was told to report for instructions to Colonel Roberts, commander of the CCB of the 10th Armored Division, instead of General McAuliffe.

Meanwhile Irzyk was ordered to call back Ezell, who was receiving instructions for employment from Roberts, and immediately the Task Force set out again to rejoin their CCB. It was shortly after noon.

On their way back they saw some strange things: first a GMC truck in a ditch on the side of the road. The truck was undamaged, the driver still sitting behind the wheel, but the top of his head had been blown off above the eyes, apparently by an amour-piercing round. Then Ezell's men noticed two tank-tracks running across the pavement, the largest they had ever seen. A little further on, they came upon another strange sight: the vehicles of two battalions of U.S. artillery stopped along the road. The equipment seemed intact, but there was no sign of any American troops! Probably the artillery units had been attacked or they had been "spooked" by the sight of the two German Panther or Tiger tanks.

Apparently a German force had cut across the road just prior to Ezell's return, but now the road was clear and the Task Force continued its way, hauling back as much of the abandoned artillery equipment as they could handle. The Task Force met no resistance, slipping probably through a gap in the German troops, as McAuliffe was going to do a few hours later.

In the afternoon, the CCB was ordered to move to the rear towards Leglise, where they arrived after dark.

Next day orders were received for the attack that was to take place the following morning. The Division would have to fight bitterly, paying a high price in order to break through the German ring and cover the same distance.

If somebody had thought of ordering Task Force Ezell and the rest of the CCB to take up positions in this area, the Germans would not have been able to cut off the Neufchâteau Road, and the costly fighting which was to take place later to reach Bastogne again would have been avoided.

However, General Patton and General Gaffey, commander of the 4th Armored Division, did not want to scatter the troops they were going to need for the main attack they were preparing, and the confusion was such, in and around Bastogne, that they did not want to sacrifice, unnecessarily, key units of the 4th Armored.

This fascinating episode of the Battle of Bastogne has been completed thanks to Brigadier General Albin F. Irzyk, whom I wish to thank sincerely.

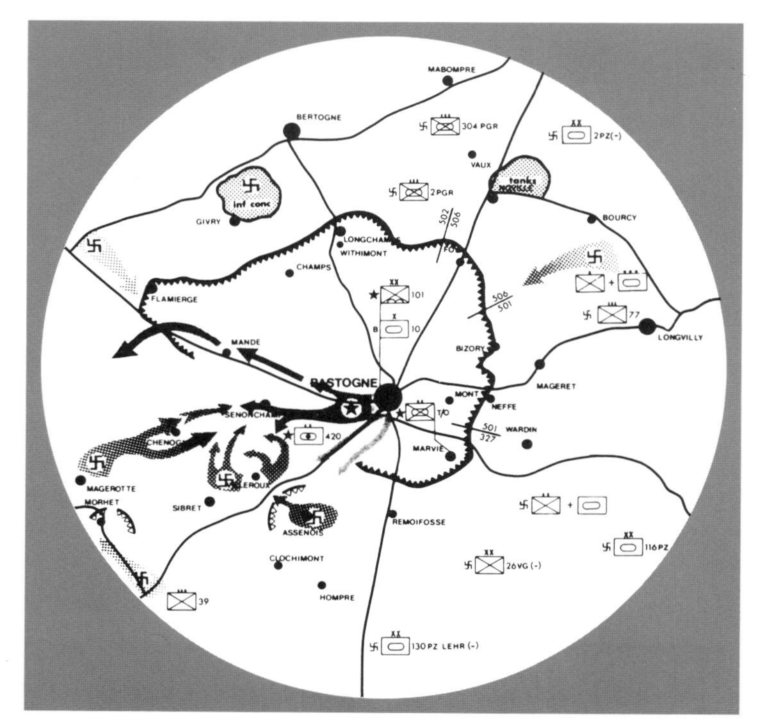

21st December

The 2nd Panzer began to move towards the west.

THURSDAY 21st DECEMBER 1944

During the night, the grenadiers of the Panzer Lehr removed the trees which formed O'Hara's road-block on the Bastogne-Wiltz road, near Marvie.

On the other side of Bastogne, the 2nd Panzer began to move towards the west. Being short of petrol, only a few vehicles had been able to reach the main Bastogne-Marche road during the night where the vanguard had the luck to capture intact the Ortheuville bridge across the Ourthe. The Division was at present stretched out in small groups between Tenneville, the crossroads of the "Barrière Hinck" and Bertogne, while the major part of its vehicles were stuck, lined up on both sides of the road between Bertogne, Noville and Bourcy.

A German group which occupied the "Barrière Hinck" crossroads, near Sprimont, had ambushed some resupply trucks of the 28th Infantry Division. A hundred men had been made prisoner, wounded or killed; only nine had managed to escape. They came to recount their adventure to Lieutenant-Colonel Allen, commander of the 3rd Battalion of the 327th Regiment. They informed him that the Germans had now established a road-block at the "Barrière Hinck". He informed headquarters and received the order to send a company to clear the crossroads and to recover the men who had escaped the ambush as well as the wounded. The Americans had to keep this resupply route open.

12 p.m. Company B of the 3rd Battalion of the 327th Glider Infantry Regiment was commanded by Captain Robert J. McDonald, a 23 year-old, surprisingly tall, thin man, who was a fierce individualist, and a field commander full of imagination and initiative. The company advanced towards the crossroads, and every 1500 yards a radio-operator was posted, in order to ensure continuous contact with base. Led by two scouts, walking on the road in order not to lose their way, the infantrymen moved along the ditches which bordered it.

After three miles, they started to hear the noise of horns and guttural laughter. The scene appearing before them was lit up by the flames of burning American vehicles.

The assailants organized themselves to surprise the Germans. One platoon, led by Lieutenant Selvin Shields, slipped off to the left of the road-block, to control the Sprimont Road, while

The 101st Airborne Hospital before its capture.

The Americans established road-blocks in all directions.

a second group led by Sergeant Mike Campano went to the right, thus blocking the road from Bertogne.

McDonald and the remainder of the troops stood on the Bastogne road along which they had come. When everyone was in position, the signal was given: two rifle shots.

The Americans opened fire on the Germans who were less than 35 yards away. Some of them fell to the ground instantly, but most ran away towards the Herbaimont Wood, crossing an open stretch which was covered by Campano's platoon's fire.

More than 50 Germans were killed, none was captured. There were no American casualties. On the contrary the Americans recovered three men, a black driver and two white, who had been taken prisoner by the enemy.

Near the crossroads, the Americans found the charred remains of the hospital captured by the Germans, as well as a large number of trucks, all burnt out, loaded with medical supplies, mail and explosives. And they discovered the bodies of two parachutists, probably patients from the hospital. Their throats had been cut.

Once the surrounding area had been cleared of Germans, the Americans established road-blocks in all directions, including a very strong one on the Bertogne road. They used a light tank, recovered from the enemy's booty, as well as .50 calibre machine-guns removed from the trucks.

7.00 am At seven o'clock, some vehicles of the 2nd Panzer which had received a small amount of petrol in the night, left Bertogne for their objective which was the river Meuse. As they approached the road-block between Salle and the "Barrière Hinck" crossroads, the noise of the vehicles was heard by the Americans who quickly perceived 9 half-tracks, 7 light vehicles and a column of 75mm guns.

McDonald was with his men on a bank overlooking the road, so well camouflaged that the German column was less than 25 yards away when they opened fire. Only one light vehicle escaped.

A short while later, two tanks, reinforced by infantrymen, tried to by-pass the road-block. One of the panzers was stopped

They took the on-coming Germans by surprise.

...a large enemy force using American vehicles and wearing American uniform.

by an armour-piercing shell while the other one retreated still covering the remaining infantrymen.

The Bourcy-Bastogne railway line, along which the Germans had tried to infiltrate Bastogne, was still a worry to Colonel Robert F. Sink. Early in the morning, he despatched Companies A and C of the 1st Battalion of the 506th to make contact with Company D which was guarding the position known as La Halte.

8.15 a.m. Sink's three companies started advancing carefully on the left side of the track towards Bourcy under cover of the woods bordering the railway line; while, on the right of the track, men from companies A and D of Ewell's 501st Regiment were doing the same thing.

They took the on-coming Germans by surprise, who, in the ensuing confusion, made worse by the fog, managed to escape Sink's men, only to throw themselves in front of Ewell's party, which they mistook for their own reinforcements.

Sink's force lost 6 men but captured 100 Germans and killed 51. The remaining 80 Germans who thought they were escaping were killed or captured by the Geronimos.

On the Neufchâteau Road, which had been cut the previous day by the parachutists of the 5th Division of the 7th German Army and by Kampfgruppe Kunkel, an American patrol from Troop D of the 90th Reconnaissance Squadron, under Lieutenant Arthur B. Arnsdorf, set off early in the morning in the direction of Sibret. Consisting of one tank-destroyer and two infantry squads, they met a group from the 101st Airborne at Isle-le-Pré, 1 1/4 miles from Bastogne. Pushing further ahead, the reconnaissance patrol encountered a strong, well dug-in enemy force and it disengaged.

Another patrol, led by Captain Keith J. Anderson, was able to observe a large enemy force at Clochimont, using American vehicles and wearing American uniforms, which proved that the road had been cut. These pseudo Americans were the spearhead of a parachute company from the 5th Division, reinforced by tanks and self-propelled guns of the Panzer Lehr's 901st Regiment and elements of the 26th VGD. This column,

Unpublished photographs taken by Bud Lauer, 907th Glider Field Artillery Batallion, 101st Airborne Division. The battery was set up around noon, December 19, and began to fire at 1.30 p.m. Both photographs were taken on the 22nd of December.
Above, from left to right: Harvey Grevatt, Sergeant Baumgardner, Willard Philips.
Sitting: Roy Strand, a Colorado farmer, and Michiel Coladnato.
Below: Sergeant Blumgardner holding a rifle. The two sitting men are eating. K ration boxes can be seen on a large wooden box.
The guns are turned towards Marvie. The pile of empty shell boxes indicates that the battery has just stopped to fire. The empty boxes were always taken away from the battery as soon as possible in order to reduce the risk of being spotted by enemy aircraft.

closing on Sibret, destroyed the three howitzers which were defending the village.

9 a.m. At nine o'clock, Sibret was captured by the Germans, who then pressed on towards Villeroux, a mile further on, thus hoping to slip towards Senonchamps by a side road and reach Bastogne without using the main Bastogne-Neufchâteau road.

At Senonchamps, learning of the fall of Sibret, Lieutenant-Colonel Barry D. Browne, commander of the 420th Armored Field Artillery, requested help. Team Pyle was sent, named after its commander, Captain Howard Pyle, who usually commanded a tank company, but who was now at the head of a group composed of 200 men and 14 medium tanks recovered from the area of Neufchâteau.

On approaching Senonchamps, the Germans saw an American column in front of them, a "real" one this time. It was the 333rd Field Artillery Group of the 771st Artillery Battalion.

Before the Americans could react, the German column had scattered their vehicles along the side of the road and made room for a self-propelled gun which opened fire. The drivers of the American gun-tractors took cover in the ditches and abandoned about twenty 155mm howitzer guns to the Germans.

11.30 a.m. At that moment, Team Pyle arrived, joining forces with Browne's men and attacking the Germans with supporting fire from the 755th and 420th Artillery Battalions. Immediately, one of the U.S. tanks destroyed one of the enemy's 75mm guns, but as the tank chased the Germans into a glade, one of its tracks was hit by an armour-piercing shell. Even with all the available help and under cover of smoke screen, it was impossible to move it, so it was destroyed on the spot.

The 969th Field Artillery Battalion equipped with medium howitzers had been recovered just as it was preparing to leave Bastogne. Lieutenant-Colonel Hubert D. Barnes, the officer commanding, took up position close to the batteries of the 755th and 420th Battalion near Villeroux, from which point they could control all the Bastogne perimeter.

Towards 11 o'clock, the defenders of the Salle road-block were reinforced by two of Colonel Templeton's tank-destroyers.

... the pseudo-American forces...

12 a.m. The Germans restarted their attack against the road-block with tank gun fire. The two 705th tank-destroyers came into action and, soon, the panzers were silenced.

The officer of the German spearhead sent a rather alarming message to his superior, describing the road-block as being a "strong enemy concentration".

The consequences of the German officer's error of judgement were to lead him to hesitate and mess about for two days, thus losing valuable time for his division – although the defenders evacuated the road-block quietly at the end of the afternoon. The order had been given to abandon the crossroads when the patrols from Company B informed the commander that all the bridges had been blown and that the road had become useless for resupplying the division.

Let us look again at those pseudo-American forces after they left the Senonchamps road. During the day, they checked the strength of the village defences, but that turned out to be a disaster for them, because they were mown down by the American quadruple machine guns (meat choppers) of Battery B of the 796th Anti-Aircraft Artillery Battalion, which produced devastating results when fired on infantry-men.

By the end of the day, Colonel Browne was commanding a force of 300 infantrymen from different units with 16 light and medium tanks in addition to his artillery battalions, and defending a front stretching from south of Senonchamps to the Bastogne-Neufchâteau road, a length of about 3 miles.

They were part of the semi-circular front held by Harper's 327th Regiment which defended Bastogne, stretched out from the left flank of Steve Chappuis' 502nd, north of Mande-St-Etienne, to the east side of Marvie, south of Bastogne. From this latter point, Team O'Hara closed the ring to the right flank of Ewell's 501st.

It is during that day that a second exceptional event, previously unknown, happened in Bastogne.

Efforts of the Combat Command R (Reserve) of the 4th Armored Division to contact the 101st Airborne Division in Bastogne by radio had been fruitless, so around noon Lieutenant-Colonel Thomas D. Gillis, X.O. of the CC-

Lieutenant-Colonel Thomas D. Gillis, Executive Officer of the Reserve Combat Command of the 4th Armored Division. (Photo taken in 1944) also present on the photograph page 310.

R of the 4th A.D. volunteered to drive INTO Bastogne to determine the situation first hand.

Arriving at the Command Post of the division, Lieutenant-Colonel Thomas D. Gillis met Brigadier-General Anthony McAuliffe and had a reunion with Lieutenant-Colonel Harry W.O. Kinnard, whom Gillis had not seen since they were boyhood chums in the Presidio at Monterey, and with Lieutenant-Colonel Hank Cherry, Commanding Officer of the 3rd Tank Battalion, 9th Armored Division, who was a West Point classmate of Gillis. Those old acquaintances determined that the 101st was in dire need primarily of medical supplies and ammunition.

The Airborne and Tank officers asked Gillis where he was going ? Gillis said that he was returning to his outfit, CC-R, by the route he came, the main highway south of Arlon.

They told him then that Bastogne was SURROUNDED !

Gillis did not change his plan and when arriving at the perimeter defences, he told his jeep driver, Harry Moritz, a gung-ho lad from Chicago, to put the pedal to the metal and not to stop for anything. With his carbine cradled in his arms Gillis and Moritz were going fast, their backs bent low in the jeep, the forest was a blur of green as they sped southward.

NOT a shot was fired at them !

Gillis is convinced that the Germans figured his jeep was the point of a larger force and that they planned on ambushing the main body.

Gillis and his driver were not aware that they were going through the lines of the German 5th Parachute Division.

As soon as Gillis' report reached the 4th Armored Division headquarters, telling that the 101st had lost its collecting station, along with most of its surgeons and medics, and that it was in dire need of ammunition, the division G-4, Lieutenant-Colonel Bernie Knestrick, started planning the composition of the relief column for the 101st Airborne Division.

Harry Kinnard adds a postscript to this saga :

"I was worried as hell about how you would fare dodging krauts on the way back to Arlon. But our needs were so desperate that I wouldn't have tried to dissuade you even if I could. I only wish I had seen you to thank you when you arrived with the manna from heaven. But if late is better than never, let me say all these years later, from the bottom of my heart :

"THANKS FOR YOUR SUPERB DELIVERING OF THE LIFESAVING GOODS! WELL DONE!" (His caps).

At the end of the day, the senior officers in Hitler's entourage reassessed the situation and, for the first time since the beginning of the offensive, felt some optimism.

Von Rundstedt had read a favourable report from Oberkommando West and was convinced that the moment had come to take Bastogne by a concerted attack. He let von Manteuffel know that Bastogne MUST fall on the 22nd, permitting the development and progress of their advance towards the Meuse.

The general commanding the 5th Panzer Army had not waited for the orders from the Supreme Headquarters. During the evening he had visited the command post of the XXXXVIIth Corps to ensure that everything was ready for the attack the following day.

Von Lüttwitz had organized his attack without his mobile armoured forces, which had to continue to by-pass Bastogne in direction of the Meuse.

Kokott, who now had the responsibility of taking the town, hoped for assistance from the 5th Parachute Division, which protected his left flank. This aid would depend on the degree of American resistance on that side. German air reconnaissance had signalled intense American activity on the roads near Luxembourg. The 26th VGD was reinforced by the 901st Combat Group detached from the Panzer Lehr, by 15 Panthers and some artillery battalions.

Kokott's natural optimism was increasing.

It was reinforced by the capture of American supplies near Sibret, thanks to which his vehicles had sufficient fuel and his troops something in the

The Americans covered their fox-holes with pieces of wood.

stomach. Further, he had noted that the tempo of the firing of the American artillery had changed – and he deduced that they were short of ammunition.

As they had not been able to break through either in the north or east, they should be able to do so in the west. Their reconnaissance at the end of the day had indicated that the defence was weak and badly organized there.

Meanwhile, the cold became more and more biting which did not please the thousands of men on both sides dug into their fox-holes or hidden in the woods.

Both sides prepared for a siege.

The Americans covered their fox-holes with pieces of wood taken from farms or from the Bastogne saw mills. These were then covered with grass and earth and called "dugouts". The Germans constructed huts from branches in the woods. Those who had the luck to occupy a farm cellar or a stable hung on firmly, braving the danger, making fires with anything they could get their hands on, light furniture being the first victim.

In the headquarters of the besieged American troops, it had been decided to move the operations' room and the communications' centre to a cellar under the building. It had a height of roughly 6 feet. The ceiling consisted of the floor of the rooms above. There were three small rooms on either side of a narrow corridor to which the access was difficult by a narrow staircase. The rooms, originally whitewashed, now dingy and grey, were damp and encumbered by coal reserves, and the light was from bulbs powered by a generator on the ground floor. A disagreable smell of mouldiness did not improve matters, but the officers were glad to be sheltered in case the building was hit by a shell.

An unexpected result of the siege was that great cohesion formed among the different units who were forced to face the enemy together. The early dissensions between the Tigers and the Eagles, the lack of liaison, personal rivalry between officers, disappeared as if by magic, and an outstanding collaboration began. Colonel Roberts, a veteran of the first World War, left the Lebrun Hotel to join McAuliffe's headquarters. His experience was of great assistance to the paratroops.

When Lieutenant-Colonel Paul Danahy confirmed to General McAuliffe that the 101st was surrounded, the reply was characteristic and well reflected the spirit of the paratroops and their leader, "Well, that's one problem solved – now we can attack on all sides".

It was during that night that the first heavy covering of snow fell on Bastogne.

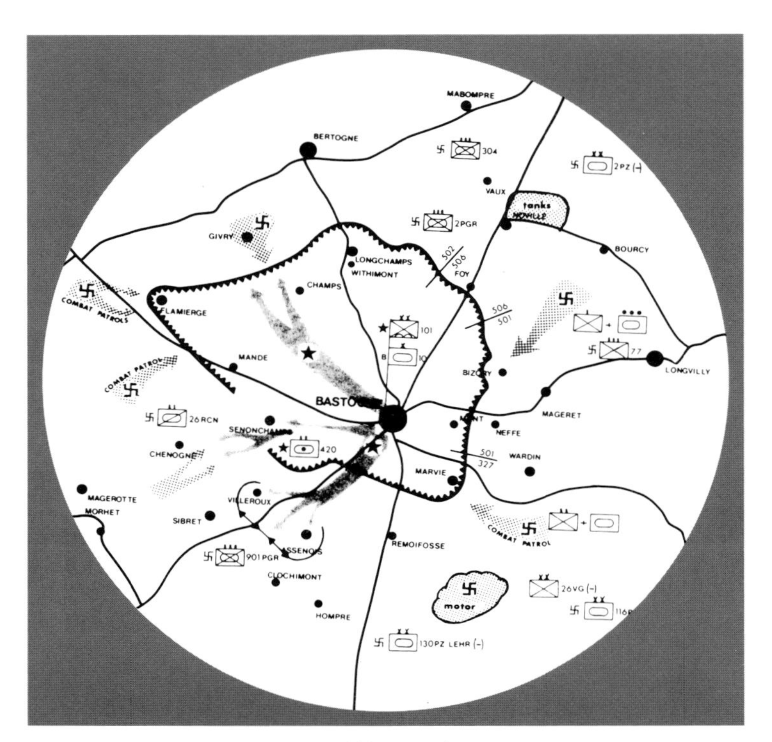

22nd December

The Combat Commands of the 4th Armored Division left the Anlier Forest.

FRIDAY 22nd DECEMBER 1944

6.00 a.m. The Combat Commands of the 4th Armored Division left the Anlier Forest, near Habay-la-Neuve, for Bastogne, reinforced by the 26th and 80th Infantry Divisions. The Combat Command A started to drive pushing to Burnon and the Combat Command B to Martelange.

The 4th American Armored Division had made a good reputation for itself during the push across France. Now, however, Patton's favourite division was not in good shape. It was badly short of tanks, and those it had were in a bad state, breaking down frequently. Furthermore, many of the crews were made up of raw recruits without combat experience. The commanding officer, General Gaffey, had only just taken over, and it was to be his first combat at the head of an armoured division.

Major-General Hugh Gaffey, 50 years old, was well known for his riding trousers and superbly shining boots. The Texan was also nicknamed "Gimlet-eyed Gaffey". He was going to need good vision.

At Marvie, in Team O'Hara's sector, something strange happened at dawn. An unknown patrol was seen marching in front of the American outposts. Everyone saw it, but no one was able to identify it for certain. Nobody fired. This phantom patrol came as close as 100 yards to the command posts of both the 327th and 54th Armored Infantry Regiments. The soldiers dressed in white did not seem to carry any weapons, and they disappeared as quickly as they had appeared. The only point commonly agreed by the Americans who saw the patrol was that it consisted of eleven men. The eleven phantoms of Bastogne!

7.30 a.m. At first light, a German panzer battalion, reinforced with self-propelled guns, made a fresh attack against the 420th Armored Field Artillery Battalion, whose guns had repulsed so fiercely the other German attacks in the preceding days. Major Kunkel who led the attack realized quite soon that the

They were rejoined by the tanks and half-tracks of the 25th Cavalry Squadron.

This hitherto unpublished photograph was taken on the 22nd December in the morning on the top of a hill, to the left of Mont, and which the photographer identifies as being the Mardasson hill where the American Memorial and the Bastogne Historical Center now stand. The photo, given by Frank Carpenter of California, shows the snow which had fallen in the night. The soldiers are grouped around a fire made with K ration boxes. They are heating snow to make instant coffee.
On the left, Johnnie Cippola; Frank is second from the right without a helmet, but with a scarf wrapped round his head. The three men behind are not identified, as Frank did not know their names. They all belonged to Company C of the 501st of the 101st Airborne. One of the three at the back was killed shortly afterwards on patrol in the woods.

intensity of the fire returned by the enemy would not enable him to enter Bastogne via Senonchamps.

9.30 a.m. A reconnaissance group from the 704th tank-destroyers of Combat Command A, 4th Armored Division, made its way along the Arlon-Martelange road and went down the long hill which leads to the bridge of Martelange. They crossed it with an M8, an armoured wheeled reconnaissance vehicle, and some GMC trucks. Here the scouts left the main road and headed towards Marnach where they were rejoined by the tanks and half-tracks of the 25th Cavalry Squadron while they were resting. They were then recalled and again crossed the undestroyed Martelange Bridge to go and guard a depot which was being set up.

Meanwhile, a German group had cut off the Mont road south-east of Flamizoulle, the next village to Mande-St-Etienne. The outpost, which reported the incident, said that "the Germans had set up a road-block consisting of two half-tracks and one salvaged jeep and trailer".

11.30 a.m. Just before midday, Colonel Allen sent his men to clear the road. They captured 25 men and repulsed the others. The vehicles used by the Germans to block the road were pushed aside. A platoon from Colonel Templeton's tank-destroyers patrolled the road and reported that all was clear.

The Germans decided that the time was right to demand the town's surrender, an idea that had already occurred to them previously but which had been rejected after due consideration by von Manteuffel. But General von Lüttwitz took the chance without consulting his superior. He felt that the moment had come to try to bluff the Americans.

Major-General Heintz Kokott let it be known that he was not keen on the idea, less so as he knew that he would be the one to have the "honour" and heavy duty of carrying out the threats in case of refusal. Lieutenant-General Fritz von Bayerlein bowed to von Lüttwitz's decision although he was not convinced of the success of the initiative.

11.30 a.m. Sergeant Carl E. Dickinson of Company B of the 327th Glider Infantry Regiment was in his fox-hole directly in front of the Kessler farm. Shortly after half past eleven, Carl saw a group of Germans approaching. There were five in all. The one in

Lieutenant Helmuth Henke, Panzer Lehr division.

Sergeant Carl. E. Dickinson Company B, 327 Glider Infantry Regiment.

the centre was carrying a large white flag. Following him at a short distance behind two other soldiers, one on each side of the road, each carrying a smaller white flag. Behind them, came two officers. Carl went to meet them. One officer could speak English, it was the Lieutenant Helmuth Henke. He said that according to the Hague and Geneva Conference it gave them the right to deliver an ultimatum and wanted to be taken to a superior officer. Each German officer had a clean handkerchief so the English speaking officer blind-folded the other officer and Carl blind-folded the English speaking officer.

At this time, Private Ernest D. Premetz of the 326th Medical Detachment came down to the meeting point not knowing anyone could speak English, for he could speak German.

The officers were well dressed in long leather coats and shined boots. The others were just ordinary soliders in their standard Army coats. All were very polite.

Carl Dickinson left the three soldiers at BAR position held by Pfc. Leo Palma. The fox-hole of Palma was just on the side of the road Arlon-Bastogne in front of the Kessler farm.

The German officers were taken to the platoon command post at the Kessler Farm where Technical Sergeant Oswald Y. Butler and Lieutenant Leslie E. Smith of Company F of the 327th were positioned.

Carl Dickinson and Ernest Premetz asked them what they should do with the two German officers. Sergeant Butler told them to take the Germans to the Comany Command Post which was about a quarter of mile away in the woods on the left of the Kessler Farm and Arlon-Bastogne road when looking to Arlon

The two Americans started out with the German officers, and as they went over the hill they turned them around several times so that they would not be familiar with the location of the Company Command Post station.

When the group arrived at the command post, the Captain James F. Adams called the 2nd Battalion command post in Marvie, then the headquarters of the 327th Regiment. Major

*Story by Carl E. Dickinson

22.Dezember 1944

An den amerikanischen Kommandeur der eingoschlossenen Stadt Bastogne.

Das Kriegsglück ist veränderlich, diesmal sind die amerikanischen Truppen in und um Bastogne durch starke deutsche Panzerkräfte eingeschlossen. Wietere deutsche Panzerkräfte haben die Ourthe bei Ortheuville überschritten, Marche genommen und über Hompré-Sibret-Tillet vorgehend St. Hubert erreicht. Libramont ist in deutscher Hand.

Es gibt nur eine Möglichkeit die eingeschlossenen amerikanischen Truppen vor völliger Vernichtung zu bewahren: die ehronvolle Uebergabe der eingeschlossenen Stadt. Hierfür wird eine Bedenkfrist von zwei Stunden gegeben, die mit der Uebergabe dieser Note beginnt.

Wenn dieser Vorschlag abgelehnt werden sollte, stehen ein deutsches Artillerie-Korps und sechs schwere Flak-Abteilungen bereit, die amerikanischen Truppen in und um Bastogne zu vernichten. Der Befehl für die Eröffnung des Feuers wird sofort nach Verstreichen der zweistündigen Frist gegeben werden.

Die durch dieses Bombardement entstehenden hohen Verluste der Zivilbevölkerung sind mit der bekannten Humanität der Amerikaner nicht zu vereinbaren.

Der deutsche Befehlshaber.

December 22nd 1944

To the U.S.A. Commander of the encircled town of Bastogne.

The fortune of war is changing. This time the U.S.A. forces in and near Bastogne have been encircled by strong German armored units. More German armored units have crossed the river Ourthe near Ortheuville, have taken Marche and reached St. Hubert by passing through Hompré-Sibret-Tillet. Libramont is in German hands.

There is only one possibility to save the encircled U.S.A. troops from total annihilation: that is the honorable surrender of the encircled town. In order to think it over a term of two hours will be granted beginning with the presentation of this note.

If this proposal should be rejected one German Artillery Corps and six heavy A. A. Battalions are ready to annihilate the U.S.A. troops in and near Bastogne. The order for firing will be given immediately after this two hours' term.

All the serious civilian losses caused by this artillery fire would not correspond with the wellknown American humanity.

The German Commander.

This is the original document given to McAuliffe. It had obviously been typed by the Germans on a captured American machine.

Alvin Jones, 327th Duty Officer, received the following message*:

"Four Krauts have arrived at Company B. They came along the Arlon Road. They are carrying a white flag and declare themselves to be emissaries. You'd say they want to surrender!".

As Major Jones could not find the regimental commander, Colonel Joseph H. Harper, he rang the 101st Airborne headquarters and asked for further instructions. With the Division's approval, he went to Company B's command post.

The German officers were waiting for him there, and handed Jones a message which he took to Bastogne. While he was travelling, rumours spread throughout the fox-holes that the Germans had had enough, and that they had sent a party to discuss their surrender. So many of the Americans used the temporary cease-fire as an opportunity to have a wash, a shave or to stretch their legs.

General McAuliffe was on his way to an outpost to congratulate the men who had done particularly well during a recent attack, when Major Jones came into the operations room where some of the headquarters' officers were present. There was no tension or nervousness. Jones saluted and informed General McAuliffe that he had a message for him. In a hurry, McAuliffe asked:

"What is it?"

"It's an ultimatum, sir", replied Jones who had started to read the English translation of the message.

McAuliffe cut him off and turned towards Moore, "What does it say, Ned?"

"They want us to surrender"

"You mean American surrender? Aw, nuts!"

The message read:

"To the U.S.A. Commander of the encircled town of Bastogne.

The fortune of was is changing. This time the U.S.A. forces in and near Bastogne have been encircled by strong German armored units. More German armored units have crossed the river Ourthe near Ortheuville, have taken Marche and reached

Colonel Joseph H. Harper,
Commander of the 327th Glider Infantry Regiment.

St. Hubert by passing through Hompré-Sibret-Tillet. Libramont is in German hands.

There is only one possibility to save the encircled U.S.A. troops from total annihilation: that is the honorable surrender of the encircled town. In order to think it over a term of two hours will be granted beginning with the presentation of this note.

If this proposal should be rejected one German Artillery Corps and six heavy A.A. Battalions are ready to annihilate the U.S.A. troops in and near Bastogne. The order for firing will be given immediately after this two hours' term.

All the serious civilian losses caused by this artillery fire would not correspond with the wellkown American humanity.

The German Commander"

McAuliffe took the message, glanced at it briefly and then left it on the table. He turned to Jones, "What are you doing with these people?"

"Colonel Harper is holding them, sir."

Silently Higgins, Moore, Kinnard and Danahy watched as the General sent Jones back to his post and then left the room without a word. On his way to the forward post McAuliffe thought over the arrogant ultimatum that he had just received. He found it totally out of place and he was infuriated by the reference to humanitarian sentiments for the civilian population. The Germans should have thought of this themselves earlier.

On his return, someone asked McAuliffe for his reply to the ultimatum. In fact, the Germans had stipulated that the Americans had two hours in which to reach a decision, that the messengers had to be returned within two and a half hours and that the Germans would attack at 3 p.m., if the Americans did not surrender!

Not usually talkative, McAuliffe was trying to think of an answer without success, "I don"t know what to tell them".

"That first remark of yours would be hard to beat", answered Lieutenant-Colonel Harry W.O. Kinnard.

"What was that?"

General Patton decorates General McAuliffe with the DISTINGUISHED SERVICE CROSS on December 30, 1944.

"You said nuts".

"That's it", exclaimed a smiling McAuliffe.

The officers in the room applauded while the General sat at a table to write his reply.

As soon as Harper arrived, he was handed the ultimatum by McAuliffe.

"Have you any suggestion to make, Bud?". As Harper could not think of anything to say, McAuliffe, grinning, showed him the sheet of paper which had just been typed:

"To the German Commander.

NUTS*.

The American Commander."

Then McAuliffe asked Harper to ensure that the message would be delivered properly. Harper said, "I will deliver it myself. And with a real pleasure".

* The famous answer NUTS is not to put to the credit of McAuliffe; in his mouth it was just a simple exclamation, said without thought, which made Mrs. McAuliffe say when she heard it, "That's Tony all over".
If it was used as the official reply to the German ultimatum, it is entirely thanks to Harry Kinnard, the ingenious colonel, who was the only one to think of it. However, history recognized McAuliffe as its author.
It is worth knowing what happened to the original of the reply sent to the Germans. This document, which might have been in its place at the Bastogne Historical Center with the Christmas message that I managed to track, has not been lost. It has been carefully kept by General von Lüttwitz who, though he might not have been very proud of his initiative in asking for the surrender, did fully understand the historical value of the reply and kept it carefully. It must still be in his family.

German artillery round Bastogne.

1.50 p.m. He went to the Kessler farm, where the two officers, still blindfolded and under guard, were waiting. Harper addressed the Lieutenant who could speak English, "I have the American commander's reply". "Is it written or verbal?" "It is written", said Harper , and turning to the Major, added, "I will stick it in your hand". "Is the reply affirmative or negative? If it is affirmative I will negotiate further".

Fearing that the Germans might not understand the good old American English, Harper said, "The reply is decidedly not affirmative. If you continue this foolish attack your losses will be tremendous".

Harper sat both German officers in his jeep and drove them along a narrow snow-covered track to the outpost, where the German soldiers were managing to talk with signs to the Americans.

In this sector, Harper had been subject to several attacks over the previous days, so he did not want the Germans to think they had control of the situation. While removing their blindfolds, he said to the German Major,

"If you don't understand what NUTS means, in plain English it is the same as "Go to hell". And I will tell you something else: if you continue to attack, we kill every goddam German that tries to break into this city".

The Germans saluted very stiffly, and Henke said, "We will kill many Americans. That is war".

"On your way, Bud", Harper jeered, thoughtlessly adding, "and good luck to you".

While Harper bit his tongue for wishing good luck to the Germans, the whole Division discovered their General's answer and enjoyed the joke.

The atmosphere improved, too, following the promise of an air-drop of supplies and that "Hugh was coming": General Hugh Gaffey's 4th Armored Division was hurrying to Bastogne.

3 p.m. Towards three o'clock, the German emissaries drove back to their lines in their Kübelwagen. A non-equivocable translation was handed to the German commanders.

Major Kunkel renewed his attack against Team Browne.

General McAuliffe sent a company of the 327th Glider Infantry Regiment as reinforcements.

Bayerlein, who had suffered more blows than he had given, was pleased that he could turn the tables, while gloating over the affront suffered by von Lüttwitz.

However, Kokott felt that the dubious honour conferred on him, of making the Americans eat their words and punishing Bastogne, was a hard task for his 26th Volksgrenadiers who did not have the same punch as the 26th Panzergrenadiers whom they were supposed to have replaced.

The snow had continued to fall, more and more heavily.

The result of this episode was a cease-fire of four hours' duration, in direct contradiction to Generalfeldmarschall Gerd von Rundstedt's strict order to capture Bastogne on the 22nd.

3.30 p.m. At the end of the cease-fire, Major Kunkel renewed his panzer attack against Team Browne. He was, however, stopped dead in his tracks by the combined fire of the American tanks and artillery.

5 p.m. Shortly before nightfall, a further German attack was attempted but without success: half of the men from a panzer battalion and half of the self-propelled guns were lost.

With the snow falling, it seemed as though the fighting was diminishing. However, Team Browne was hit badly, in turn, by the German artillery which was concentrating all its fire on predetermined zones. Unable to manoeuvre because of lack of room, Browne had to submit to the German fire as many others had done. Wounded, he was taken to a house in the village, where he died when a shell scored a direct hit, destroying it.

At dusk, worried by Team Browne's situation, General McAuliffe sent a company of the 327th Glider Infantry Regiment and a hundred men from Team SNAFU as reinforcements.

6 p.m. A reconnaissance unit of the CCA of the 4th Armored Division was sent to verify the exact situation at the Martelange Bridge. It ran into the German 5th Parachutists who inflicted severe losses, several vehicles being destroyed and 12 men put out of action.

The day's fighting had taken place principally on a curved front line from Villeroux, on the Neufchâteau road, to Mande-St-Etienne, on the Marche road. The situation was complicated in this sector, and the two adversaries sometimes held positions behind each other, there being no exact front line. This had made the battle confused, which had been to the Americans' advantage – except in certain cases.

Colonel Ewell's 501st Regiment had not been lucky with its resupply convoys. Their remaining trucks were parked in the assembly zone near Mande-St-Etienne, the area which had served as a base for the 101st Airborne on their arrival. As there had been combat in this locality that day, the drivers had decided to return to Bastogne. They had tried to do this via Sibret, but had been captured by Kunkel's combat group.

This incident was typical of the reigning confusion, but it also had more serious consequences for the Geronimos. The trucks held all of their gear and especially their precious sleeping bags and blankets. The officers had to collect blankets in the front line to warm the wounded who were filling up every available space in the town. Added to their losses when the divisional hospital was attacked at the Hinck Barriere, the regiment had now lost most of its transport.

However, despite the apparent confusion, the American defence was being organized by an expert, Kinnard, whose importance continued to grow. The defence line installed originally by McAuliffe and Higgins had been transformed by the young colonel into a circular defence which was both efficacious and simple. He had imposed strict limitations on the use of reserves without permission of headquarters. He insisted on being informed immediately of all enemy movements. He knew all the officers commanding front line positions well and could not hide a weakness for his former regiment and his old friend Ewell.

As the cold and snow increased, the Americans' situation became very uncomfortable. They were short of winter equipment, and their cotton jackets offered poor protection against the biting cold. Very few had overcoats. But the wounded were suffering the worst effects of the winter. Lying, in most cases, on the ground without medicines to treat them, except for parsimonious sips of brandy, it was difficult to keep them warm. The situation was so serious that after having visited the wounded the first time, General McAuliffe decided not to do so again for fear that his decisions might be influenced by their suffering.

When the able-bodied men heard their commander's response to the German ultimatum, they burst with pride and laughter. It is supposed that the German soldiers were not told of the affair.

In the official journal of the 101st Paul Danahy wrote: "The commanding general's reply, expressed so sarcastically and humourously, was totally negative. The catastrophic loss of life from an immense artillery barrage promised by the enemy, did not happen".

Nothing could better conclude that day than the comment of a parachutist of the 101st Airborne on look-out in his fox-hole at the edge of a wood when his food and ammunition were brought to him. The man who brought his supplies told him that they were surrounded, "So they're got us surrounded, the poor bastards!". This remark, as well as the belief during the truce that it was the GERMANS who were surrendering, perfectly illustrates the state of the besieged men's morale.

But the increase of the cold favoured the Germans. They were used to fighting in the snow, had suitable clothes, and the hardening of the earth would permit them to leave the country and secondary roads on which they had only been able to move slowly because of the heavy traffic.

However, the day had been bad for them. Von Lüttwitz' decision to ask for the town's surrender had made him look ridiculous, not only because of the stinging reply he had received which was to immortalize the battle of Bastogne, but also because it showed a total misunderstanding of the situation. A belief that encircling the Americans would be sufficient to make them surrender was to misunderstand the enemy, which is always an expensive mistake. Further, by making threats that could not be carried out, he had given further confidence to an adversary who was not short of it before. In brief, he had suffered an affront, and along with him, all the German Army also.

Feldmarschall von Rundstedt had personally visited the Führer to beg him to stop the Ardennes offensive and to send reinforcements where they were needed, to the Eastern Front. General Guderian was in fact very worried to see that essential material and equipment needed to prepare to contain the Russian offensive had been reserved for the Ardennes operation.

The Germans had failed in their threat to destroy Bastogne but there had been hard times.

During the night the Luftwaffe bombed the town for the first time, starting the destruction of buildings which had already been damaged by artillery fire.

Late in the night, the main force of Combat Command A of the 4th Division reached Martelange, but the bridge had been destroyed, which stopped their progress. Combat Command B had made better progress along the secondary roads that it had taken and had reached Burnon at nightfall, only

Colonel Sherburne, the artillery commander, had spent the rest of the day taking stock of the remaining ammunition.

6 miles from Bastogne. But there too the bridge had been destroyed, and their progress was stopped. Combat Command Reserve was following.

The crisis occurred during the night of **the 22nd to 23rd of December.**

General McAuliffe had distributed his men fairly evenly between the front lines and the reserves. The losses in infantrymen were light. The Germans had not launched a general attack around the perimeter, making instead local attacks, often in strength, which could be countered by concentrated artillery fire.

This method, although extremely efficient, was costly to the Americans, and by midday on the 22nd, the 463rd Field Artillery Battalion, whose task was to support the 327th Infantry Regiment, had raised the problem of the shortage of ammunition. In fact, they had only 200 shells left, and many other battalions were facing a similar situation.

Colonel Sherburne, the artillery commander, had spent the rest of the day taking stock of the remaining ammunition; the results were not promising. Some batteries of Roberts' Combat Command B had only ten rounds per gun left; some of the 101st had twenty. McAuliffe decided that firing should only take place when the gunners could see the whites of the enemy's eyes!

This did not suit the front line infantry officers, who requested that at least two rounds be fired during each attack.

Colonel Kinnard listened to the appeal and relayed McAuliffe's reply:

"If you see 400 Germans in a hundred yards area, and they have their heads up, you can fire artillery at them – but no more than two rounds".

The ammunition shortage was illustrated quite well by the remark of Steve Chappuis (Silent Steve), "The road intersections in front of us looked like 42nd and Broadway after a football game. Most of the traffic seemed to be moving to the west. They were in easy reach, but we could do nothing about it, because we did not have the artillery ammunition".

The situation was at its worst when small arms ammunition became dangerously short also. Even Middleton's statement that "Hugh is on his way", plus the promise of resupply by air, did not help their confidence. Although the paratroops had been trained for this eventuality, all the small units reinforcing them were doubtful.

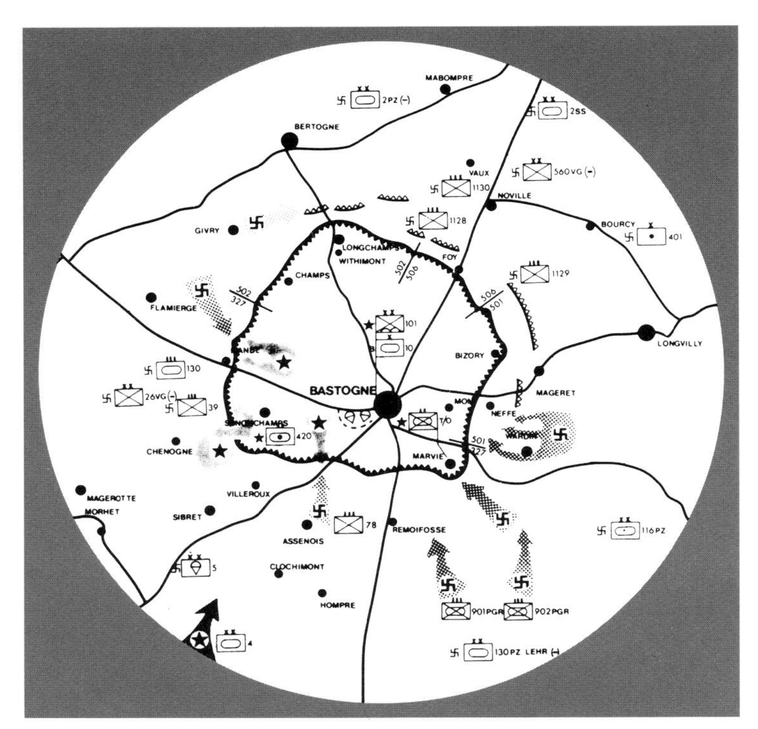

23rd December

A short while later, the German columns were under fire.

SATURDAY 23rd DECEMBER 1944

8 a.m. From daybreak all the guards on duty at Bastogne continued to peer at the sky, now clear, with unlimited visibility, searching for the promised aircraft.

8.30 a.m. Two teams of pathfinders from the 101st Airborne, trained in England, jumped into a field to the south-west of the town where they set up their equipment to control the expected parachute drop.

9.45 a.m. First Lieutenant Gordon O. Rothwell, commanding the pathfinder teams, telephoned Colonel Kohls to say that the supply planes would arrive in about 90 minutes.

10 a.m. Captain James E. Parker, the US Air Force coordinator who had arrived on the 19th, heard on his radio at last that the support aircraft were in the air. These included fighters and light bombers which were homed in immediately on the "hot-spots" in the 502nd's and 327th sectors where the artillery was now powerless.

A short while later, the German columns were under fire.

The flyers were able to trace all vehicle movements thanks to the snow covering the ground. From the sky, the flyers could see the trails left by panzers taking cover in the woods, and they were able to bomb them there. They used napalm which burnt both the vehicles and the woods that were hiding them. Soon the perimeter was surrounded by smoke which replaced the fog.

"This was better hunting than the Falaise Pocket, and that was the best I ever expected to see", said McAuliffe later on.

During the early attacks, the German anti-aircraft guns did not fire back immediately because they did not want to give away their positions, but subjected to the punishment inflicted, the German flak was to come into full action.

The Germans set up a line of outposts on the hills overlooking the roads from Champs and Givry. They also set up roadblocks using farm machinery and dug numerous trenches.

A first wave of 16 aircraft started the drop.

These remarkable photographs (unpublished until now as well as those on page 180) have been taken by 1st Navigator Lieutenant Max W. Demuth of the 85th Squadron, 437th Troop Carrier Group, at the risk of his life; his right arm holding the camera outside the plane was hit by a bullet. The pilot of the C47 was 1st Lieutenant Jim Shive. On the photograph below, to the right, can be seen the barracks where the 101st Airborne Headquarters were set up.

10.30 a.m. Further south, the news for the Americans was not very good either. The 3rd Battalion of the 327th Glider Infantry was posted in defensive positions in the area between Flamierge and Flamizoulle and on the road, west of Mande-St-Etienne. Colonel Allen decided to pull back Companies B and C into high ground west of Champs and Grandes-Fanges. Company A was in the front line.

Lieutenant-Colonel Allen, a small and wiry man, was "a hell of a good soldier", his men said. Full of vitality and very resourceful, he obviously relished the hazards of the battlefield and the problems of command there.

Opposite the barracks where the headquarters had been established, in a part of the cemetery away from the civilian tombs, a group of German prisoners under the watchful eye of their guards, was digging perfectly rectangular graves in the frozen ground. Nearby a dozen bodies of American soldiers lay in the grotesque positions in which they had been frozen.

Suddenly, the deafening sound of a cargo plane filled the cemetery, and the men looked up, interrupting their funerary work.

11.50 a.m. All the signalling equipment was ready, in position, when the defenders saw the arrival of the C47's (the famous Dakotas*). A first wave of 16 aircraft started the drop; it was the most heartening spectacle of the whole siege.

Hundreds of parachutes, each in a different colour to indicate the nature of its burden, opened in the sky. The large loads landed softly in the fields beyond the cemetery.

12 a.m. In Colonel Allen's sector, a patrol from Company A of the 3rd Battalion signalled the approach of 12 panzers coming from the woods south of the St. Hubert Road followed by infantrymen dressed in white overalls. This was the 39th Regiment of the 26th VGD.

1.30 p.m. The outposts of Company A retreated without fighting. The panzers halted on a hill and started to fire on the positions held by Company C. However, they were forced to retreat under the fire of the American artillery, and two tanks were destroyed. Even though they had fallen back, they were to continue pounding at the sector of Company C all afternoon.

A veteran C47 can be seen in front of the Victory Memorial Museum.

This photograph shows a great part of Bastogne.
In the foreground the railwaystation and the pond near by.

How the ground looked from the air, the tracks of the vehicles being visible in the snow.

Templeton's six tank-destroyers were in trouble; with the help of a reconnaissance platoon, they had supported Company C since the beginning of the fight, then, as they were trying to disengage, they exposed their flank to the German tank guns which were hidden in the woods, and immediately, they lost two tank-destroyers. The survivors, careful, formed a road-block, while the accompanying scouts dug in round the position.

4.06 p.m. General Kokott and his officers saw the drop from some distance away and thought they were dropping men, thus increasing the confusion among the attackers.

Two hundred and forty-one aircraft dropped 144 tons in 1446 containers in an area of half a square mile with such accuracy that it was possible to retrieve 95 percent of the supplies, prompting Kinnard to say, "That's close enough for government work".

This excellent work was carried out in part by men of the 53rd and 60th Troop Carrier Wing. Purely by chance, they had been based a few miles away from one of the camps of the 502nd Regiment in England prior to the invasion of Europe. When they heard that their "buddies" were surrounded, they wanted to fly immediately to help them. But the atrocious weather grounded the C47's. The friendship between the parachutists and the flyers in England had often seemed questionable expressing itself most often in fist fights. But this is, after all, one way of showing mutual appreciation.

The headquarters officers watched the parachute drop with emotion. One of the soldiers, standing not far from McAuliffe, said to him, "We'll beat the Krauts now, sir".

5 p.m. Already some of the ammunition which had been dropped was being used. However, the supply problem was far from being resolved. There were too many .50 calibre bullets, which were not required, and not enough .30 calibre bullets, which were in great demand. Also, there was a shortage of 75mm and 76mm APC shells.

The Division had a dire shortage of penicillin, stretchers and blankets, even after door-to-door collections had been made of all available equipment from the town.

C-47 cargo planes returning after having dropped supplies. In the background behind the trees: Bastogne. Date unknown.
(Unpublished photograph taken by Luther E. Barrick from his battery position).

The white-clad grenadiers.

5.25 p.m. At Marvie, the 2nd Battalion of the 327th, was bombarded heavily by the shell-fire of panzers hidden in a small wood near the village of Martaimont. From their position, they could shoot directly into Marvie.

As night fell, the help afforded by the fighter-bombers during the hours of daylight decreased.

5.35 p.m. The attack was launched by the panzers and infantry moving out of the woods and developed quickly, the fine snow, which was still falling, affording ideal camouflage for the white-clad grenadiers and the whitewashed tanks.

The U.S. 54th Armored Infantry Battalion spotted two enemy machine-guns that were firing into Marvie and silenced them immediately. But strong automatic fire swept the American defences continuously. No enemy could be seen, so the men of the 54th held their fire except for one heavy machine-gun on the left. A few minutes later, a grenade dropped next to the gun, killing the gunner and wounding one other man. The rest of the crew retreated.

The wounded man was not found until the next morning, when he was in such a frozen state that only by nodding his head was he able to indicate to the stretcher-bearers that he was still alive. Later, he reported how the Germans had searched him and his dead comrade before going away.

6 p.m. Colonel Allen was informed after dark that the Flamierge road-block manned by Company C was occupied by whiteclad infantrymen who had come along the St Hubert road with four panzers. The Germans had been able to do this easily because Allen's men confused the Germans with the expected 4th Armored Division. It was too late by the time they realized their error, and they were mown down. The survivors managed to escape.

Colonel Allen judged that his positions were in danger and ordered a withdrawal as they had planned previously. It was very difficult to achieve because of the confusion of Company C.

When the men reached their new position, Allen told them, "This is our last withdrawal. Live or die, this is it".

He was right. They did not withdraw again.

Another white-clad German group attacked Marvie from the south.

...the Germans were working through the houses.

6.40 p.m. The battle was developing in the Marvie area. One platoon of Company G of the 327th became surrounded on Hill 500, south of the village. The Germans had moved furtively through the fields and through the houses into their positions round the hill. A few men managed to withdraw before the ring was closed, but most were trapped. Of the 98 defenders of Hill 500, many were either wounded or killed.

Another white-clad German group, supported by 12 panzers, attacked Marvie from the south. Lieutenant Stanley Morrison, commanding the surrounded platoon, told his men to dig in on the sides of the hills or to pull back to the houses to resist.

Harper asked him on the telephone: "What is your situation?" "Now, they are all round me. I see tanks just outside my window. We are continuing to fight back but it looks like they have us".

Harper thought he was very calm. Three minutes later he called back again. "We are still holding on", was all that Lieutenant Morrison was able to say before the line went dead.

Looking at Harper's face to guess what had happened, Lieutenant-Colonel Thomas J. Rouzie murmured: "Well, I guess that's the end of Morrison".

Morrison had not been very lucky. He had already been made prisoner in the attack on Marvie the previous Tuesday, but had managed to escape.

7 p.m. His end came towards 7 o'clock when his platoon was overrun by the men of the 901st Panzergrenadiers of the Panzer Lehr.

Team O'Hara was so busy that it was unable to do anything to help Company G of the 327th.

Four tanks followed the grenadiers and added their fire to that directed at Marvie from the woods.

Major Galbreaith, executive officer of the 2nd Battalion of the 327th, who took command when Lieutenant-Colonel Inman was seriously wounded, reported to Colonel Harper that the Germans were in the south end of Marvie and were working through the houses. He asked for help.

Reinforcements arrived, sent by Team O'Hara. Infantrymen and grenadiers started house-to-house fighting while a tank-

O'Hara's command post on the Wiltz-Bastogne road at Marvie. The German tank in the picture was destroyed on the night of 23rd December.
(Photo taken in the spring of 1945).

destroyer kept the panzers at bay so that they could not intervene.

Colonel Harper had always been very worried by this weak point in his defences. Early in the morning he had asked O'Hara to send a tank to Hill 500. A 57mm gun was sent instead. The half-track towing it arrived at the hill as is was being attacked, so the driver turned back towards Marvie. The village defenders, alerted by the noise of the battle, saw the half-track coming from the battle zone and mistook it for the enemy. They fired on it with all their available guns, destroying both the vehicle and the crew.

Though tragic, this mistake turned out to be useful, for two German tanks, arriving a short while later, saw the road obstructed by the half-track and turned back.

The fight which had started with a series of cautious approaches now changed its tempo. O'Hara's men saw tracer bullets flying about them in all directions slowly surrounding them; in addition, a self-propelled gun rushed at them from the direction of the Wiltz road. It was set ablaze and destroyed by the fire from a medium tank. The flames lit up all the surrounding area. The Germans used this opportunity to adjust their fire, and O'Hara's men and tanks had to withdraw 100 yards back to the cover of darkness.

Harper had no more reserves. The Germans on Hill 500 were in an ideal position to overrun the centre of his sector and rush on into Bastogne. Once more, however, the Germans made the tactical error of attacking only one point of the defensive line in force.

Near by, Ewell had fresh troops available.

9.45 p.m. A platoon from Company A of his 501st, under Captain Stanfield A. Stach, came to reinforce Company F of the 327th Glider Infantry which was in bad shape. But its centre had not moved an inch.

Gradually the ruptured line north of Hill 500 was patched and strengthened before the badly informed German High Command could exploit their success. A platoon of Company F took up position to the east of the Bastogne road.

The 327th was also reinforced, at Kinnard's orders, by Batteries D and E of the 81st Airborne Anti-Aircraft Battalion and by guns from Team Cherry. These 12 guns were sited in an arc, on the hillcrests above Marvie, about half a mile from the junction of the Wiltz and Arlon roads at the entry to Bastogne. Under Colonel Rouzie's orders, 24 men from Company F and the Geronimos reinforcements formed a defensive line in front of the artillery.

During the night of the 23rd and 24th, General von Lüttwitz himself went to the famous Hinck Barrière road-block on the Bertogne Road. The officer who had attacked it on the 21st maintained, still, that the road was blocked by a large American force.

However, von Lüttwitz was dubious. He reached the road-block without being shot at, so his doubts were confirmed. He even started to have the tree trunks removed. He realized that the road-block had been undefended for two whole days, and he was very angry. Part of the Division had lost its chance to advance further because of a frightened officer. Subsequently, this man was court-martialled and shot. Meanwhile, von Lüttwitz joined the 2nd Panzer, which had finally been fully refuelled and was advancing towards Marche-en-Famenne.

Colonel Kinnard reported this to VIIIth Corps at the end of the day:

Concerning our situation, things are getting rather tight around us. We could do with some help. The enemy has been attacking along the southern defensive line, and some tanks have got their noses into our positions. You'd better tell the 4th Armored Division of our situation and tell them to hurry".

The day's events had shown that the American defence lines were still too stretched out. The tank men complained that they did not know where the parachutists were positioned, and the paratroops moaned that they did not have a clear idea where the tank men were...

However, things were changing. The weather factor alone was in favour of the besieged Americans. The fog and the cloudy skies had helped the Germans in the first few days, but when the skies cleared, aircraft were brought in posing a serious threat to the Germans both on the ground and in the sky, and some spectacular fights with the Luftwaffe pilots took place.

Viewed from the sky, the roads leading to Bastogne looked like the spokes of a wheel; they were in good condition, and the Germans had had unrestricted use of them for a long time – but no longer, because Allied air supremacy was absolute, and the punishment of the Germans had begun.

What were the German generals concerned with the taking of Bastogne thinking?

Von Manteuffel, Lüttwitz and Kokott no longer had any hopes of taking the town without considerable reinforcements.

Hitler's decision to send two reserve divisions, the 9th and the 15th Panzergrenadiers, let Manteuffel think he might be able to make use of them. But Generalfeldmarchall Model had only designated one regiment of the 15th Panzergrenadiers to reinforce the Bastogne attackers. Even with the supplementary tanks and artillery, this extra regiment would not be enough.

The 4th Armored Division had made little progress during that day. The difficult terrain, the blown bridges and the stiff enemy resistance had halted the three columns. They had not been able to build a new bridge at Martelange, because the paratroopers of the 5th Division held the bridge approaches under fire and ruled out any attempts at construction.

The interest of the world was now focussed on Bastogne. Since McAuliffe's stinging reply to the German demand for surrender, the world's press was neglecting all the other points of the German offensive.

Bastogne had become a symbol of resistance in the eyes of public opinion, which obliged the Americans to hold the town at all costs, and the Germans to capture it.

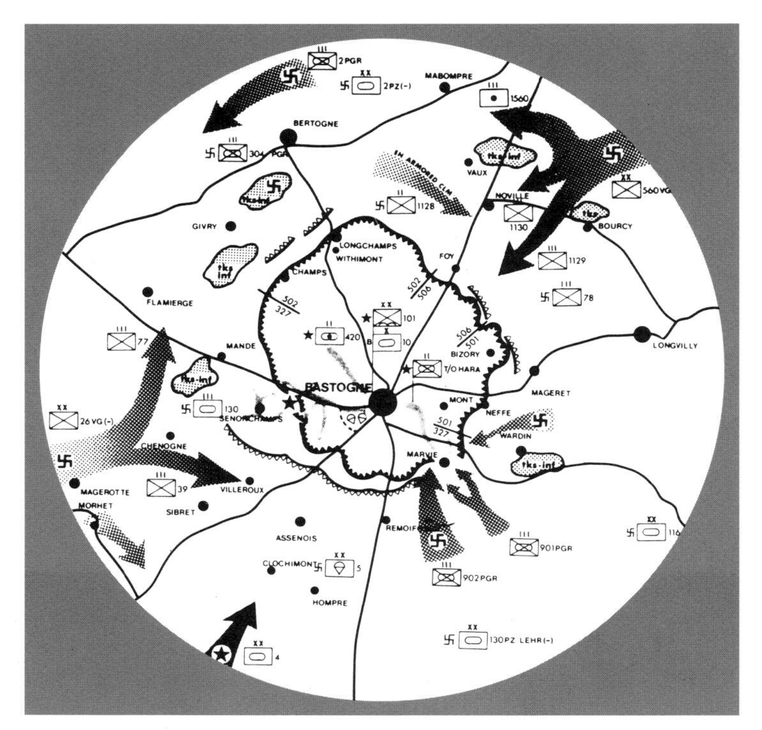

24th December

The two American tanks made their way through the village...

SUNDAY 24th DECEMBER 1944

In his command post installed in a farm a few miles from Bastogne on the road to Arlon, Major-General Kokott was very badly informed of the situation following the attack on Marvie. His intelligence services informed him that the village was in their hands, but the Americans had repaired the gap in their lines.

So he decided to continue his attack on two axes: along the Arlon-Bastogne road and, beginning at Marvie, along the Wiltz-Bastogne road. Following the two routes, he hoped to break through to the town on the wedge formed by the two roads.

12 p.m. At Marvie, two Shermans, which had been called for by Harper, in the commander's name, from Team O'Hara, arrived in the village which was occupied in the south by German infantry, and from where tanks and grenadiers were launching a violent attack. But the Sherman crews could only see this by the light of the gunfire.

The survivors of the 327th Infantry were dug in at the foot of the houses, hidden by their shadow, while the snowsuited Germans were highlighted as they came across the open spaces by the light from burning buildings and explosions. Very few managed to reach the shelter of the walls and to dig in.

The two American tanks made their way through the village on the main road and could now clearly see the flames coming from the German tank guns which were firing at point-blank range from the route coming from the south.

The first panzer to reach the village crashed into the half-track which had been destroyed the previous night and which again saved the situation. While the tank was trying to extricate itself, the two Shermans took aim, as if on an exercise, and destroyed it.

The intensity of the German attack began to lessen. The grenadiers who had managed to take up positions in the ruins of the first houses of the village, attempted to move forward, but were to be stopped by the men of Company G leading to

...they were repulsed by heavy firing or bazooka fire.

a bloody fight with close-combat weapons in the ruins or the rooms of the remaining houses.

12 p.m. – 1 a.m. The arc-shaped defence line formed by the twelve guns of the 81st, under the orders of Colonel Rouzie, was reinforced between midnight and one o'clock by 60 men. Rouzie thought that his forces were insufficient to take back Hill 500, so he secured the gap with the help of Captain Adams who, for his part, reorganized Company F.

The German panzers attacked the left flank twice during the night along the Bastogne-Arlon, road, each time they were repulsed by heavy firing from two platoons of Company F, led respectively by Lieutenant Smith and Sergeant Butler.

In one of these assaults, two panzers got to within fifty yards of the American fox-holes and hit Smith's command post with 15 rounds. They were eventually repulsed with bazooka fire.

During the night, the Germans of the 901st Regiment shelled Marvie with captured mortars. This barrage was to continue until the early morning, when the Germans asked for a cease-fire in order to collect their dead and wounded lying in front of Company F.

Later, when the men from the U.S. intelligence services tried to collect information from the dead Germans' papers, they found no bodies. The German medical services had been very thorough.

American losses were light – 5 killed and 7 wounded during the night's fighting round Marvie.

In other parts of the defence, the results of the fighting were still unclear. Two of the Panzer Lehr's tanks managed to slip past Harper's force, entering Bastogne and shooting up houses around his command post. They were quickly destroyed.

It became evident in Kokott's headquarters that yet another battle had been lost. The attack was abandoned because they had to prepare Hitler's Christmas present – the taking of Bastogne the next day.

From the first crack of dawn of a day which was to be perfect for the air force, the P47's from 512,513 and 514 squadrons of the XIXth Tactical Air Command took off for Bastogne. Like

Like faithful guard dogs, they flew over the Bastogne perimeter all day.

...gliders to increase the resupply of shells.

faithful guard dogs, they flew over the Bastogne perimeter all day, intervening at the slightest German movement.

General von Manteuffel, who was becoming increasingly frustrated with Bastogne, the abscess in his lines of communication which blocked essential roads, sent a message to Marschall Model, asking whether he should turn all his forces against Bastogne to take the town or whether he should continue to push towards the Meuse. Though Hitler had said that Bastogne had to be taken, he seemed to have lost his interest in the area for the moment. The reply to von Manteuffel was unchanged: he was to use all available forces for the push towards the Meuse.

7 a.m. Harper inspected the lines at dawn. Hill 500 was still in German hands, but his men were holding Marvie in spite of the fact that the Germans were occupying some of the houses in the southern part of the village.

8 a.m. Bastogne was bombed by the Luftwaffe.

8.30 a.m. Colonel Kohls asked the VIIIth Corps for additional quantities of ammunition for the 75mm pack howitzer and also 105mm shells. He suggested that gliders should be used to increase the resupply of shells.

9 a.m. A patrol from O'Hara discovered the old road-block abandoned except for two Germans sitting on the tree trunks. A brief salvo sent them running away. O'Hara's men recovered the wounded as well as material and vehicles from the area taken by the Germans the previous night.

12 a.m. After that the bridge at Martelange had finally been replaced, Combat Command A of the 4th Armored Division took and cleared the village of Warnach on the Arlon-Bastogne road. They were now some 8 miles from their objective – the besieged town. Combat Command B was still making progress along the side roads and was 4 miles from Bastogne. But they had just come up hard against the German 653rd Heavy Tank Destroyer Battalion equipped with the dreaded Ferdinand, a tank-destroyer consisting of the dangerous 88mm gun mounted on a Tiger tank chassis. This was a hard nut to crack for Patton's tank men.

Meanwhile, Combat Command R had cleared out Bigonville and was now moving towards the Molinfaing-Bercheux area.

Thunderbolt-Republic P47

Several aircraft were shot down. (This is a C47).

1 p.m. VIIIth Corps passed on a message from General Patton: "Christmas present coming. Hold tight!".

1.30 p.m. Six American P47 Thunderbolts bombed Marvie, dropping six 500 pound bombs on the American positions, following this with machine-gun fire, in spite of the fact that the proper cerise-coloured panels were visible, clearly denoting the limits of the American sector.

Harper spotted a German tank hidden in a haystack between two houses south of the village, with only its gun muzzle showing. The only remaining Sherman and O'Hara's light tank fired on it, removing the hay with the first salvo. The panzer escaped.

During the afternoon, the 704th tank-destroyers were sent to the Martelange Bridge for the fourth time. They managed to cross it at night, seriously hindered by the Germans para-troopers.

3 p.m. The 160 C47 Dakotas, which had bravely dropped 100 tons of material during the morning, completed their task courageously despite heavy fire from German flak, several aircraft being shot down. Eleven gliders had been able to land near Savy, at the vicinity of the "B" Battery position of the 327th Parachute Field Artillery Battalion, carrying medical personnel including four surgeons. But the loss of planes was added to a number of other deficiencies, such as petrol, for only 445 gallons had been parachuted, and K rations*. The 26.406 rations received were only enough to supply the defenders for a little more than a single day! The men had to forage for any food supplies in their area, and their Christmas dinner was a K ration – for those who were lucky enough to have one...

It is necessary to stress the heroic work carried out by these American aviators. Colonel Harper said: "Their courage was

* K rations, devised in 1941 by Dr. Ancel Keys at the University of Minnesota, were contained in small waxed cardboard boxes. There were three types: lunch, dinner and supper. Weight 5 pounds, 3000 calories.
The difference between the meals was the main part of the meal, either a box of meat, cheese or meat paste. There was also a choice between a bar of crystallized fruit, chocolate or vitamin tablets. The drinks varied between coffee or fruit juice in powder form or concentrated soup. In each type of ration were also 3 pieces of sugar, 1 packet of 4 cigarettes, 1 tin opener, 1 packet of chewing gum, two packets of cracker type biscuits and toilet paper or handkerchief.

"Their courage was tremendous..."

...creating havoc among the German positions with explosive bombs, napalm and machine-guns.

tremendous and I believe that their example did a great deal to encourage my infantry".

4 p.m. Second bombing of the town by the Luftwaffe

4.45 p.m. At Marvie, there was yet another erroneous attack by P47 Thunderbolts on the American lines...

6 p.m. Harper was given command of the sector from Marvie to the north-west of Hemroulle. "Look at it! This is half of the perimeter", he exclaimed to Higgins who replied: "It's all yours. Do what you can with it, Bud. There isn't any other solution".

Beginning at the western boundary of the 506th Regiment outside Recogne the front line of the 502nd Regiment ran westward about 4 miles, joining the 327the Regiment just south of Champs. Then ran 5 miles south and east around and below Bastogne meeting the 501st Regiment near Marvie. The circle was completed there where the front line of the 501st met that of the 506th near Foy north of Bastogne.

This reorganization was the result of Kinnard's fine tactical sense, sacrificing Flamierge, Mande-St-Etienne and Senonchamps, thus reducing the perimeter to 16 miles, held by four regiments – the 501st, the 502nd and the 506th Parachutists and the 327th Glider Infantry, supported by the remainder of Roberts' CCB and SNAFU.

7 p.m. A huge hall in one of the buildings in the barracks had been turned into a chapel. A hundred men had assembled to take part in a service for Christmas. The altar was lit by candles, and the service conducted by a young chaplain, assisted by two parachutists. Another played Christmas carols on a portable field organ while the men sang. The atmosphere was extraordinary. The priest gave a short sermon, reminding the congregation of the suffering which is demanded of man and of the necessity of keeping their trust in God.

The Americans had made numerous air attacks during the day, creating havoc among the German positions with explosive bombs, napalm and machine-guns.

8.30 p.m. But the Lufwaffe was not idle. A dull noise, very different from the noise of the Allied aircraft, that everyone knew in Bastogne, began to shake the town.

A hospital installed in a big shop situated in Neufchâteau Road.
This photograph, taken after the battle, shows the ruins of the building were the hospital was located (on the left).

The barracks were not spared.

First, flares were dropped, and their burning magnesium lit the perimeter as if it were daylight. This was followed by a terrible bomb attack which mixed explosive and incendiary bombs and destroyed, among other buildings, a hospital of the 20th Battalion of Armored Infantry of Combat Command B of the 10th Armored Division. This was installed in a big shop situated in Neufchâteau Road, close to the Place du Carré and to the Neufchâteau-Arlon-Marche crossroads. It was in this hospital that a young nurse from Bastogne, Mademoiselle Renée Lemaire, was killed along with a large number of American wounded.

Team Cherry's command post received a direct hit in this attack, and Lieutenant Hyduke and Captain Ryerson who had held the Germans five days ago near Longvilly were killed together with two other officers. Although the 2 tons of bombs dropped by the German Junker 88's could not compare in quantity with the weight of the Allied air bombing, the damage caused was considerable. The Place du Carré was half wiped out, which added to the desolate look of the town.

The barracks containing the headquarters were not spared from damage either. The men, who were more numerous than usual in the corridor which separated the different rooms in which the headquarters were installed, squatted down instinctively when three terrifying explosions took place. A few seconds later, there were three more a little further away, and the noise of a plane accelerating. The first to react was Colonel Moore, hurrying out of the operations' room to maintain calm. But he was unable to stop fat Corporal Olney, Kinnard's driver, from rushing outside with his blankets. The fresh air calmed him and from the shelter of a wall he could see the planes disappearing in the distance, while the roofs were outlined and the sky lit up by a large burning building from which flames were rising higher and higher. It was the Small Seminary in which was installed the command post of the 501st whose wounded and sick, with a great many civilians, had sought shelter in the cellars.

10 p.m. The advance party of the 15th Panzergrenadier Division arrived on the outskirts of Flamierge and Givry. The force was made up of two artillery battalions, a tank battalion of about

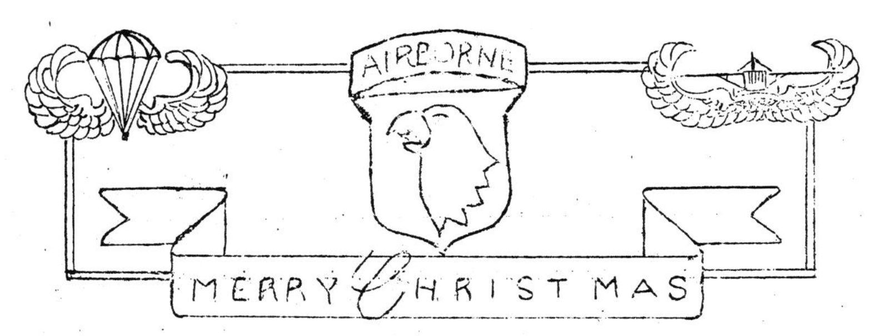

HEADQUARTERS 101ST AIRBORNE DIVISION
Office of the Division Commander

24 December 1944

What's Merry about all this, you ask? We're fighting - it's cold - we aren't home. All true but what has the proud Eagle Division accomplished with its worthy comrades of the 10th Armored Division, the 705th Tank Destroyer Battalion and all the rest? Just this: We have stopped cold everything that has been thrown at us from the North, East, South and West. We have identifications from four German Panzer Divisions, two German Infantry Division and one German Parachute Division. These units, spearheading the last desperate German lunge, were headed straight west for key points when the Eagle Division was hurriedly ordered to stem the advance. How effectively this was done will be written in history; not alone in our Division's glorious history but in World History. The Germans actually did surround us, their radios blared our doom. Their Commander demanded our surrender in the following impudent arrogance:

December 22nd 1944

"To the U. S. A. Commander of the encircled town of Bastogne.

The fortune of war is changing. This time the U. S. A. forces in and near Bastogne have been encircled by strong German armored units. More German armored units have crossed the river Ourthe near Ortheuville, have taken Marche and reached St. Hubert by passing through Homores-Sibret-Tillet. Libramont is in German hands.

There is only one possibility to save the encircled U. S. A. Troops from total annihilation: that is the honorable surrender of the encircled town. In order to think it over a term of two hours will be granted beginning with the presentation of this note.

If this proposal should be rejected one German Artillery Corps and six heavy A. A. Battalions are ready to annihilate the U. S. A. Troops in and near Bastogne. The order for firing will be given immediately after this two hour's term.

All the serious civilian losses caused by this Artillery fire would not correspond with the well known American humanity.

The German Commander"

The German Commander received the following reply:

22 December 1944

"To the German Commander:

N U T S !

The American Commander"

Allied Troops are counterattacking in force. We continue to hold Bastogne. By holding Bastogne we assure the success of the Allied Armies. We know that our Division Commander, General Taylor, will say: "Well Done!"

We are giving our country and our loved ones at home a worthy Christmas present and being privileged to take part in this gallant feat of arms are trully making for ourselves a Merry Christmas.

/s/ A. C. McAULIFFE
/t/ A. C. McAULIFFE,
Commanding.

Christmas Message distributed in the fox-holes to all the besieged men in Bastogne. (the original document can be seen at the Bastogne Historical Center).

30 medium tanks and tank-destroyers, two armoured infantry battalions and a pioneer company.

McAuliffe telephoned Middleton to say, "The finest Christmas present the 101st could have would be a relief tomorrow". "I know, old chap, I know", replied Middleton in a fatherly way.

Higgins was worried about the Germans' intentions and feared Christmas day: "The Germans are a sentimental people, and they are probably thinking of giving a present to Hitler".

The Americans in their fox-holes received a message from McAuliffe, written out by Lieutenant-Colonel Kinnard:

"Merry Christmas!

What's Merry about all this, you ask? We're fighting, it's cold, we aren't home. All true, but what has the proud Eagle Division accomplished with its worthy comrades of the 10th Armored Division, the 705th Tank Destroyer Battalion and all the rest? Just this: We have stopped cold everything that has been thrown at us from the north, east, south and west...

Allied Troops are counterattacking in force. We continue to hold Bastogne. By holding Bastogne we assure the success of the Allied Armies. We know that our Division Commander, General Taylor, will say: "Well done!".

We are giving our country and our loved ones at home a worthy Christmas present and being privileged to take part in this gallant feat of arms are truly making for ourselves a Merry Christmas.

A.C. McAuliffe
Commanding".

Christmas night always has a special effect on people. Perhaps it was for this reason that the officers reported that many of their men were sure that the end was imminent. They shook hands or hugged each other, certain that it was their last night.

General McAuliffe went out to get a breath of fresh air, walking between the brick buildings which made up the Bastogne barracks. Near the one which housed the German prisoners, he stopped to listen to their carols "Stille Nacht", and "O, Tannenbaum", rendered as only the Germans can.

Impressed by the atmosphere, McAuliffe went into the prison where he was met by the kind of comments which showed the morale of the troops engaged in the Battle of Bastogne: "We'll soon be freed, and it is you who will be the prisoner. You will like it there, General, it is most comfortable and cozy. And we'll be in Antwerp in a few weeks".

Taken aback, the General let them talk and then, leaving, said: "I was just here to wish you a merry Christmas".

Towards the end of the evening, the General got into his jeep and drove out of Bastogne. He had decided to spend Christmas Eve with his artillery friends. He went to Savy, a small village a short distance away, where the Battalion Headquarters of the 377th Parachute Field Artillery Battalion was installed in a huge stone building. Across the road was the Battery Command Post in the home of Arthur Leroy. A midnight mass was celebrated in the presence of McAuliffe and all the gunners who were not on duty elsewhere.

Kinnard and Danahy stayed at the headquarters. The only visible change in the routine was MERRY CHRISTMAS written in green crayon on the operations' map.

During the day, the headquarters of the XXXXVIIth Panzer Corps was visited by an envoy from Hitler, Major Johann Mayer. His mission was to discover why what Hitler considered to be a weak force could hold out against his troops' efforts to take Bastogne. By the time Mayer left the headquarters, von Lüttwitz had convinced him of the strength of the Americans. Nevertheless, Mayer insisted that Bastogne had to be taken on Christmas day, by order of the Führer.

That night, General von Manteuffel visited General Kokott in his forward command post on the Martelange-Bastogne road. He told him that OKW was worried about the Bastogne resistance. The capture of the town had become more urgent as the pressure from the south from the 4th Armored Division against the 5th Parachute Regiment was increasing hourly. And further, Hitler wanted the town captured, his determination being reflected by his decision to authorize Feldmarschall Model to send the Führer Begleit Brigade as reinforcements. This force was part of the famous Grossdeutschland Division and formed part of his reserves. It could be used only with Hitler's signed permission.

This decision showed clearly that the original plan had been changed, because it modified the objectives of an elite unit.

Von Manteuffel and Kokott decided to attack from the north-west, which was a suitable region for using tanks, but also because their attempts at other points of the perimeter had failed. They hoped that the resistance would be less obstinate there. Manteuffel was categorical: Bastogne must be taken at any cost. Kokott was also to receive reinforcements from the 15th Panzergrenadier Division, which continued to arrive.

However, by then, the brilliant Panzer General did not believe it possible, and he had already telephoned Feldmarschall Model, informing him that "he could not take Bastogne", and that because of the delays so far, the total plan of the offensive had become impossible to realize. He had advised the retreat of the German forces to their original departure point to avoid considerable and useless losses. Hitler had refused.

On that day alone, the whole plan had been upset.

And Bastogne had now moved to the centre of the stage.

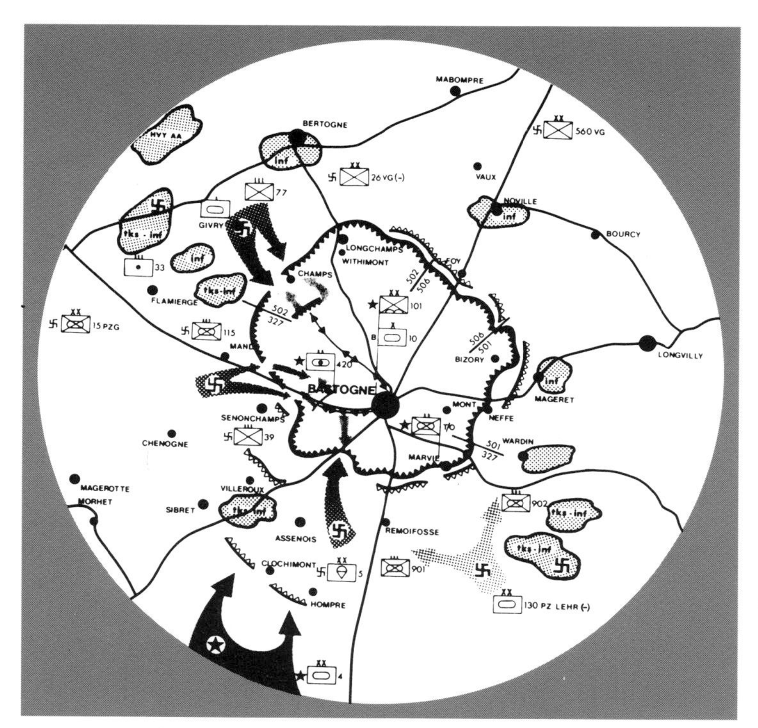

25th December

Tired, cold and hungry.

CHRISTMAS DAY, MONDAY 25th DECEMBER 1944

General von Manteuffel had ordered Kokott to attack very early.

The attack was planned to start at 3 a.m. on Christmas day. As was his habit, Manteuffel hoped that he was going to obtain a psychological and military advantage: the Germans hoped to give Bastogne as a Christmas present to Hitler, and the Americans would be surprised by an attack on this day of peace.

The attackers had to take Bastogne by 8 o'clock at the latest; otherwise, it would be impossible to continue to fight once Allied air power came into action at daylight.

Colonel Wolfgang Maucke, commander of the 115th Regiment of the 15th Panzergrenadier Division, considered that he had not enough time to prepare for the attack or to feed and rest his grenadiers who were tired, cold and hungry.

The attack was to be led by the two battalions of the Panzergrenadier Regiment, who were already there, with two battalions of self-propelled artillery and 18 Mark IV and Panther tanks. This large force was to be reinforced by a regiment of Volksgrenadiers of the 26th Division and by the divisional artillery.

The plan of the commander of the 26th VGD was to take the defenders of Champs in the jaws of a huge pincer shaped attack. The 77th Regiment of the 26th VGD was to attack from Givry, the left jaw of the pincer, while the 115th Regiment of the 15th Panzergrenadiers was to move via Flamizoulle towards Champs and Hemroulle, the right jaw of the pincer.

He was thus to be fighting the 502nd and 327th Regiments, with his main thrust being at the link between the two forces once again. Diversionary attacks were to be staged at other points on the perimeter to tie down the American defenders and to stop their sending reinforcements to the breach in the line as they usually did.

2 a.m. The Reserve Combat Command was ordered to pull out of the line on the east flank of the Fourth Armored Division and march from Bigonville around the division's rear to its west flank at Bercheux, preparatory to launching a surprise attack north to relieve the beleaguered 101st Airborne Division surrounded in Bastogne.

Lieutenant-Colonel Steve Chappuis,
Commander of the 502nd Parachute Infantry Regiment.

A patrol of the 502nd Regiment ready to leave Rollé.

2.45 p.m. While the waning moon lit the snow-covered fields, the impressive silence of the night was broken by the characteristic drone of German aircraft. The American positions near Champs were bombed while a heavy artillery barrage fell on the fields where the parachutists were dug in. However, well protected in their fox-holes, they suffered few casualties. Then, a second wave of bombers followed to complete the job of the first, hitting the barracks and other buildings.

3 a.m. Company A, commanded by Captain Wallace A. Swanson, formed a screen between the village of Champs and the enemy to the north. In front of them, they observed intense activity as grenadiers dressed in white moved from Givry towards Rouette and their objective: Champs.

Swanson telephoned Lieutenant-Colonel Patrick J. Cassidy, duty officer of the 502nd Regiment, whose command post was installed in the Rollé Château, on the left of the Champs-Hemroulle road. He informed him that he was under fire from troops on the road from Rouette, but he could not state either the strength or the objective of the attack.

3.30 a.m. Cassidy called Swanson to find out how the situation was developing. The Captain barely had the time to say that his men were fighting with the grenadiers before the telephone line was cut. Cassidy then awoke the regimental commander, Lieutenant-Colonel Steve A. Chappuis. At that moment, all telephone lines with their units had been cut, leaving only communication by radio.

Chappuis contacted Major John D. Hanlon, commander of the 1st Battalion of the 502nd, whose command post was in a house in the village of Hemroulle at the limit of the sectors held by the 502nd and 327th. The command post of the 3rd Battalion of the 327th was only a short distance from Hemroulle, commanded by Lieutenant-Colonel Roy C. Allen, who occupied an isolated farmhouse on the right of the Champs-Hemroulle road.

Chappuis ordered Hanlon to prepare companies B and C to move to the front line and to come to Rollé urgently. "Silent Steve" then contacted Swanson by radio who confirmed the attack on Champs by the grenadiers who were fighting a furi-

...the armoured vehicles and men of the 115th Regiment of the 15th Panzergrenadiers.

ous house-to-house combat against the parachutists, often using bayonets and other close-combat weapons.

When Hanlon reached Rollé, he was ordered to send Company B towards Champs, to occupy the ground to the west of Rollé and then to enter the village to assist Company A.

The Champs defenders had the help of two tank-destroyers from the 705th Tank Destroyer Battalion. One was stationed at the centre of the village while the other was strategically placed to the west to cover the road and the surrounding hills. Machine-guns had been placed in front of the tank ambush in the village to force back the grenadiers while the gun of the tank-destroyer stopped their advancing through the houses: when they occupied one, it was destroyed with a shell.

In Bastogne, only Colonel Moore was on duty at the operations' centre. In his command post, however, Colonel Harper had stayed awake, because he was still very worried by the weakness of his overstretched lines of defence.

At Rollé, Chappuis remained very calm. He was waiting to be sure of the strength and purpose of the German attack before committing his forces prematurely. The positions held by Company A had been attacked from the front, but grenadiers were infiltrating to the east of Champs on the left flank of the 2nd Battalion, at exactly mid-distance between Champs and Longchamps. Alerted to this menace, the commander of the 2nd Battalion, Lieutenant-Colonel Thomas H. Sutliffe, swung part of his forces round to face the danger.

5 a.m. Major Hanlon was ordered to send a platoon of Company B to reinforce this threatened flank.

Around Mande-St-Etienne on the Marche-Bastogne road, panzers were manoeuvering and preparing to attack. These were the armoured vehicles and men of the 115th Regiment of the 15th Panzergrenadiers.

In Bastogne, the headquarters' duty officer had decided to wake General McAuliffe. The size of the attack now under way was being confirmed.

5.45 a.m. Hanlon hesitated to send the men of Company B into Champs. In the darkness and in the extreme confusion of combat, house by house, it was impossible to distinguish friends from enemies, so the Americans ran the risk of killing each other.

...the enemy tanks were assembling to the east of Mande-St-Etienne for an attack.

...the grenadiers who were clinging to them.

Chappuis agreed with this decision and told him to hold his present positions.

Company B formed a solid line behind Champs and could contain the attack if the Germans were to take the village.

In their command post, Chappuis and Cassidy felt that another major attack would develop, but they did not know from which direction it might come. Like Harper, they were worried about the link between their regiment and the 327th – justifiably, because it was there that the second phase of the German offensive was to take place.

Harper sent two Sherman reinforcements that he had received to protect Company C at Hemroulle. He had known since 5 a.m. that the enemy tanks were assembling to the east of Mande-St-Etienne for an attack. They were in the sector defended by Company A of the 3rd Battalion of the 327th.

7 a.m. In the feeble light of the moon reflected on the snow, the men of Company A, commanded by Lieutenant Bowles, saw coming towards them 18 panzers painted white followed by foot-soldiers dressed in white. This seemed to be a ghost attack, but it was most real. Company A occupied a hill top while Company B, under Captain McDonald, was positioned on the edge of a wood.

7.10 a.m. The German armour supported by grenadiers reached the American lines. They moved forward in a single column winding in between the woods. The tanks were firing with all their weapons as were all the grenadiers who were clinging to them. Some were equipped with flame-throwers which loosed great jets of fire towards the American positions, more to intimidate than to destroy because their range was too short. Screaming and shouting as they advanced, the grenadiers seemed to be drunk. The head of the column moved towards the command post of the battalion. The Germans broke through the line but the 463rd Parachute Field Artillery Battalion, under Lieutenant-Colonel Cooper, began to fire on the tanks with their 75mm guns.

7.15 a.m. Harper received a telephone call from Colonel Allen, commander of the 3rd Battalion of the 327th, informing him that the Germans had arrived at his command post. "How close?" asked Harper. "Right here", asnwered Allen, "They are firing

...who held a line of fox-holes...

The major part of the German armour charged straight into the positions of Company A...

point-blank at me from 150 yards'range. My units are still in position but I've got to run".

At that moment, he saw the sinister barrel of an 88mm gun in front of his window. He ran out of the back door with two other officers as the tank crew fired a shell which passed over their shoulders. Having got away by the skin of their teeth from the German fire, they were then shot at by the men of the 502nd who mistook them for Germans rushing towards their positions. They changed direction, fleeing towards Hemroulle, where they were in turn shot at by the infantrymen who held a line of fox-holes protecting the artillery of the 463rd. But their adventure ended happily, and they were able to get to the village by waving their white handkerchiefs.

On the ground, Captain McDonald of Company B of the 3rd Battalion of the 327th had followed the incident on his walkie-talkie. He called the 3rd Battalion's companies and sent them the following message:

"The battalion commander has had to get out. I can see you from where I am. Your best is to stay where you are. Hold tight to your positions and fight back at them".

And that was exactly what they did.

Harper sent Major Jones with his radio to the command post of the 463rd Battalion near Hemroulle, where his mission was to assemble the remnants of the 3rd Battalion.

Followed by the grenadiers, the major part of the German armour charged straight into the positions of Company A, who had been ordered not to give way by Lieutenant Howard G. Bowles, their commander. Deep in their fox-holes, they watched with horror as the enormous panzers passed next to them or right over their heads. They lost 4 men killed and 5 wounded, but the 68 survivors were up and fighting, setting up a murderous fire against the tanks with their bazookas and against the grenadiers with their automatic weapons. Taken from behind, the tanks were defenceless, and the German infantrymen fell under their fire.

Nevertheless, the attack did break through the 327th's lines. The German column immediately began to fan out. Part went to the left to attack Champs from the rear on the road from

The Rollé Château.

The Germans were in difficult position.

Hemroulle, while the rest of the force continued straight on and to the right towards Hemroulle.

Colonel Chappuis was informed of the armoured threat by Lieutenant Samuel B. Nickels, who ran into the château crying, "There are seven enemy tank and lots of infantry coming over the hill on your left".

The château was emptied almost before Nickels had finished speaking. Even cooks, clerks, drivers, and chaplains were collected under Captain James C. Stone who sent them up a slope bordering the road, where they set up a line of defence. Even the walking wounded joined in, led by the divisional surgeon, Major Douglas T. Davidson, who himself took up arms.

The Germans were 600 yards from the château. Cassidy called Hanlon, commander of the 1st Battalion, and ordered him to stand firm with Company B, while Company C took the full frontal shock of the attack.

Now, Templeton's tank-destroyers came into action. Two, which were hidden in a wood behind Company C's position, remained silent, while the two more advanced ones put two panzers out of action with their first shot as the German tanks appeared over the brow of the hill. But this did not stop the German advance, and the two tank-destroyers retreated towards Rollé. Encouraged by this, the following panzers came forwards and blew up the tank-destroyers during their manoeuvre.

The grenadiers approached Company C's lines, and Captain Cody, unaware that he had two more tank-destroyers behind him, decided to pull back to the edge of the woods to ensure better protection for his men. Once in place, his men hit the grenadiers with a torrent of fire from machine guns, riffles, automatic weapons, while the bazookas took care of the tanks. This violent defence stopped the German advance which turned instead towards Champs.

This manoeuvre presented the attackers' flank to the tank-destroyers, which had still not opened fire. The Germans were in difficult position, because they were now being fired on from four sides. Three panzers were immediately knocked out while the column encountered the men of Company B who stood between them and Champs. One Mark IV was destroyed by

A single tank got through to Champs...

...the fields were covered with grenadiers.

bazooka fire. A single tank got through to Champs, where it was stopped by the combined fire of a 57mm gun and the bazookas of Company A.

Captain James J. Hatch of the 502nd was in the command post of Company A, when the tank came to a halt in front of the farm. Intrigued by the noise, Hatch took out his pistol and opened the door cautiously. Less than 15 yards away, the barrel of a 75mm gun was pointed at him. He closed the door carefully and told the stupified officers, "This is no place for my pistol".

At Champs, the grenadiers of the 77th pulled back from the houses where the fighting was too murderous. They bypassed the village to advance towards Hemroulle, but were cut to pieces by the crossfire of the three companies.

Before leaving the village, one of them had written the following message on the school blackboard:

"May the world never again live through such a Christmas night! Nothing is more terrible than meeting one's fate, far from mother, wife and children. Is it worthy of man's destiny to bereave a mother of her son, a wife of her husband, or children of their father? Life was bequeathed us in order that we might love and be considerate to one another. From the ruins, out of blood and death shall come forth a brotherly world.

A German officer".

Company C alone took 35 prisonners, and the fields were covered with at least 60 grenadiers, lying next to their destroyed tanks.

While the fighting was taking place around Champs, the situation was fairly well communicated to the headquarters of the division, and for the first time since the beginning of the siege, McAuliffe was worried. There was a real danger this time that they would be overrun. The men of the barracks' staff began to get ready to go to the front line. Drivers, cooks and clerks ran everywhere to find weapons. Many of the headquarters' staff were veterans from the Normandy landings. One of them, Corporal David W. Bernay, attempted to get together as many bazookas as possible.

Daylight brought back the fighter bombers of the 9th Air Force...

Christmas Mass in 1944.

During this time, a few tanks under the command of Colonel Cherry went towards Hemroulle to meet the Germans. But it was not to be necessary, because, in the meantime, knowing the terrain perfectly, McDonald had sent a radio message to Towns, explaining the plan for the counter-attack. Caught between the two companies, the Germans surrendered. Their attempt to take Hemroulle had failed, and only one panzer was able to get there, where it was captured intact. 98 Germans were taken prisoner.

Kokott had failed again. His plan to take Bastogne before 8 a.m. had come to nothing.

9 a.m. McAuliffe and his staff knew that this battle was won. The telephone lines were functioning again thanks to the skills of the signal men who had not stopped working in the dark and during the fighting.

Daylight brought back the fighter bombers of the 9th Air Force who began their habitual death dance, severely punishing the Germans. From their fox-holes and at the barracks, everyone closely watched the diving attacks of the planes, some of which did not appear again, shot down by the very active German anti-aircraft defense. But the quickfiring guns and the Luftwaffe fighters could not, however, stop the terrible punishment inflicted on the concentrations of men and material around the battlefield.

10 a.m. Colonel Maucke began to regroup the remainder of the 1st Battalion of the 115th Regiment in the shelter of a hill to the south of Flamizoulle, a short distance from the main Bastogne-Marche road. They had only just reassembled, when the survivors of the morning's fight were violently attacked by fighter bombers. The reserve battalion was hidden in a wood to cover the 1st Battalion's northern flank, which enabled it to escape the massacre.

12 a.m. Kokott asked XXXXVIIth Corps headquarters for permission to stop the attack in order to regroup his troops. This was categorically refused. He had to take Bastogne, because the menace of a break-through on the left flank was becoming more and more alarming.

1 p.m. The combat ground to a halt by itself for lack of troops. Kokott threw no new troops into the battle. Those who had escaped

Christmas dinner round a table in the mess.

Christmas carols in Bastogne, just before the German air attack.

were going to wait for the cover of darkness to regain their starting point.

2 p.m. The lines of defence had been reestablished under the protection of the force sent by Team Cherry, by order of the 101st Airborne, and were now in a dominant position along the edge of a wood, south of the position of the 502nd.

The air force took over the task of keeping the Germans at bay for the rest of the day.

It was thanks to this airborne control that a serious hoax was exposed; a column of American tanks was seen proceeding towards Bastogne. It was spotted by an American observer, when it had no trouble in crossing German lines! It was annihilated by the US Air Force. It was really a disguised German column sent to attack Bastogne.

During the afternoon, General McAuliffe visited Ewell's command post on the Neffe road. At the entrance, an unexploded bomb hampered the passage. "Julian, don't you think you ought to have that thing removed?" said McAuliffe. "Well, I don't know, General. It's kind of a good thing. Sort of keeps us on our toes".

6 p.m. A Christmas dinner brought together round a table in the mess General McAuliffe, Roberts, Moore, Higgins, Sherburne, Kinnard, Kohls, Danahy and Renfro. Sergeant Herman Smith had done his best to produce a good Christmas dinner. On the round table was a tree decorated by images cut out from tin cans and silver paper used by the planes to jam enemy radar. The menu: ersatz coffee, tins of sardines and biscuits from the K rations. But it was the dessert that was the greatest success, and the officers applauded the arrival of a magnificent lemon meringue. But they had only just been served, when the building was shaken by violent explosions, and they were obliged to rush down to the cellar, some even taking their precious dessert with them. But alas, they could not even taste it, because it was covered with plaster.

The same thing happened to the civilians hiding in their cellar shelters. They also had tins of sardines which came from the shop stock accumulated by the mayor. Monsieur Léon Jacquemin had wanted his fellow citizens to have a Christmas dinner which was out of the ordinary, and he had ordered a

Christmas dinner in the front line.

general distribution of tins of fish. But sadly, most of those opened for Christmas dinner were inedible after the bomb attack.

For most of the tank men who were fighting in order to liberate the town, it was a sad Christmas dinner too, consisting of frozen potatoes which had to be cut with a bayonet in their container to get out as frozen blocks which the soldiers sucked in a melancholy way before chewing and swallowing them.

Although the siege was by no means over, the Americans had gained an advantage. Two battalions reinforced by artillery units had destroyed the third and last chance that the Germans were to have of entering Bastogne before it was reinforced.

Hitler himself paid homage to McAuliffe:

"I would like to see a German general who would fight on with the same stubborn, tough resistance in a situation which seemed just as hopeless".

What did his officers think?

General von Manteuffel knew that all hope of crossing the Meuse had been lost. Bastogne had become the prinicpal objective of the 5th Armored Army and of the whole offensive, because the two other armies were being held up.

And this was to be the tragic conclusion of the Ardennes offensive.

General Kokott knew that it was all over from as early as 10 a.m. At midday, he had asked permission from XXXXVIIth Corps to break off the attack and minimize his losses, but he had been refused. High Command's orders were firm. He had, therefore, continued to attack knowing that the only result would be additional and useless wastes of troops and equipment.

McAuliffe, however, was bitter. He rang Middleton, who was celebrating Christmas with a meal prepared by the nuns, who occupied the top floor of the school where VIIIth Corps had its headquarters in Florenville.

"We have been let down", he said, expressing his disappointment at not having received the anticipated Christmas present – the arrival of the 4th Armored Division.

Even so, on the morning of the 25th, clear and cold, Patton commented "Lovely weather for killing Krauts".

However, he had not followed the advice Middleton gave him at their Arlon meeting of the 20th December to take the shortest route, the Neufchâteau-Bastogne road. He had decided instead to break through along the Arlon-Bastogne highway, and for six days, his tanks had slipped and skidded about on icy or muddy roads often sliding into ditches, while having to put up a hard fight. Nevertheless, on Christmas Day, the leading tanks of Combat Command A, led by Brigadier-General Herbert L. Earnest, were less than 7 miles from Bastogne, having made only a painful 2 miles the previous day. Combat Command B under Brigadier-General Holmes E. Dager was moving towards Chaumont, and the Combat Command Reserve was now on the Neufchâteau-Bastogne road. Its column of 400 vehicles stretched right back to Vaux-sur-Sure, scrupulously respecting the rules for convoys at night: 8 miles an hour, 50 yards between vehicles, 1 minute between companies and 5 between battalions.

In the open half-tracks, the "Dough boys" (infantrymen, a term which dates from the 1914-1918 war) were freezing. The 30 miles, in spite of the beauty of the night and the brilliance of the moon, were a torture for the G.I.'s illy equipped for such a biting cold.

They stamped their feet on the floor of the vehicle trying to restore the circulation in their feet. Even those who were lucky enough to wear mittens sewn from three thicknesses of a blanket and fleece lined boots, many of them had their hands and feet frost-bitten.

In the G.M.C. trucks, covered with canvas but just as cold, the "Redlegs" or artillerymen, were no better off.

At a sudden stop in the column, Colonel Wendell Blanchard was projected through the windshield of his jeep.Lieutenant-Colonel Gillis in the following jeep jumped from his car to help his commander. With great difficulty because of his stiff fingers, he was able to remove the helmet of Blanchard and work his head back between the shards of glass without suffering any more cuts. Blanchard refused medical attention until 06.00 that morning when the command surgeon sewed up his neck and forehead in the new command post at Bercheux.

Blanchard's CCR was made up of three battalions. The 37th Tank Battalion was commanded by the twenty-nine-year-old Lieutenant-Colonel Creighton W. Abrams, nicknamed Abe. He had become famous since the landings in France and was well known for his unlit cigar which pointed from his tank "Thunderbolt IV" like a second gun. His principle was simple, "Go east, it's the quickest way home". The 53rd Armored Infantry Battalion was under the orders of Lieutenant-Colonel Georges L. Jaques, nicknamed by his men "Jiggers Jakes", but affectionately called "Sadsack" by Abrams. The 9th Armored Field Artillery Battalion under Lieutenant-Colonel Parker, supported by a battery of 155mm howitzers detached from the 177th Field Artillery Battalion, completed Combat Command R.

While the tankmen were progressing towards Bastogne, what was the parachutist in his fox-hole doing? Between skirmishes, he had a little fun reading the "Para-Dice Minor", a news sheet published by Private David J. Phillips, which contained the following social note:

"Miss Champagne Belch, your Society Editor, offers the following tips on where to go for dinner and dancing on your night out,

"The Bastogne Bar and Grill" is featuring a tasty little luncheon consisting mainly of "Ratione de Kay avec Café GI". Gerald Kraut and his 88 piece band furnish lively and varied entertainment during the cocktail hour. After sundown, the club occasionally bills Mr. Looft Waffe and his famous "Flare Dance".

"The Blue Boche" up the street furnishes a clever program of native folk dances. The most entertaining of these is the renowned German War Waltz in which the chorus performs in intricate circles with hands overhead while singing the hit number of the show, as popularized by the Wehrmacht playboys, entitled, "I'm Forever Shouting Kamerad".

Perhaps the most popular of the Bastogne bistros is the invariably crowded "Cellar Club"."

And these were the men that the Germans were supposed to beat.

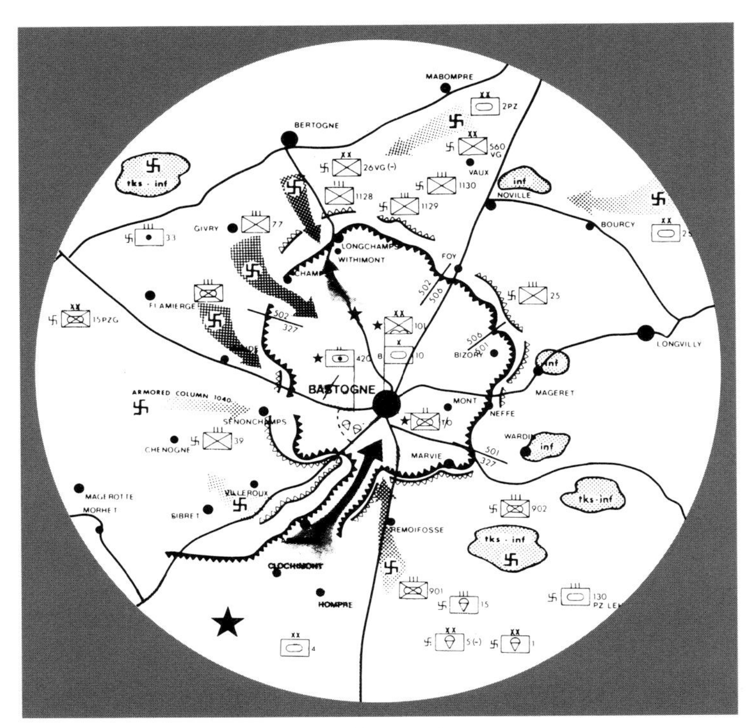

26th December

Team B of the CCR set out across the frozen ground.

TUESDAY 26th DECEMBER 1944

If the Americans besieged in Bastogne had impatiently awaited the arrival of the 4th Armored Division for a week, the Germans feared its coming. Since disembarking in Normandy, it had achieved a very revealing nickname among its opponents: "Roosevelt's Butchers". And these "Hell Buggies" were now getting nearer to the block.

During the night, a patrol from the CCB of the 4th Armored managed to cross the German lines and reach the barracks where Colonel Kinnard gave them a plan of the American lines round the town. Thanks to this, the risk of the Americans killing each other when they broke through was considerably reduced.

What was the general situation of the Division?

Combat A and B led the main attack, with their left flank protected by Combat Reserve, on whose side, however, events were going to move fast.

During the night, the command posts of the 37th Tank Battalion and the 53rd Armored Infantry Battalion were set up in Cobreville. Colonel Blanchard, commander of the CCR, had set up his headquarters in Vaux-sur-Sure, where he summoned Abrams, Jaques and the second in command of the 53rd, Major Crosby. Blanchard told his subordinates that the CCR had to attack via Remichampagne and Clochimont, where they were to turn left towards Sibret to rejoin the main Neufchâteau-Bastogne road. But Sibret was very strongly defended, and the battalion commanders were opposed to making a frontal attack on the village. They proposed to make their way via the small backroad on which their forces were located, to reach Bastogne via Assenois. Although he was a little worried about the protection of his own left flank, Colonel Blanchard agreed with this plan.

3 a.m. The commanders immediately gave verbal orders, not bothering for once to fill in the five paragraphs of written campaign orders.

Team B of the CCR, under Captain Jimmie Leach, set out across the frozen ground. Teams A and C had to provide covering fire from Remichampagne and the Cohet Wood.

8 a.m. Just as the guns of the two Teams were about to open up with supporting fire, P47 planes from the 362nd Combat Group appeared in the marvellously clear sky. They had not been requested, and there was no ground coordination, but they

P47 planes from the 362nd Combat Group appeared...

Kokott attempted a last desperate effort.

were very welcome. They hit at the German lines, machine-gunning and bombing a few hundred yards in front of the American tanks, clearing the way for them.

Despite this precious help, the infantrymen had to fight house by house to conquer Remichampagne. It took them two hours to clear the village.

10 a.m. At Bastogne, Kokott attempted what he called "a last desperate effort" to get into the town. Starting from Senonchamps, he sent a small, very heavily armed group composed of men from his division and supported by 10 tank destroyers. His plan was to try fo force a new passage, on the La Roche-Bastogne road. The group had to slip between Bastogne and Hemroulle, then move to Savy from where it was to rush into Bastogne. He hoped to pass without many problems between Bastogne and the advanced defences of the 327th and 502nd Regiments, which he had come up against the previous day.

But it turned out to be a failure, the group was literally cut to pieces by the howitzers positioned to the west of Bastogne. Nevertheless, four tank-destroyers managed to get as far as Hemroulle, where a large ditch forced them to turn broad side on. The Americans took this opportunity to fire at them at point-blank range with their artillery and tank-destroyers, annihilating the force.

So, as not to be left behind, the besieged troops themselves launched a punitive counter-attack against Assenois, and, with the assistance of a dozen tanks, destroyed the command post of a regiment of the 26th VGD.

10.55 a.m. At the Remichampagne crossroads Colonel Abrams went accross to "Blockbuster III", the tank of Captain Leach. He ordered Team A to take the hill on their left. But the moment the tanks began manoeuvering to execute the order, several antitank shells, fired from a position ahead of the group, burst around them. Abrams, who was by now back in his "Thunderbolt IV", calmly took his microphone: "Gunner, steady on! Twelve hundred. Fire". "Target. Cease fire".

Once again, Abe had proved that his crew was the best in the 37th Tank battalion.

While Abrams and Jaques were working out their plans of attack for the remainder of the day, hundreds of C-47's flew

...flew very low over their heads like great geese.

"Get to those men in Bastogne".

very low over their heads like great geese. Soon, the sky was full of red, yellow and blue parachutes. The German anti-aircraft fire was very intense, and many cargo planes were shot down. The relative ease with which Leach's Team B had reached their objective and the direct trajectory followed by the planes convinced the two men that they should head straight for Bastogne even though the other Teams had barely progressed half a mile since the morning. They could feel that their chance had come.

Yet the two battalions were a relatively weak force. In fact the 37th and 53rd had lost 20 tanks and 230 men since they set off a few days before.

2 p.m. Abrams called his commander Hugh Gaffey and told him of their plan. Gaffey called "the Boss", and without a moment's hesitation, Patton agreed.

Thirteen batteries, these of the CCR and some of the CCB, were organized to bombard Assenois. The left flank was protected by Teams A and D of the 37th, because they feared a tank attack coming from Sibret. Abrams called his S-3, Captain William A. Dwight, universally called Bill, and ordered him to form a well armed team with plenty of ammunition from Team C. A short meeting was held at the Clochimont crossroads with Lieutenant Charles P. Boggess. They had not carried out any reconnaissance, but they knew that the enemy defence was strong. Abrams said simply:

"Get to those men in Bastogne".

Boggess, who had commanded Squadron C for only 2 days as a replacement for Captain Trover, who had been killed in combat, brought together his eight tank commanders and informed them briefly what they had to do.

"I"ll lead the attack in my tank "Cobra King". You all know we've got to get to those men in the town. All you've got to do is keep rollin' and follow me. It won"t be any picnic, but we'll make it".

4.20 p.m. Abrams waved his hand, his usual way of signalling a departure, "Let 'em roll". The nervous drivers picked up speed, tracks squealing, and charged right through Clochimont towards Assenois, guns firing, with Cobra King in the lead. They had to cover 3 miles.

Lieutenant Chamberlain's jeep was hit...

The Shermans were supposed to have been followed by the half-tracks of Walt Green's Company C.

Boggess fired straight ahead, the tank following fired to the left and the next to the right, the Shermans using their 75mm guns like machine-guns.

During this time, Abrams had sent the following message to the artillery: "Concentration number 9, take it easy with no mistakes". Almost immediately the village of Assenois literally exploded, and the barrage cleared the road for the tanks, the shells exploding just in front of them. And so, as not to slow his advance, Boggess had to ask them to fire 200 yards further ahead, otherwise "You'll get me".

But the Germans were also firing. The jeep belonging to Lieutenant Chamberlain, who was directing the artillery fire, was hit and blown into the ditch. Lieutenant Billy Wood took over with a small spotter plane.

Charging literally through their own artillery barrage, the Americans ran into Assenois in the middle of the explosions with farm buildings crumbling and pieces of shrapnel ricochetting on the tanks' armour. Usually the tank commanders kept their torso outside the tank turret to see as much as possible, but here it was impossible, and the hatches remained firmly closed, the tank commanders keeping their eyes to their periscopes.

Boggess was not content with what he could see like this and opened the hatch, exposing just his helmet and eyes. It was not through carelessness, but because he had to guide his driver whose periscope had been damaged by a piece of shrapnel.

As his tank arrived in Assenois, one of the tank tracks locked, and they shot off on a side track, followed closely by two other tanks obeying orders to the letter.

The Shermans were supposed to have been followed by the half-tracks of Walt Green's Company C, but the artillery barrage was too intense for the light armoured vehicles. Two of the half-tracks had already been destroyed. The infantrymen of C Company rushed into the houses to find shelter, but the Germans were hiding in the cellars, and bitter fighting followed. All the night, the Americans' armoured infantry fought in the ruins of the houses and in the cellars against German paratroops of the 5th Division and Volksgrenadiers of the 26th.

The road was open again. On we go!

There were many outstanding acts of bravery. For instance, Jimmy Hendrix, a soldier of nineteen, armed with an automatic M1 rifle, forced the crew of an 88mm gun to surrender. Then he shot up two machine-gun nests before he threw himself forward to rescue a GI who was burning to death in the flames of a half-track. For his heroic acts, he was awarded a Congressional Medal of Honour.

But the situation was very confused when Colonel Abrams arrived in Assenois. A tank was blocked by a telephone pole, and Abrams and his crew had to jump out of their tank to help remove the obstruction and get the tracked vehicle moving again.

The road was open again. On we go!

In the general confusion, Boggess had managed to get his tank into the right road and continued towards Bastogne followed closely by the other Shermans. But there was again a gap opening up between the leading tanks and those following as they left Assenois, which gave the Germans the chance to place mines between the tanks on the road, and when the first half-track left the village to join Boggess, it blew up running over the mines. Dwight, who was following, stopped his tank and jumped onto the road, removing the mines and throwing them into the ditch. Then, he got back, unhurt, into "Tonto" and charged forward again in a hail of light arm and anti-tank rocket fire. Four more halftracks were destroyed.

Dwight tried to call the 101st: "Tony! This is one of Hugh's boys. Over!". But channel 20 which was reserved for commanders did not reply.

Leading the attack, Cobra King was still charging forwards. The gunner Milton Dickerman put three shells into an old concrete pill-box camouflaged in the pine trees and occupied by a group of German machine-gunners. His assistant, Harold Hafner, machine-gunned everything that moved on the edge of the woods which bordered the road. He saw white silhouettes falling like ducks in a shooting gallery.

Then, the tanks were out of the woods in open country. The snow-covered fields were decorated with immense blue, yellow and red flowers, standing out from the white background

Then, the tanks were out of the woods in open country.

Photo of the first tank to reach Bastogne: Cobra King.
From left to right: Harold Hofner - chief gunner, Hubert J.S. Smith - driver, Milton Dickerman - gunner, Charles P. Boggess - tank commander, James G. Murphy - loader. (Photograph given by Charles P. Boggess).

and made unreal by the falling night. They were the parachutes from the last resupply mission.

4.45 p.m. Boggess ordered his tank to slow down, because he saw a line of fox-holes in front of him, "Come on out, this is the 4th Armored". But there was not a word or a movement in reply.

Finally, after what seemed a long wait, a paratrooper got out of his hole. On his shoulder was an eagle's head. "I'm Lieutenant Webster of the 326th Engineers, 101st Airborne Division. Glad to meet you".

At 4.45 p.m., the following simple phrase may be read in the CCR journal: "A breach has been made in the circle which enclosed Bastogne". Cobra King was the first tank to break through the German lines and to link up with the besieged troops.

When the parachutists, now reassured, were milling around the tanks, Dwight standing up in his turret murmured, "It would not have been as bad as all that round here". The men of the 4th Armored were covered with grease, unshaven, dirty and blackened with powder, whereas the parachutists were trim and fresh-looking. They had scrupulously respected the rule that they should be clean shaven to maintain discipline and morale at a high level. But the contrast was surprising.

One of the young parachutists asked a battalion veteran if all the tanks were commanded by officers. This was not generally the case, but it is worth noting that the head of the valorous 4th Armored Division was in fact composed of tanks commanded by officers.

McAuliffe observed the scene from the top of a small hillock near by. Dwight approached him, saluted and shook his hand.

"Gee, I'm glad to see you", said the taciturn McAuliffe. Abrams joined them a few minutes later.*

6 p.m. Two hundred and sixty seriously wounded left Bastogne in twenty-two ambulances and ten 2 1/2 ton GMC trucks for the village of Villers-devant-Orval.

* This account of the liberation of Bastogne by the 4th Armored Division has been made with the help of Professor A. Harding Ganz of the State University of Ohio, USA, author of Breakthrough to Bastogne.

260 seriously wounded left Bastogne in 22 ambulances.

428 Germans had been captured...

7 p.m. By 7 o'clock, all the seriously wounded who could be transported had been evacuated.

8 p.m. Company B of the 53rd Battalion of Armored Infantry, under Lieutenant Robert "Potsi" Everson, completed the cleaning up of Assenois. Four hundred and twenty-eight Germans had been captured along with numerous pieces of artillery including four 88mm's and a battery of 105mm howitzers.

They had then to clear out the very dense woods to the north-east of the village. Although wounded in both legs, Lieutenant Frank Kutak directed the operation from his jeep.

The protection of the flanks of this narrow corridor was undertaken by Companies A and B of the 37th Tank Battalion.

During the night which followed, the G-4 of the Division, Lieutenant-Colonel Knestrick, headed the first supply column to Bastogne, containing food and ambulances, escorted by the light tanks of Company C.

For their part, the CCA and CCB did not stay inactive.

The CCB had fought hard with the 15th Panzergrenadier Division at Hompré. During the night, the advanced elements of the CCB established contact with the lines held by the 101st Airborne.

The CCA, which was further from the town, had captured the commander of two battalions of the 15th Regiment of the 5th Parachute Division. Despite the information they had managed to extract from him, the advance of the 51st Armored Infantry Battalion was stopped, when they attacked towards the village of Sainlez, by German paratroops well dug in on a hill.

The Shermans had to intervene and destroy part of the village to force out the Germans who slipped away towards Livarchamps, where they ran into the 1st Battalion of the 318th Regiment of the 80th Infantry Division, which had cleared out the village a short while before. The fighting did not stop until late in the night.

Bastogne was relieved, but the 4th Armored had paid a heavy price for the exploit, losing more than 1000 men since its departure from Habay-la-Neuve.

... but the 4th Armored had paid a heavy price for the exploit.

It was in fact the beginning of the end.

During the evening, General Patton wrote to his wife Beatrice: "The relief of Bastogne is the most brilliant operation we have thus far performed and in my opinion the outstanding achievement of this war".

During this time, five hundred and forty German prisoners were driven to Neufchâteau under the guard of glider pilots and men of the 28th Division.

For them, the war was over.

It was in fact the beginning of the end, even if there remained much to do. The breaking of the siege of Bastogne presaged the defeat of the German army in the Ardennes offensive.

But if General Kokott was to say later of this moment that "It was all over", the German Press Agency DNB gave out a very different version of affairs in its radio communiqué:

"The enemy forces surrounded in Bastogne are on the verge of annihilation. Despite their intense air activity in the last few days, the enemy cannot stop the progress of the German offensive".

However, the better informed Adolf Hitler screamed that Bastogne had to be taken, because the defeat was like having a fish bone caught in his throat!

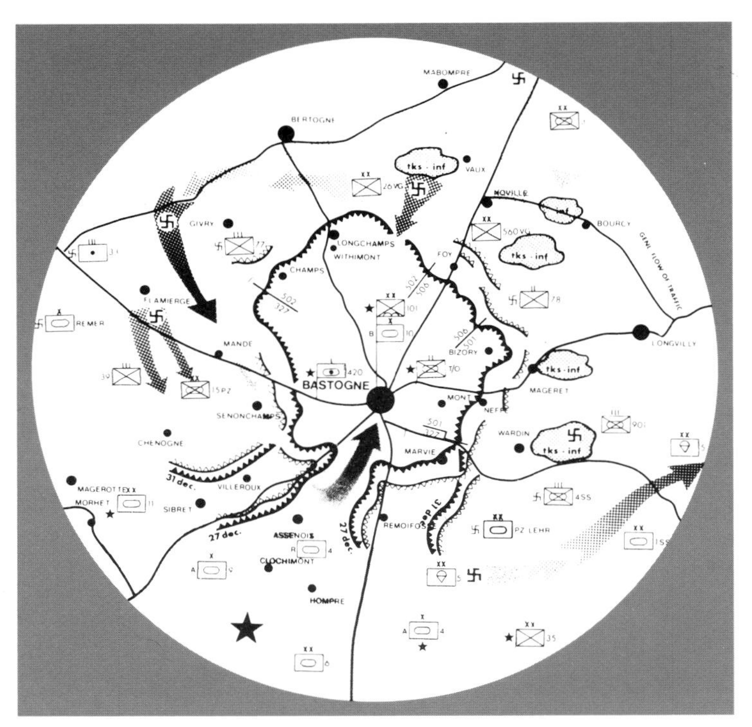

27th-31th December

There was a great activity on the newly opened road, and trucks, tanks and ambulances were driving bumper to bumper in both directions.

WEDNESDAY 27th DECEMBER 1944

Bastogne was bombed twice by German JU 88 bombers, just after midnight and shortly before dawn, causing considerable damage to houses in the town. A 500 pound bomb was dropped on the command post of the 501st Regiment, installed in the town's small seminary, but it did not explode.

1 a.m. A large American force was sent to reinforce Bastogne. There was a great activity on the newly opened road, and trucks, tanks and ambulances were driving bumper to bumper in both directions: towards Bastogne, reinforcements and supplies, and from the town, ambulances, trucks filled with prisoners as well as the first civilians.

The defence of this narrow corridor was the responsibility of the CCB of the 4th Armored Division which was later assisted and then replaced by the CCA of the 9th Armored Division, which covered the left flank while the 35th Infantry Division covered the right.

Despite the bad conditions – cold weather, fog and snowstorms – seventy ambulances evacuated another 964 wounded men in record time, those who could not be moved being treated in Bastogne by personnel recently flown in by gliders. In fact, during the day one hundred and thirty C47 cargo planes and thirty-two gliders of the 447th Troup Carrier provided the town with further supplies. The German anti-aircraft defence and fighters were also very active. The gliders were lucky to escape their barrage, whereas nine out of the thirteen C47 Dakotas flying behind them, were shot down.

General Taylor, the commander of the 101st Airborne, finally arrived in Bastogne. Grounded by the bad weather in Washington, he had jumped onto the first plane leaving for Europe and had flown to Orly among the crates and barrels of the C47's cargo. Then, he went straight to see General Eisenhower at his headquarters in Versailles. He had great difficulty in getting there because the guards were on red alert for German parachutists. He was told by his old friend Bedell Smith that he could get to Bastogne by the road which had

General Taylor was received joyfully on his arrival in Bastogne by McAuliffe.

Sappers of Company B, 326th Battalion of Airborne Engineers, photographed at Bastogne on the 27th December 1944 by M. Bando.
From left to right: Joe Halderman, unknown, Landery; below: unknown, Packy and John Tocco.

just been cleared by the 4th Armored Division and that he did not need to be parachuted in. But first of all he had to see Generals Bradley and Patton in Luxembourg.

He went via Mourmelon to pick up his combat gear and winter clothes and continued in a jeep to Luxembourg, arriving on the morning of 27th December after a difficult journey caused by overcrowded roads and numerous checkpoints, on the outskirts of each town and village. He spoke over the telephone with Bradley and Patton and finally managed to reach the 4th Armored Division, who offered him a tank for the rest of the journey as they were not sure if the road was still open. But Taylor preferred the mobility of his jeep to the security of a tank.

A couple of miles from Bastogne, he met some journalists who had taken shelter in a farm and invited one of them to join him in his jeep. (They were Joseph Driscoll of the New York Herald Tribune, Norman Clark of the London News Chronicle, Cornelius Ryan of the London Daily and Walter Cronkite of United Press). They politely declined his invitation... there was stilll a good deal of shooting going on!

4.10 p.m. He was received joyfully on his arrival in Bastogne by the staff and by McAuliffe, who handed back the command of the Division. Taylor's first question was: "How does it feel to be international heroes?".

They were astonished, "Who? Us?". And these officers protested when they were told that the break-through of the 4th Division had been painted as a "rescue".

Then, when he had heard McAuliffe's report, Taylor informed IIIrd Corps to which the Division had just been attached, that they were ready to attack.

Before the day ended, the Germans attacked twice, but two hundred grenadiers and three panzers were halted by the American artillery before they reached the lines of the 327th Glider Infantry. The tanks were destroyed and the grenadiers either killed or wounded.

Against the recommendation of General von Manteuffel, OKW ordered the continuation of the battle to take Bastogne using all available divisions.

The losses of the two panzer divisions, the Panzer Lehr and the 2nd Panzer, amounted at that time to 2500 killed, 1000 prisoners, many wounded, and 81 tanks, 81 guns and 674 different vehicles. And it was far from finished. For the most murderous fighting was only just about to start.

Bastogne had become the main objective.

What did Bastogne look like?

What did Bastogne look like?

Lieutenant-Colonel Ralph Ingersoll* described it as follows:

"I had gone up to see the attack on Bastogne – it was launched an hour's creep over the ice from Luxembourg. It was a hard, stark thing. The wind swept through the broken trees along the roads and the armor in the field, even the tanks that had been smeared with white paint, stood out in sharp relief, cold and naked. The troops built little fires of anything that would burn, even within sight of the enemy, to try to warm themselves. The infantry fought down one hill and up the next. The tanks were not much good then except as artillery. The dead lay frozen and stiff and when the men came to load them in trucks, they picked them up and put them in like big logs of wood. The frozen arms and legs got in their way when they were piling them. But everyone who had come through the summer before commented on how nice it was that the battlefield didn't stink...

On the edges of the town you could see, like a picture-story in a book, where the German columns had broken through the perimeter defence and come right up to the edge of the houses themselves. You could see this from the burnt-out panzers the Germans had left behind. One by one, their tanks had been shot through until, standing on a high place, the trail of them was almost like a snake cut into little pieces, winding across the hill on which Bastogne stands.

Mixed in with the wrecks of tanks were the wrecks of the gliders that had brought the medics in when the garrison was surrounded – and here and there, black in the sun, were the little basketfuls of charred junk, that is all that's left of an aircraft when it goes into the ground at three or four hundred miles an hour...

Riding through the Ardennes, I wore long underwear, a woolen uniform, armored force combat overalls, a sweater, an armored force field jacket with elastic cuffs, a muffler, a heavy lined trenchcoat, two pairs of heavy woolen socks, and combat boots with galoshes over them – and I cannot remember ever being warm!

Not that the temperature was so low, but there seemed a mean dampness in the air and the cutting wind never seemed to stop".

* Lieutenant-Colonel Ralph Ingersoll in his book, *Top Secret*.

A final supply by gliders brought in 10 tons of medical supplies.

THURSDAY 28th DECEMBER 1944

The morning began with a German air attack on Bastogne. The day was misty so that observation planes – both American and German – were unable to watch the lines, forcing both sides to send out numerous foot patrols to note enemy movements and to warn of any attack.

9.30 a.m. The advance party of Combat Command A of the 4th Armored Division reached the outposts of Company G of the 327th Regiment, accompanied by the 318th Regiment of the 80th Infantry Division.

12.30 a.m. Combat Command A of the 9th Armored Division reached Bastogne by way of the Neufchâteau road.

The 705th Battalion was rejoined by two platoons of its Company A and the Sappers Platoon, both of which had been unable to rejoin before the ring had been closed.

That afternoon, Lieutenant-Colonel X.B. Cox, Commanding Officer of the 101st's anti-aircraft battalion, was appointed as coordinator of all anti-aircraft defences in Bastogne.

A final supply by gliders brought in ten tons of medical supplies.

5.45 p.m. The Germans threw in a surprise attack against the 3rd Battalion of the 327th near Lutremange. The fight lasted for about an hour, the attackers being supported by heavy artillery and mortar fire. However, the 3rd Battalion was so well dug in that the attack failed. This was to be the main action of the day.

Throughout the day, the German DNB boasted on the radio that, "the 101st Airborne had suffered enormous casualties", while the German press announced that "the 101st Airborne had been annihilated" or that "very few had survived", or that "the enemy forces in encircled Bastogne were facing their annihilation. Despite the intensified enemy air activity in the past few days the enemy could not prevent the German offensive from progressing satisfactorily."

8 p.m. A column of sixty-two vehicles drove into Bastogne, twenty-five loaded with ammunition, nine with rations, one with engine oil and two with mail and parcels from home.

Grave registration Service

Nineteen of these trucks belonged to various units of the 101st Airborne who had been unable to join up before the siege, and six of them belonged to the Grave Registration Service. As soon as these arrived, the Bastogne cemetery was closed, and those killed after the 28th were taken to the rear area for burial.

The 101st Reconnaissance Platoon rejoined the Division also.

Towards the end of the day, the fog lifted to reveal a beautiful clear sky. The icy cold night which followed was quiet, the whole zone now being protected from the air by American P61 Black Widow night fighters, flying high in readiness to intercept any air or ground attack. The German aircraft did not take any risk...

9 p.m. Generalfeldmarschall Model signed an order of the day to restore a stable situation round Bastogne, which was to be carried out in two stages on and after the 29th December.

Genralfeldmarschall Model

Members of the 101st Airborne moving into the line on the 29th December.

Tons of food, ammunition and winter clothes accompanied the stream of arriving men.

FRIDAY 29th DECEMBER 1944

From daybreak, the weather was excellent and visibility perfect.

The whole day was to be quiet except for two incidents.

Between Monaville and Recogne, a thirty-strong German patrol clashed with an outpost of the 502nd Regiment. In the ensuing fight, they were turned back by the Americans.

4.30 p.m. The 801st Airborne Ordnance Maintenance Company which had left Mourmelon for Bastogne on the 19th December finally arrived.

Just before dusk, Company E of the 501st Regiment was attacked with some losses, its Captain, Frank "Foxy" Gregg, being wounded.

But the Americans were under the impression that the Germans were planning something. Throughout the day, the German patrols had pushed back the American ones, preventing them from entering the German lines, to see what was happening. Observation aircraft were under continuous fire from very alert German flak. It appeared that the Americans' eternal adversary, "the old 26th" (as the Germans had nicknamed the 26th VGD), was being regrouped in the vicinity and that the 3rd Panzergrenadier Division had been sent to reinforce them.

6 p.m. Night had just fallen when three JU 88's bombed the town, destroying a gun, two half-tracks and a light tank and damaging more houses. One of the aircraft was shot down by Colonel Cox's anti-aircraft defences. The town was bombed twice again during the following night.

Supplies continued to arrive by road. Tons of food, ammunition and winter clothes accompanied the stream of arriving men. The 506th and the 501st were strengthened by men who had previously been unable to reach Bastogne.

The besieged troops received a new weapon too, called the Pozit or VT rocket, which was an artillery shell that could explode at a preset height and which, up to then, had been

...the newly arrived and arriving reinforcements.

top secret. It was to inflict considerable physical and moral damage on the Germans, demoralizing their troops and giving the American artillery an important advantage*.

During the afternoon, General von Manteuffel summoned all the commanders under his orders, both those who had fought at Bastogne and those commanding the newly arrived and arriving reinforcements, notably three commanders of the Waffen SS. He began with a few remarks about the error of judgement concerning Bastogne at the beginning of the offensive. He then explained that the initial aims had been abandoned, and that Bastogne had become the "main problem".

The German High Command considered that the impending battle was an opportunity to score a spectacular psychological victory or at least, to smash the enemy divisions which were to be thrown at them. This was to be achieved in three phases:

First: reimpose the blockade. Second: drive the Americans back towards the south. Third: using reinforcements that were on their way, take Bastogne.

Lüttwitz' Army Group would lead the attack with the XXXIVth and XXXXVIIth Armored Corps. The XXXIVth would attack from east to west via Lutrebois towards Assenois, and the XXXXVIIth from west to east. This attack was to be the stronger, spearheaded by the Führer Begleit Brigade, through Sibret to close the circle. It was to be supported by the 3rd Panzergrenadier Division on the left flank, while the survivors of the 26th VGD and the 15th Panzergrenadiers would cover the north and west of Bastogne. The main problem was that they did not know when the reinforcements were arriving – the 12th SS Armored Division, the 9th SS Armored Division and the 340th VGD Division.

But once again, their orders were explicit: no delay was permitted.

* In the head of the rocket was a proximity fuse and a miniature radio which emitted radio waves when it left the gun barrel. As it approached the target, the radio waves were reflected and amplified by a thyratron tube which caused the shell to explode at a predetermined height.

The civilians were terrorized and decided to take advantage of the supply trucks to evacuate the town.

The 1st Panzer SS.

SATURDAY 30th DECEMBER 1944

12 p.m. – 4 a.m. It was a most troubled night. At midnight and again at four o'clock in the morning, Bastogne was bombed by the Luftwaffe. Then silence fell again on the town and the thick carpet of snow which covered the area muffled any noise.

7 a.m. Suddenly, the silence was broken by what was to be the most severe bomb attack that the town was to sustain during the whole battle. The civilians were terrorized and decided to take advantage of the supply trucks that were returning empty, to evacuate the town.

They left, lying on the freezing floors of the GMC's, while machine-gun fire tore the canvas covers and punctured the trucks' metal bodies. If calm had returned to Bastogne, the surrounding areas were alive with gun-fire.

General Patton had insisted on an attack for that morning. Middleton had to carry it out at any cost, because Patton did not want to see the Germans strengthen their position around the town thanks to the reinforcements which were coming in on the northern flank. The attack was to be led by the 11th Armored Division which had never been under fire and the 87th Infantry Division which had seen some action in the Sarre but which was also a "green" division. The 11th Armored Division was reinforced by the 602nd Tank Destroyer Battalion (less Company C) equipped with the famous M-18 tank destroyer with the high velocity gun (76 mm) known as the "Hellcat".*

The men of the 11th Division, which was supposed to attack from Vaux-les-Rozières, were exhausted and frozen after a difficult 85 mile journey over frozen roads to reach the assembly zone. They did not know the nature of the terrain, nor did the 87th Infantry Division which had assembled in the area between Bertrix and Libramont, their attack beginning from Bras, a small village to the north.

Their objective was to push forward between the Ourthe River and Bastogne to reach Houffalize.

* A superb M18 is shown at the Victory Memorial Museum, E25/E411 near Arlon, Belgium..

The men of the 11th Armored Division were exhausted and frozen after a difficult journey.

As luck would have it, the flank of this attack ran up against one of the two attacks organized by Lüttwitz. The one which was to run into the American offensive from the west was led by Major-General Walter Denkert, commander of the 3rd Panzergrenadier Division, and by Colonel Otto Remer at the head of his Führer Begleit Brigade. In addition, on this side of the perimeter were the 26th VGD and the 15th Panzergrenadiers. Denkert had planned his attack to start at 7.30 a.m. so as to surprise the Americans who, he maintained, never moved before 9 a.m.

The other attack saw the 1st Panzer and the 167th VGD attack in the region of Lutrebois.

The aim of the two attacks was to reimpose the blockade on the town by cutting the supply route which the 4th Armored Division had opened on the 26th December.

To give as clear a picture as possible of this decisive battle for Bastogne, the two attacks will be described separately.

The first contact between the opposing forces was anecdotal. An American patrol saw a shadow in the fog and early dawn which they took for an American. One of the soldiers gave a happy "Good morning" to receive a deep "Guten Tag" in reply. But the surprise was going to be even bigger for the Germans.

7.30 a.m. In fact, the 11th Armored Division's attack had only just begun when it ran up against the flank of Denkert's attack. The Major-General's plan was to pass between Chenogne and Senonchamps to take Villeroux with the armoured grenadiers. Remer was to follow with the tanks to take Sibret. Then, the two forces were to attack Assenois and Hompré jointly, linking up with the 1st Panzer SS and the 167th VGD.

The grenadiers advanced with great difficulty towards Sibret in the snow, while the tanks, loaded with men, waited at Chenogne to attack in their turn via Flohimont. The fog was so thick that neither side could see the other, and the American and German attacking troops moved forwards ignorant of their enemy.

The grenadiers surprised Task Force Collins of the CCA of the 4th Armored Division against whom they had already fought the night before and pushed them back towards Sibret. But

The leading tanks of Combat Command B of the 11th Armored Division.

The tanks had been able to get out of the village in time...

during the fighting, the German commander was killed, hence the German advance slowed. Behind them, their tanks had begun to move. They arrived at Flohimont when the fog suddenly lifted to reveal thirty Shermans in the distance.

10 a.m. These were the leading tanks of Combat Command B of the 11th Armored Division. Colonel Yale had divided his CCB into two groups: Force Poker, which the tank commanders of the Führer Begleit Brigade had just spotted, and Force Pat, which was made up largely of armoured infantrymen supported by Shermans.

Force Poker's tanks avoided Lavaselle, which was located in an unpropitious valley, and its commander, Major Wray F. Sagaser, headed them towards the villages of Houmont and Brul on the tops of the hills to the north. The two hamlets were weakly held by infantry and were taken without any problem. The Task Force was now on Remer's right flank, but he decided to ignore this threat and to continue towards his goal. However, when he learned that the Americans had run up against his flank defence at Lavaselle, he decided to go and see the gravity of the menace himself. But his men had established a strong barrage, and, reassured, he returned to Chenogne to find his grenadiers decimated by the intense American air and artillery attack that they had just sustained. The tanks had been able to get out of the village in time, and Remer left to find them, having informed Denkert of the situation and requested reinforcements.

Not far from Chenogne, part of the tank force had meanwhile come up against Company B of the 22nd Tank Battalion which accompanied Force Pat. Remer's men had destroyed seven enemy tanks, and the Americans had requested a truce to recover their wounded. After this collision, the two forces retreated.

At the end of the day, Remer regrouped his forces, while the 3rd Panzergrenadier Division, which had not been able to do much that day, paralysed by the enemy artillery, moved its troops towards the ruins of Chenogne.

Combat Command A of the 11th Armored Division and the 87th Infantry Division attacked far away from the perimeter.

During a difficult journey they had been serverely punished by the American aviation.

The objective of the 87th was to cut the Panzer Lehr's supply route near St.Hubert.

On the other side of the perimeter, to the south-east of Bastogne, the 1st Panzer SS and the 167th VGD attacked early in the morning. The 1st Panzer SS had led the attack of the 6th SS Armoured Army at the beginning of the offensive on the 16th December, and it had suffered serious losses of men and material. Its state had not been improved during the difficult journey towards Bastogne, especially near Houffalize, where they had been caught in a natural trap on a narrow winding road in a deep valley and had been severely punished by the American aviation. Furthermore, SS Oberführer Wilhelm Monke's division had not yet grouped its remaining forces for the attack. The reinforcements which had been made available, the 14th Regiment of the 5th Parachute Division and the remains of the 901st Regiment of the Panzer Lehr did not nearly replace their losses. Finally, there was discord between the Waffen SS, the Luftwaffe, and the men of the Wehrmacht.

The 167th VGD, commanded by Lieutenant-General Hanz Kurt Hoecker, was a good division which retained a nucleus of veterans from the Russian front despite massive losses. The gaps had been filled by men from the Luftwaffe. The Division was very badly equipped in artillery and suffered from the unreliability of its transport, most of which had been recovered from the Italian army and which could not be kept in working order because of the shortage of spare parts.

The purpose of their attack was to link up with the Führer Begleit Brigade beyond the Bastogne-Arlon road.

The two divisions were separated by a defensive line centred on Lutrebois. This village had been taken the previous day by the 35th Infantry Division, and it was now defended by three companies of the 3rd Battalion, commanded by Lieutenant-Colonel W.C. Wood, while the hilltops from Lutrebois to the Bastogne-Arlon road were held by the 2nd Battalion under Major C.F. Dannel. These two battalions were part of the 134th Regiment, while the 137th defended the village of Villers-la-Bonne-Eau.

The first attack was stopped dead by a concentrated artillery barrage.

The Losange Château.

The 1st SS Panzer had assembled its tanks on the Tarchamps-Lutremange road, and it was from here that it was to launch the attack against Lutrebois and Villers-la-Bonne-Eau, to try to break through to its objective.

4.45 a.m. The first attack was stopped dead by a concentrated artillery barrage, and both tanks and grenadiers were stopped. They made another attempt to attack via the north of the village, but the German armour ran into concentrated bazooka fire, and the grenadiers who came from the west were cut down by machine-gun fire.

The day began badly for the Waffen SS, who had already lost a large number of men and two tank-destroyers, which had been destroyed by anti-tank fire, while a third had exploded on a mine.

Meanwhile, Villers-la-Bonne-Eau had been attacked by seven tanks and grenadiers with the lines being infiltrated by small groups of German infantry wearing white uniforms.

Before dawn, the tanks near the two villages began to destroy the farm buildings one after the other with gunfire. The villages were burning.

6.35 a.m. Informed of the attack, Brigadier-General Herbert L. Earnest, commander of the CCA of the 4th Armored Division, sent reinforcements urgently needed to the 35th Division.

8.45 a.m. Villers-la-Bonne-Eau was in the hands of the Waffen SS. Only one of the 169 defenders escaped, Sergeant Webster Phillips.

10 a.m. The reinforcements from CCA began to arrive. The first half-tracks filled with the infantrymen of the 51st Armored Infantry Battalion raced to reinforce the lines being held with much difficulty by Dannel's 2nd Battalion and which the grenadiers of the 2nd Regiment of the 1st Panzer SS were bypassing by going through the woods.

The Americans began to pull back towards the Losange château to the south-west of Lutrebois where the command post of the 3rd Battalion was installed. The SS grenadiers tried to take it, but the half-tracks of the 51st arrived firing all their .50 machine-guns, forcing the SS to retire to the woods.

Attacking in columns, using all the small routes and lanes, the 167th VGD reached and cut the Bastogne-Arlon road, then

The fighter-bombers had come into action and destroyed seven panzers.

But the German menace was becoming more and more serious.

moved into the woods to the south-east of Assenois where they were eagerly awaited. The head of the German attack was decimated by machine-gun fire, and the rest of the division was given a rough handling by the U.S. aviation and artillery which nailed them to the spot.

11 a.m. More than 25 German tanks moving along the Lutremange-Lutrebois road were spotted by the F.O.*, who warned the air force.

1 p.m. The fighter-bombers had come into action and destroyed seven panzers, the rest taking shelter in the woods. The "green" G.I.'s of two companies who were without anti-tank weapons and excited by the fighting, opened fire on the tanks with their rifles and machine-guns. The effect on the armoured monsters was like mosquito bites on a rhinocerous, but the noise reassured them.

But the German menace was becoming more and more serious.

The companies retired towards the Losange château.

A spotter plane had closely watched the retreat of the thirteen panzers which had pulled back to the cover of the woods between Losange and Lutrebois. The observer informed Lieutenant John A. Kingsley of Company B of the 35th Tank Destroyers. With the assistance of a platoon from the 701st Tank Destroyers and his own six Shermans, Kingsley laid an ambush. When everything was in place, everyone laid low. Unsuspecting, the Germans began to move.

The six first presented their flank to Kingsley's guns. The first shot destroyed the leading tank which was the platoon commander's. The others were pulverised one after the other before they could escape from their vulnerable position. When another wave of panzers arrived, six were put out of action by the Shermans, while the tank destroyers dealt with the self-propelled artillery and grenadiers which followed.

* The F.O.: Artillery Forward Observer, the advanced "eyes" of the artillery. The mission of these specialists is to spot the fall of artillery shells and correct their aim. They use either tanks or jeeps to get around, with powerful radio equipment.

His jeep had passed through the two main combats of the day.

General Patton had arrived in Bastogne.

But, despite this sucess, the Germans had occupied both Lutrebois and Lutremange by the end of the day.

This was a small result for the heavy losses which had been sustained in the attacks. Their attempt to isolate Bastogne again had failed totally. Firstly, Denkert's attack had not developed as expected and had been practically stillborn. Secondly, the attack launched by the 1st Panzer SS and the 167th VGD had not reached its objective, the two divisions sustaining heavy losses. The two jaws of the pincers had not closed.

General Patton had arrived in Bastogne during this time. His jeep had passed through the two main combats of the day, but Patton had total contempt for the danger.

Even though the sky had been heavily overcast since midday, he wanted to see every detail of the battlefield; and, in addition, he wanted to be seen everywhere. He took McAuliffe in his special jeep with a high windscreen and side screens, comfortably seated on a red leather seat, his legs well wrapped with several blankets. He had everything explained to him and frequently stood up in the jeep to look at a particular point through his binoculars or to take photographs of the wrecked German tanks which littered the countryside.

He was most interested by the point which the Germans had chosen for their Christmas attack and insisted on a description in the minutest detail of the American positions and of the places where the 115th Panzergrenadier Regiment had attempted to break through the line.

When he returned to Bastogne and got out of his jeep, he was wearing his magnificent Colts with ivory handles hanging from a belt, over a fur-lined air force jacket with the armored army insignia on the left sleeve. After a long conversation with General Taylor, he pinned the Distinguished Service Cross on the chests of McAuliffe and Steve Chappuis.

This visit of their famous general remained in the minds of all the American fighting men at Bastogne. Though few had actually managed to see his well-known silhouette, they had just learned the good news – there was to be an issue of brandy to celebrate the new year.

Patton was pleased with his men. But he was also conscious of the danger which remained; and at the end of the day noted in his diary, "Unquestionably this was the critical day of the operation as there was a concerted effort on the part of the Germans, using at least five divisions, to again isolate Bastogne".

He was convinced that without his order to attack that morning, the Germans would have broken through and occupied Bastogne on the 30th December. The fact that they had fallen on the German attack from the flank was one of those pieces of luck which changed the course of events.

Besides being a genius, Patton was lucky.

Napoleon, already, preferred luck to glory!

General McAuliffe, Colonel Chappuis and General Patton in Bastogne.

The American press on 30th December was asking why the Germans were being allowed to call the shots.

In Washington, the situation was studied at the highest level. The Secretary of War, Harry L. Simpson, and General George C. Marshall lunched together and calculated the consequences of an eventual German success.

They reckoned that the Germans still had an equivalent number of divisions to the Allies. Marshall thought that if the German offensive achieved its goals, and if the Russians did not move, they would have to reexamine the whole strategy of the war and take up defensive positions along the German frontier, at best, until the American people could be persuaded to furnish the fresh troops which would be indispensable.

Antwerp had become the key point, and it was now essential that the city remained in Allied hands.

As we can see, from this distance, the issue of the battle was hardly resolved.

On the German side, General von Manteuffel was surprised to see the quantity of reinforcements that he was being sent to take Bastogne, and he compared them with bitterness to the feeble forces that he disposed of to cross the Meuse...He deplored the fact that he was obliged to throw them willy-nilly at Bastogne as soon as they arrived at the front. He knew that at present even a massive attack with the considerable forces at his disposal would probably not succeed in taking the town. But his orders were definite, and the new arrivals continued to wear themselves out uselessly against the solid American positions.

The fact that the best divisions had now been concentrated around Bastogne was an admission by the High Command that their last hope of taking Antwerp had slipped away. Further, it was known that General-Oberst Jodl had told Hitler, "My Führer, we must face the facts squarely and openly; we cannot force the Meuse river".

General Kokott, whose famous 26th VGD was down to 2000 men at that time, must have regretted his boast at the beginning of the offensive when he had declared, "I don't need tanks. I shall take Bastogne with the MP44 pistol". It was, indeed, an excellent machine pistol...

This aerial photograph taken on the 25th December by the American aviation shows clearly the area where the major fighting took place:
The Assenois-Bastogne road that the CCR of the 4th Armored Division had used and the Arlon road used by the CCA to reach Bastogne. The Kessler farm where the emissaries had been taken to present the surrender ultimatum. The Arlon and Wiltz roads which join before entering the town, and the area where the fighting took place on the 30th December. The Neufchâteau-Bastogne road by which the CCB of the 6th Armored Division tried to reach Bastogne, and which was crowded with the vehicles of the 11th Armored Division.

SUNDAY 31st DECEMBER 1944

It snowed throughout the night.

The comparative breathing space enjoyed by the Bastogne defenders seemed now to come to an end. The most recent fighting had taken place beyond the perimeter between the Germans who were besieging the town and the newly arrived American reinforcements, but it was now to increase in intensity at different hot spots, and the American defenders of Bastogne were engaged again. The difference now was that the Germans were attacking in several different places simultaneously.

Despite the fighting, a number of large troop movements took place. The 6th Armored Division arrived to reinforce the units already in place, especially the 4th Armored which had only forty-two tanks fit to fight.

Combat Command A of the 6th Armored Division, commanded by Colonel John L. Hines Jr., arrived without serious problems along the road which had been used by the CCR of the 4th Armored to relieve Bastogne. That morning, it took up position in its assembly zone to the south-east of Bastogne after crossing the town with difficulty and the lines held by the 101st Airborne.

But things did not work out so well for the CCB, commanded by Colonel George Read. It used the Neufchâteau-Bastogne road, which was thought to be free but which was totally obstructed by the vehicles of the 11th Armored Division. The road was covered with a layer of ice which made it impossible to manoeuvre, and it was 10 a.m. before the first elements managed to reach their assembly zone near Clochimont.

8 a.m. Early in the morning, Lutrebois was bombarded by artillery batteries from several points on the perimeter. The 2nd and 3rd Battalions of the 134th Regiment watched the devastating results of the shelling. As soon as it was over, the 2nd Battalion attacked to the east. But no sooner had the infantrymen left the shelter of their fox-holes and begun to cross a small valley than they became ideal targets for the Waffen SS who were well dug in on the edge of the wood. Under the deadly fire of light automatic weapons, ninety American sol-

Some sixty grenadiers managed to attain their objective which was the first houses of Champs.

diers were mown down, and the survivors pulled back quickly. The 3rd Battalion had approached Lutrebois but it was also pinned down by fire coming from the woods covering the hills to the north-east. Access to the village was denied.

On the north-west of the perimeter, the 1st Battalion of the 77th Regiment of the 26th VGD attacked the positions held by the 1st Battalion of the 502nd. Some sixty grenadiers managed to attain their objective which was the first houses on the outskirts of Champs, where they took up positions.

Simultaneously, the 2nd Battalion of the 77th threw fifty grenadiers into an attack on a hill to the west of Champs. Assisted by artillery, mortar and machine-gun fire they took it and set up an artillery observation post on the top.

Several Americans were taken prisoner, an officer and two men were killed and four wounded.

10 a.m. But the 1st Battalion of the 502nd did not give in so easily. They launched a counter-attack, and heavy fighting took place for two hours in the deep snow. The Americans managed to retake the houses occupied by the Germans, freed the prisoners and in their turn captured an officer and four soldiers. The houses were full of dead grenadiers and the area around littered with bodies.

Despite the late arrival of the CCB of the 6th Armored Division, Hines and Major-General Robert W. Grow, the divisional commander, decided on a limited attack. The vehicles of the CCA were assembled outside Bastogne on the Neffe road without any natural cover and were suffering increasingly from German artillery fire.

A Task Force was put together with the 69th Tank Battalion, commanded by Colonel Chester E. Kennedy, with mission to take Neffe and clear the surrounding woods. Another Task Force consisting of infantry was made up from the 44th Infantry Battalion commanded by Colonel Charles E. Brown. Its mission was to follow the first force, to assist in the clearing of the woods and to take the hills overlooking Wardin, coming from Neffe.

12 a.m. The CCA moved off at midday, troubled more by the snowstorms than by the enemy. The air force was unable to assist them, and their advance slowed rapidly.

Combat Command A had skidded around all day.
This aerial photo gives a good idea of the nature of the terrain on which the fighting took place.

The armoured column had hoped for support from the 35th Division on their right, but they were much too busy themselves, spending the morning in a fruitless attack against Lutrebois where all their efforts were of no avail against the Waffen SS, who threw them back again and again.

Near Morhet, Combat Command A of the 11th Armoured Division moved forwards on the Sibret-Flamierge road through the positions occupied by the CCB in the area of Brul and Houmont. But they could not leave the road because the snow was so deep.

At Rechrival, they came up against a defensive line held by the 3rd Panzergrenadier Division, supported by antitank artillery and assault guns. As the engagement started, the 3rd Panzergrenadiers were quickly reinforced by the 115th Regiment of the 15th Panzergrenadiers. The destruction of the tanks of the "green" American division had begun.

Finally, the U.S. Air Force was able to intervene during a sunny spell, and when the tanks arrived in Rechrival, the village was empty... The fighter-bombers had driven off the grenadiers yet again with the help of the artillery.

Chenogne was attacked by Task Force Pat. At midday, the foot soldiers pushed forward bravely in the deep snow to confront the 39th Regiment of the 26th VGD, the men of the 3rd Panzergrenadiers and those of the Führer Begleit Brigade. Well covered by the fire of "meat-choppers", the Americans reached the first houses of the village, but they were not able to remain there long. At the end of the day, the German tank-destroyers dislodged them.

The CCR of the 11th Armored Division also ran up against Remer's grenadiers, their Shermans forcing the Germans to retreat from Magerotte to Pinsamont, where the intensity of the mortar fire compelled the Americans to retire towards Magerotte. The CCR had run into the right flank guard of the Führer Begleit Brigade. During the course of the day, the 55th Battalion lost 80 men.

5 p.m. Combat Command A of the 6th Armored Division had skidded around and made no progress all day. Just before dusk, the column was attacked on its flank by small enemy units. The artillery came into action to protect them, and Hines'

The New Year's Eve was calm in Bastogne.

armour remained under this umbrella. As always, the gunners played a decisive role. In addition to its three artillery battalions, the 6th Armored was assisted by the 193rd Field Artillery Group. It was to be very useful because the 1st Panzer SS had brought up an artillery corps consisting of 170mm long-distance batteries and rocket launchers, which were being installed to the south-east of the perimeter.

The New Year's Eve was calm in Bastogne, but the situation remained critical. There had been seventeen major attacks that day.

Patton, though an optimist by nature, said during the day, when he was informed of the situation: "Damn it, we can still lose this damn war".

"Damn it, we can still lose this damn war".

A camouflaged tank of the 6th US Armored Division moving through a wooded area near Bastogne.

The Germans ate American rations and smoked the pleasant smelling cigarettes.

MONDAY 1st JANUARY 1945

New Year's Eve was celebrated by the men on both sides of the lines, each in his individual way. The Germans, dressed in their heavy winter clothing, dug in next to their white-washed vehicles parked in the woods or copses, ate American rations they had captured, taking great pleasure in trying the unusual items: lemon drops, salted biscuits, chewing-gum, and pleasant smelling cigarettes.

The Americans, now better equipped since Patton got through, were keeping warm with their arctic boots worn over their normal footwear and fleecy linings inside their field jackets. They removed their thick green camphor smelling woolly gloves to open their parcels from home, brought to them by truck from Mourmelon. From time to time, they would sip their brandy slowly and watch the blue smoke from their Lucky Strikes rising in the air. Then, those who were not on guard tried to get a cat-nap keeping one eye open.

But Patton had other ideas, and while it was snowing heavily, the calm of the night was broken at 12.01 p.m. by a deafening noise. All the artillery of the 101st Airborne and the other divisions started their own particular celebrations. And the German lines were showered with high explosive shells.

From the advanced positions, the American troops could hear the screams of terror and pain of their adversaries between the salvoes.

On their side the German Air Force bombed Bastogne but without significant damage. It was a sad New Year's celebration.

The CCB of the 6th Armored Division had finally managed to take up its position to the left of Hines' CCA. Its first objective was to cut the German supply route from Longvilly which the Germans depended on to sustain their attacks in the Lutrebois sector.

The two Task Forces of the CCB were to attack Bourcy and Arloncourt to the left of the CCA. After taking the hills which overlooked the road used by the Germans, their objective was Longvilly. The 101st Airborne was to clear the St. Jacques Wood between the Bastogne-Noville road and Bizory. However, this order was countermanded, though General Grow was not informed.

One of the 105mm self-propelled guns of the 6th Armored Division.

...an intense barrage of 500 rounds in 20 minutes from the 212th Field Artillery.

The morning of the first day of 1945 was grey, the clouds low and gusts of wind were blowing up the snow.

Lieutenant-Colonel Harold C. Davall's 68th Tank Battalion made quick progress along the small road to Bizory, charging towards the defensive line set up by the 78th Grenadier Regiment since the beginning of the battle for Bastogne. Bizory fell without any resistance.

12 a.m. The Germans retaliated by bombarding the American right flank with their artillery.

The firing seemed to be coming from Mageret, and some Shermans went off towards this new menace. They raced into the village while the field guns dealt with the anti-tank guns that were firing from the cover of the near-by woods. The fight for Mageret had started.

3 p.m. The grenadiers gave way, after 3 p.m., under the American pressure, which allowed the 69th Tank Battalion of the CCA of the 6th Armored to come into action and to push its way east, while the CCB took the road to Arloncourt.

The sky had cleared; visibility had become excellent.

5 p.m. The 68th Battalion reached Arloncourt, where it ran into very strong opposition. The armoured infantry managed to occupy a few houses, but after dusk the Americans decided to pull back. Lieutenant-Colonel Arnold E. Wall's 50th Armored Infantry Battalion had to retire almost to its starting point. The two battalions had just run up against a very strong German defence force which counter-attacked, luckily to be stopped by an intense barrage of 500 rounds in 20 minutes from the 212th Field Artillery.

The 44th Armored Infantry Battalion of the CCA came up against the grenadiers who were well dug in in the woods to the south-east of Neffe. When the infantrymen approached the German positions, they were checked by rifle and machine-gun fire. Three times, the Americans attacked, finally forcing the Germans back and occupying half the wood.

For the next day they had to bring not only the CCR into line but also every able-bodied man, tank and gun.

At Lutrebois, things were not going well either.

The 1st SS Panzer.

While the CCA began to regroup...

All of the 134th Regiment of the 35th Division was engaged against the 167th VGD which had replaced the 1st SS Panzer.

The 1st Battalion of the 134th Regiment made a sortie from Marvie to try to chase off the grenadiers who occupied the heights of Lutrebois. But the veterans of the 167th VGD reacted quickly and filled the gap left in the American lines between the 1st and 3rd Battalion.

The 1st Battalion risked being surrounded. During the afternoon, Companies E and G of the 2nd Battalion tried an attack through the valley and the woods, but the German reply was strong, the two companies being encircled by the end of the day.

What happened to the 11th Armored Division?

12 a.m. While the CCA began to regroup, the Führer Begleit Brigade, of which a part, composed of the 31st Panzer Group and a battalion of grenadiers, was resting at the village of Fosset to the south-west of the Hinck Barriere crossroads, took the opportunity to fall on the CCB by surprise. The tanks and guns of the 31st Group destroyed a large number of American tanks.

Beginning at midday, the battle had lasted for three hours when the fighter-bombers and the artillery of the 11th Armored Division came into action to support the CCA's counter-attack designed to relieve their brother combat group.

3.30 p.m. The CCA had broken the force of the German attack, and its tanks reached Hubermont at dusk.

However, faced with the uncertain situation and the slow progress of the supporting infantry, the tanks pulled back around Rechrival and Brul.

Task Forces Pat and Poker were now able to coordinate their attacks for the first time. The Valets Wood were mercilessly bombarded by thirteen artillery battalions, and the grenadiers, who were dug in there, suffered considerable losses.

Colonel Yale thought that his CCB could easily get through to Mande-St-Etienne. As the Shermans slipped between the woods through a fire-break, the lead tank became bogged down in the marshy land and blocked the column with no pos-

The remainder of the CCB withdrew...

Prisoners taken by the 6th Armored Division.

sibility of any other vehicle's getting past. Hidden under the trees, the Germans had been waiting for this. Using their Panzerfaust, they destroyed all the platoon's tanks one after the other. The remainder of the CCB withdrew and took up positions in a semi-circle on the edge of a wood where they endured German fire all night.

Around St. Hubert, the 87th Infantry Division had tried to reach its objective which was the cutting of the Panzer Lehr's supply route from St. Hubert towards Bastogne. But the Training Division fought gallantly.

The 347th Regiment attacked from Moircy and Remagne to try to cut the road at Amberloup. The patrols of the 1st Battalion commanded by Major Cecil Chapman left Remagne towards the north. Each company was preceded by two Shermans, but the German reaction was very lively with both light weapon and artillery fire.

Lieutenant-Colonel Richard D. Sutton's 3rd Battalion for its part left from Moircy and took the village of Jenneville around midday. Bayerlein, however, refused to surrender the Libramont-Hinck Barriere, St. Hubert-Morhet cross-roads and had dug in six tanks well concealed behind piles of wood. From there, they could cover with their guns any attempt to approach.

The day was passed in skirmishing, but in the evening the Panzer Lehr brought up its tanks and forced the Americans back to Remagne.

Not being able to appreciate the situation, the two battalions ceased their attack at dusk.

6 p.m. General von Manteuffel received Gruppenführer Hermann Priess, Lieutenant-Generall of the Waffen SS.

The situation was alarming. Not only was Manteuffel well informed of the 6th Armored Division's attack, but he was also very worried by the pressure to the west of Bastogne against the Panzer Lehr and the Führer Begleit Brigade as well as the setbacks in the attacks of the 1st Panzer SS around Lutrebois. The 12th SS Panzer Division "Hitlerjugend" was on its way in support, and Baron von Manteuffel ordered Priess to take over the weak sector defended by the exhausted 26th VGD, from

Priess' Corps...

2nd January at midday. Priess' Corps was made up of the 26th VGD, the 12th Panzer SS and the 340th VGD, which came from Aachen.

On the American side the mood was better. In his press conference in Luxembourg City, Patton concluded, "I think yesterday was the crucial time in the operation. He (the enemy) could have done something yesterday; he can't do it now".

On the American side the mood was better.

Aerial view of the villages of Oubourcy and Michamps taken on the 25th December 1944 by American observation aircraft.

...the Germans suddently gave in leaving 30 dead and 7 prisoners.

TUESDAY 2nd JANUARY 1945

During the night, the Commander of the 3rd Panzergrenadiers decided to withdraw a number of defenders from the villages of Chenogne and Senonchamps as well as from the positions in the neighbouring woods

1 a.m. The Luftwaffe began to bomb the assembly zone of the 6th Armored Division. While this was happening, the 167th VGD was preparing an attack from Wardin, but the battalion involved was decimated by a barrage from nine field artillery battalions.

2 a.m. The leading units of the 340th VGD overran the forward positions of the CCB of the 6th Armored and entered Mageret. The fighting lasted two hours, and the Americans were kindly assisted (for once) by the German Air Force which carefully bombed its own troops!

Just before dawn, two battalions of the 347th of the 87th Division were ready to attack again and try to cut the road. The 1st Battalion took Gerimont and the 3rd Bonnerue, losing four tanks to the panzers lying in ambush at the crossroads.

6.30 a.m. The 1st Battalion of the 506th, in reserve at Savy, left the village to reinforce the lines of the 2nd Battalion, which stretched 1500 yards from the south to the west of the Foy-Bizory road. When they reached Luzery, on the Bastogne-Houffalize road, the column was bombed and machine-gunned by a dozen German aircraft, causing three losses.

8.10 a.m. Company F of the 327th Regiment reinforced Team Cherry which was preparing to launch an attack on Senonchamps. After the artillery barrage, the Tigers and the Eagles charged into the attack, supported by tanks. But they ran into little resistance and at 8.45 a.m. took the village.

8.45 a.m. – 9.30 a.m. The 2nd Battalion of the 506th, whose previous positions were now held by the 1st, who had come from Savy, attacked through the woods in the direction of St. Jacques Wood which was located between Foy and Michamps, their objective being to reach and occupy the Foy-Mageret road. After stiff

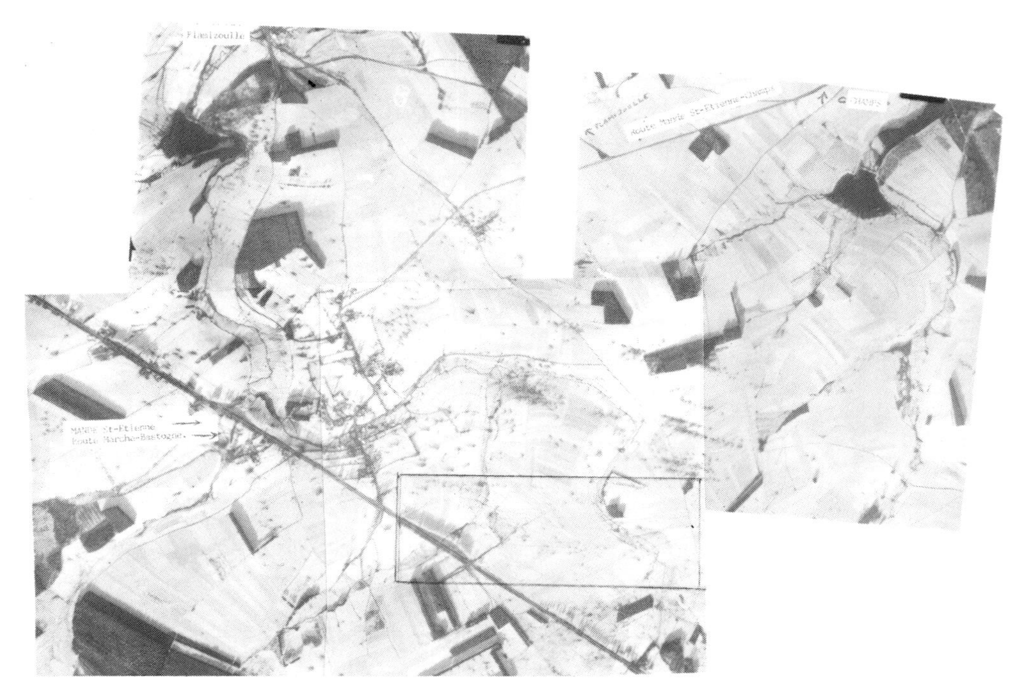

View of the village of Mande-St-Etienne and the Bastogne-Marche road. Photo taken on the 25th December at the beginning of the afternoon. The rectangle marked on the picture shows the tracks made by the tanks of the 15th Panzergrenadier Division, which had attacked towards Hemroulle in the morning. This had previously been the 101st assembly zone.

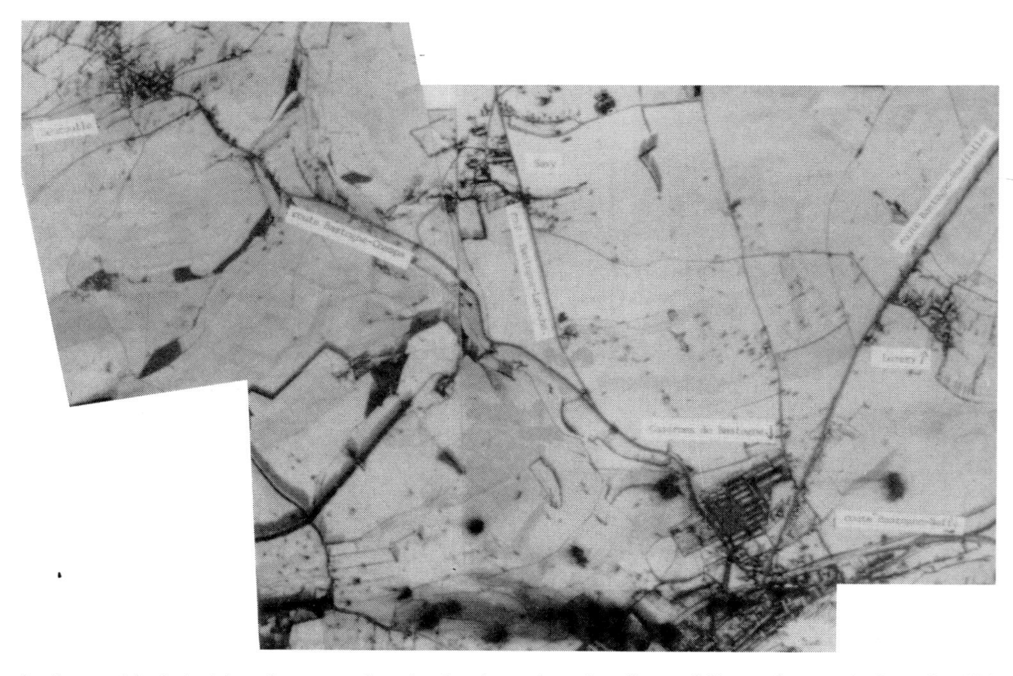

Another aerial photo taken the same day showing how close the village of Hemroulle, attacked on the 25th December, was to the Bastogne barracks and the general headquarters. Under the word Hemroulle can be distinguished the lines of fox-holes and the tracks made by the American tanks.

resistance, the Germans suddenly gave in leaving 30 dead and 7 prisoners.

12 a.m. The 68th Tank Battalion of the CCB of the 6th Armored Division continued its advance towards Arloncourt. Their tracks slipped on the ice-covered road, and the troops were obliged to throw down straw on all the slopes so that they could move forward. But the moment that the village came into view of Company B, the Germans who had been alerted by all the noise began firing with Nebelwerfers and assault guns, putting 8 Shermans out of action immediately. The Americans could not see neither the German guns which were painted white and well dug in, nor the white-suited grenadiers, invisible in the snow. So, when a company of Shermans and one of the light tanks came to the rescue, they were caught in a deluge of fire from their front as well as their flank. They extricated themselves from this trap with great difficulty, helped by an artillery barrage and a smoke-screen.

The 50th Armored Infantry Battalion had cleared a few grenadiers out of the cellars in the village of Oubourcy. They continued on towards Michamps, but just as the leading troops were entering the village, they were attacked by machine-gun, rocket and cannon fire from the hills above Bourcy. Twelve American artillery battalions opened up to silence them.

12 a.m. Lieutenant-Colonel Embrey D. Lagrey's 15th Tank Battalion had great difficulty in making its way through the defensive positions set up by Brown's 44th Armored Infantry Battalion. On the right, the 9th Armored Infantry Battalion, commanded by Lieutenant-Colonel Frank K. Britton, replaced the 44th for the attack against the woods near Wardin. The armored infantry had to clear out the Germans who were occupying the edge of the woods above Wardin, while Lagrey's armored force had to take the village from the north.

When Britton attacked, his men suffered intense fire which disorganized the attack. The firing came from the 134th Infantry Battalion – their friends. Lagrey who had no news of Britton, guessed that he had attained his objective and so began his own attack against Wardin.

A soldier of the 6th Armored Division searches prisoners from the 12th Panzer SS "Hitlerjugend".

Troops of the 320th Regiment of the 35th Infantry Division try to warm themselves.

But the Germans were securely entrenched and their anti-tank guns destroyed seven American tanks. However, a platoon of Company C of the 9th Battalion managed to fight their way into Wardin while the remainder of the battalion was pinned down by machine-gun fire, while they attempted to cross a stream which lay between them and the woods. They lost a lot of men during these repeated attacks to reach the German positions.

3.30 p.m. The Americans dug in along the Foy-Mageret road.

Combat Command B of the neophyte but stubborn 11th Armored Division had not been discouraged. Despite their reverses and losses and Middleton's advice that they should retire to regroup until relieved by the 17th Airborne Division, they insisted on taking Mande-St-Etienne, which was less than a mile from their leading tanks. Colonel Yale obtained authorization and organized his attack.

So as to take no risks, the American artillery bombarded, in 3.800 rounds, 120 selected targets in and around Mande-St-Etienne. But when the twelve artillery battalions ceased fire, the infantry was slow to take advantage of the grenadiers' disorganized state and allowed them to regroup leading to difficult house-to-house fighting which lasted all night, until the village finally fell to the Americans.

The 11th Armored had paid dearly in its baptism under fire. In the 7 miles won in four days, it had lost 220 men dead or missing and 441 wounded. In addition, 42 Shermans and 12 light tanks had been lost.

5.30 p.m. Colonel Wall decided to abandon Michamps and Oubourcy when German armour was spotted in Bourcy. He was wounded by a shell fragment in the eye and evacuated. The tanks in Bourcy were the first of the 12th Panzer SS "Hitlerjugend".

Despite heavy losses, the 6th Armored Division had won a lot of ground during the day. As always, the American artillery had been very effective, but it was to the Air Force and particularly the XIXth Tactical Air Command that the men on the ground owed a debt of gratitude.

At Lutrebois, Companies E and G disengaged with difficulty, while the 3rd Battalion again attacked courageously across

open ground. Company K got to within a few yards of the first house where they might have been protected, when a machine-gun suddenly appeared at the window and cut down the infantrymen. A platoon sergeant slid along the side of the house, climbed onto the roof and threw a grenade down the chimney. With the house now emptied, the Americans took up position there. It was to serve as a starting point for retaking the village, as the part held by the Germans was bombarded by the batteries at different points within the perimeter.

To the east of Marvie, the 1st Battalion had to clear out the grenadiers who had got round behind them in the woods. When they began this operation, they came into contact with the 6th Armored Division, exchanging fire with the men of the 9th Armored Infantry Battalion. Finally, however, the Americans recognized each other and linked up.

All day, the 347th Regiment of the 87th Infantry Division had fought hard. At nightfall, the reserve battalion joined the attack and cleared Pirompré and the surrounding woods. The 87th had reached its objective, the road now being cut at Bonnerue.

Despite having expended a disproportionate effort, von Manteuffel had not succeeded in reimposing the blockade around Bastogne, and he was definitively convinced that he could not take the town. Rather than run the risk of having his own troops surrounded and destroyed he suggested, with the support of von Lüttwitz, that they should retreat to a line based on Houffalize, which would also spare the lives of his men. Feldmarschall Model agreed strategically, but OKW had not changed its position on Bastogne.

Model was asked to submit another plan for the besieging of the town. The new plan called for the 9th and 12th SS Panzer Divisions to attack from the north-east and the Führer Begleit Brigade from the east.

This plan took into account the very limited manoeuvering possibilities caused by the weather conditions, notably the very deep snow.

Hitler agreed. He hoped that the Waffen SS would succeed where the Wehrmacht had failed.

The Allies launched a powerful general offensive in atrocious weather conditions.

WEDNESDAY 3rd JANUARY 1945

The day was to see the Allied forces launch a powerful general offensive in atrocious weather conditions. It was to be considered the most difficult of all the attacks carried out by the Allied forces on the Western Front.

This was to interfere with the Germans' plans against Bastogne, but it did not stop them completely.

12 a.m. The 2nd and 3rd Battalions of the 501st entered the St. Jacques Wood with the aim of clearing it, the Germans hidden in the thickest part of the wood forming a wedge between the 501st and the 506th American Regiments. The right side of the wedge was the Bastogne-Houffalize road and the left side was the Bastogne-Bourcy railway line. The objective was to occupy the Foy-Michamps road, so as to increase the chance of regaining Noville.

There was ground fog with occasional snow showers. The Geronimos attacked alone, without tank or artillery support, because of the ground conditions, starting from the railway line. The American advance was undertaken on the right by the 2nd Battalion, reinforced on their right flank by the 50th Armored Infantry Battalion of the 6th Armored Division – and on the left by the 3rd Battalion. The 1st Battalion was held in reserve.

From the outset, the 3rd Battalion met strong resistance but continued its advance. A few men reached the Foy-Michamps road, the remaining two companies of the Battalion being some 200 yards from their objective. The 2nd Battalion did not meet any resistance and penetrated 500 yards into the wood.

1 p.m. Captain S. Snodgrass's Company D on the left and Captain Arthur L. Cady's Company F on the right, reached their objective on the Foy-Michamps road and set up a road-block on the level crossing on the Bastogne-Bourcy railway line.

1.20 p.m. Near Champs, Sergeant Lawrence J. Silva telephoned the command post of Company D of the 502nd Regiment to report that he could see 20 German tanks facing him, and a little

The panzers had left Compogne.

while later he confirmed that there were possibly more, but he was unable to see them because a panzer charged upon him. He died in his fox-hole.

This surprise attack by the 9th and the 12th SS Divisions was directed against the 502nd's lines running in front of the villages of Champs, Longchamps, Monaville and behind Recogne. The thick fog had hidden the preparation from the defenders, who could not hear the sound made by the vehicle tracks because of the snow. The panzers had left Compogne, a village on the Houffalize-Bertogne-Salle-Sprimont road, heading for Longchamps. There were thirty to forty, mainly Mark IV's, followed by a grenadier battalion, who spread out.

Six panzers crossed the Bertogne-Longchamps road and started firing on Company D's anti-tank guns and machine-guns. Five other panzers rushed at E Company.

The fire from the eleven panzers was so heavy that the Americans could not move from their fox-holes, and eight panzers, with infantry support, were able to reach Monaville and attack the 1st Platoon of Company D, under the command of Lieutenant Thomas Bunn. Six other panzers attacked the boundary of the 2nd and 3rd Battalions, while Company F rushed to their aid.

The Germans had so many tanks that they were able to clean out each fox-hole individually, either by firing on it or by driving over it and crushing the occupants. If the hole resisted, the edges being hardened by the frost, the tank driver directed exhaust fumes into each hole to asphyxiate the occupants. If anyone survived, he could only clench his fists on his rifle which was powerless against the tanks.

In the St. Jacques Wood the 50th Armored Infantry Battalion of the CCB of the 6th Armored Division tried to position itself to the right of the 2nd Battalion of the 501st Regiment. However, they were told by a scout that eight panzers and a panzergrenadier company had arrived, so they retreated.

A gap had thus opened up in the American lines of defence and the 26th SS Panzergrenadier Regiment of the 12th SS "Hitlerjugend" Division moved towards Bastogne through the

The Germans' reply was terrible.

To guide them, Major William E. Pelham drove his jeep ahead of the tanks sent from Team O'Hara.

gap. Once again, they used the Bourcy-Bastogne railway line as had done their comrades a few days before.

2.30 p.m. A messenger arrived at the 2nd Battalion command post set up 600 yards from the level crossing where the Geronimos had a barrage. Major Sammie N. Homan, the battalion commander, thus learned of the arrival of the Germans who were already harrassing the defenders of the barrage with rifle and machine-gun fire. Homan despatched E Company, under the command of Lieutenant William P. Heaton, to the edge of the wood bordering the railway line, between the command post and the road-block. After about 15 minutes of fighting, the road-block was taken, and the Waffen SS came towards them over the open fields between Michamps and the railway line.

The Americans could not believe their eyes; the grenadiers advanced in close order with the support of four panzers and six half-tracks. The 501st opened fire, especially E Company, which was very well placed, and the Germans moved southwards in order to get behind the Americans.

The Germans' reply was terrible. Every second was accentuated by mortar rounds while their tanks and machine-guns fired as hard as possible.

The Americans called in tank support.

4 p.m. To guide them, Major William E. Pelham drove his jeep ahead of the tanks sent from Team O'Hara. He spotted a Mark IV which had penetrated between the battalion and Homan's command post and warned the Shermans which destroyed it.

O'Hara's men went into position south of the Geronimos' 2nd Battalion and repulsed the German half-tracks. During the fight, Lieutenant Joseph C. McGregor and Sergeant Dale R. Smith, leading 26 men of the 1st Platoon of Company E, attacked the Germans on the flank and knocked out one tank and two half-tracks with their bazookas.

Discouraged, the Waffen SS pulled back, while the Americans mounted the abandoned vehicles and opened fire on the enemy with their own machine-guns.

Great courage was displayed by both sides during the fighting.

Simultaneously on the American side, a machine-gunner yelled in German to the grenadiers...

This was how 65 Waffen SS surrendered to 20 Geronimos.

Some curious incidents happened, too, as for instance when, firing from less than 75 yards, an MG 42 machine-gun crew scattered about 30 Geronimos. The only surviving medic was trying to attend to his comrades when he was wounded also. Believing that the Americans were out of action, the Germans began firing in another direction. Sergeant Desmond D. Jones crawled towards the machine-gun nest, stood up behind the Germans and, when he pressed the trigger of his Thompson, was horrified to find that it failed to fire. Then, he drew a P38 "captured" from a German soldier a few days previously and took aim. It too failed to fire. Eventually, the Germans noticed and swung their guns back to him.

Simultaneously on the American side, John M. Fox, a machine-gunner, yelled in German to the grenadiers facing him to send an emissary. A man stood up, but a Geronimo who did not know what was going on, shot him. Fighting started again for a few minutes, then things quietened down. A German medic looking like a Crusader with big red crosses on his chest and back, moved towards wounded men lying between the lines. Fox called to him, asking if they wanted to surrender. The medic replied that he would find out and came back with a Feldwebel (platoon sergeant) who surrendered because of their heavy losses to Fox with his 65 men.

This was how 65 Waffen SS surrendered to 20 Geronimos and how Jones without understanding anything, came back with the machine-gun crew who had held him at their mercy.

4 p.m. The battalions started to disengage, pulling back one company at a time, in order to maintain continuous cover.

4.20 p.m. The Americans sent reinforcements to the vicinity of Champs. Team Cherry had deployed their tanks between Bastogne and the panzers. They laid mines and by 4.20 p.m. the Americans had the situation under control. So the tank-destroyers, with the aid of bazooka fire, started settling their debts with the panzers.

4.30 p.m. General Higgins started to organize Task Force Higgins, which consisted of the 502nd and 327th Regiments, Team Cherry, Companies B and C of the 705th Tank Destroyer Battalion and Company A of the 326th Engineer Battalion.

In their fox-holes the Americans in their white overalls looked little different from the Germans.

A German courier from the 9th Regiment of the 9th SS Panzergrenadier Division.

8 p.m. The original 502nd positions were retaken but losses were heavy:

Company D lost 49 men, 17 of them being killed in action.

Company E lost 14 men.

Company F lost 47 men, including the company commander and two other officers. Moreover, a whole platoon was captured by the Germans.

Battery C of the 81st Anti-Aircraft Artillery Battalion lost five 57mm guns but destroyed ten Mark IV's.

Company C of the 609th Tank Destroyer Battalion destroyed three panzers. Company C of the 705th Battalion destroyed two panzers. The 969th Field Artillery Battalion destroyed one.

During the night, the 501st reestablished a line of defence, flanked by the 6th Armored Division and the 506th. The manoeuvre was to be completed by 3 o'clock in the morning of the 4th January. The Regiment had already lost 86 men, 30 of them being killed in this action.

In their fox-holes the Americans in their white overalls looked little different from the Germans. This was to confuse a German courier from the 19th Regiment of the 9th SS Panzergrenadier Division, who tapped on the shoulder of Corporal Davis of the 2nd Battalion of the 502nd Parachute Infantry Regiment and found himself a prisoner. By this lucky chance, the American interrogators learned that another concentrated attack was to be launched in the early hours of the morning. Forewarned is forearmed: that appareared to be necessary.

The courageous men besieged in Bastogne had become known as the Triple B's, the BBB's or the 3xB - "The Battered Bastards of Bastogne".

This photo, taken on the 18th January 1945, shows the board with the new nickname of the 101st Airborne. It was nailed to a building belonging to Mr Gustave Lemaire, father of the nurse killed on the 24th December 1944.
From left to right:
Major-General Troy H. Middleton, Major-General Maxwell D. Taylor, Lieutenant-Colonel Thomas D. Gillis, Brigadier-General Gerald J. HIggins, Monsieur Léon Jacquemin, Bourgmestre f.f. of Bastogne.

Hitler finally admitted that the objectives of his offensive would not be realized. He would not cross the Meuse nor capture Antwerp – but he had not lost everything. He had weakened the Americans and could now continue to protect the Ruhr and launch other attacks. To do so, he had to maintain the bulge that he had made in the enemy lines, and to achieve this, he had to take Bastogne so as to control its important road junction and, in his turn, be able to block the roads.

Bastogne had become the final objective of the German offensive.

The Battle of Bastogne ended, and the Americans went onto the offensive.

THURSDAY 4th JANUARY 1945

2.30 a.m. Three Germans dressed in American uniforms arrived in a jeep near Bizory and drove some 300 yards into the lines held by the 501st Regiment. With the greatest of ease, they drove up next to a half-track, killed the driver and returned to their lines with the vehicle.

3 a.m. A strong artillery barrage saturated the German assembly area north of Longchamps, which threw the troops into disorder before their attack, due to be launched at 4 o'clock.

4 a.m. The German artillery started their preparatory fire.

5.30 a.m. The 104th Regiment of the 15th Panzergrenadier Division launched an attack on the sector near Champs, held by the 1st Battalion of the 327th, with eleven panzers and self-propelled guns. Firing as they advanced, they were followed by the grenadiers, who overran the lines of the 1st Battalion and killed or captured most of the Americans.

6 a.m. Champs was now in German hands, and they immediately started firing on Company C. Two Panthers making for the Hemroulle-Champs-Givry road ran over anti-tank mines set out the night before and caught fire. The crews jumped down from the burning tanks, and most were killed by men from Company C hiding behind the embankment which bordered the road.

The sight of this made the crews following hesitate. Then, the grenadiers moved forward, to be met by machine-gun fire from Company C. Hand-to-hand fighting took place in the dark, and many acts of great bravery occurred on both sides.

Four panzers and an infantry battalion broke through the lines but were thrown back in a counter-attack by men from the 502nd Regiment, who where returning to the sector from which they had been relieved by the 327th the day before.

After tough fighting in the streets of Champs, two German tanks were knocked out and the panzergrenadiers thrown back. Then, Longchamps was attacked by 15 panzers, but they were all repulsed by the artillery. The Americans suffered heavy losses.

The roads leading to Bastogne after the battle.

For the last five days, the Germans had launched attacks simultaneously against different points on the perimeter. Had they done this earlier, they would have succeeded, but it was now too late, because the American troop strength was too great.

The commander of the German 5th Panzer Army knew that all his efforts were wasted. Moreover, Model ordered him to send the 9th SS Panzer Division back to the 6th Panzer Army. Later Manteuffel also withdrew the 12th SS Panzer Division from the fighting to reorganize it in reserve.

These decisions marked the end of the fighting to take Bastogne.

OKW cancelled the order to take the town and authorized the retreat. The Americans were able to go on the offensive, but they could not stop the Germans from retiring in good order, thanks to Manteuffel's ingenuity.

A great battle had come to an end.

The Americans were able to go on the offensive.

An example of the evolution of the destruction of Bastogne: the same part of the main street at two different dates.

CONCLUSION

The Germans' original objectives were the river Meuse and Antwerp, NOT Bastogne. Therefore, their planning had not concentrated on Bastogne, because the town was supposed to fall inevitably into their hands.

General von Manteuffel had not given much attention to the town before the Ardennes offensive. Rather it had become more important as the campaign and the fighting developed. First, there was a race between the opposing forces to reach the town. That was the start of the Battle of Bastogne.

It is interesting to note the opinions of other German generals:

Jodl: "Bastogne was not important at the beginning, this was to change when it became a large pocket of resistance behind our advance".

"Bastogne could have been by-passed, not St. Vith".

Wagener: "Taking Bastogne was secondary, which was not the case with St. Vith, which was indispensable".

Lüttwitz: "If we had taken Bastogne on the 18th December, then the 2nd Panzer and the Panzer Lehr would have reached the Meuse on the 22nd. Had that been the case, Patton would have had to deal not with just three divisions, but with three more, the 9th Panzer and the 3rd and 15th Panzergrenadiers. Nevertheless, your aviation would have stopped us at the Meuse".

The most important events were to take place in the sector of the 6th SS Armored Army, which led the main attack. Stopping this very quickly, at great cost to themselves, the Americans prevented the Germans from reaching Liège.

The main role then fell on Manteuffel's 5th Armoured Army whose secondary attack became the major thrust.

Bastogne was a road junction located at the centre of an open plain but surrounded by hills and woods that had to be taken, and which forced an attacker to use the roads, especially in winter.

The speed with which the defence of the locality was organized slowed the progress of the break-through and had a decisive influence on the operation. The Bastogne pocket quickly became a menace for the left flank of the 5th Panzer Army, increased still further by the failure of the 7th Army to continue its protective advance.

Because of shortage of fuel*, Hitler committed the error of attacking Bastogne piece-meal, rather than waiting and launching a general all-out attack. This tactic suited the Americans, who were able, with the help of their dominant artillery, to use their relatively small forces to maximum advantage by moving them quickly to the point where they were most needed.

The German front-line generals knew that the war was as good as lost.

They were convinced that the offensive was a hopeless gamble, because the objectives were too far away for the available forces to reach, and unconsciously they set out as potential losers.

"The quality of the command and the commanders was that of an army worn out by six years of warfare".**

This, however, did not reflect on their valour or courage, nor on the courage and self-sacrifice of their soldiers.

From the start, the Americans had the absolute will to resist.

The indecision at the beginning in the higher ranks was quickly compensated by the men on the ground. General Middleton played a central role in the course of events, understanding and reacting with great speed as well as making the right decisions at the right time. To help him, he had under his orders exceptional troops – the courageous infantrymen of the 28th Infantry Division, the elements of the Armored divisions, and the paratroops of the 101st Airborne, all of whom offered tough resistance.

The relief of Bastogne was the most brilliant operation of General Patton and his 3rd Army, and, according to Patton himself, the outstanding achievement of the Second World War.

Whereas the German Army, since the war of 1870, usually preferred to circumvent strong points rather than to attack them directly, the Americans were used to fighting when surrounded. That had belonged to their way of life since the start of their history, for to become surrounded was their classic way of defense. This is what the weak did to defend themselves. The early American settlers formed a circle with their wagons when attacked by the Red Indians – here were the shadows of Boonesboro, Alamo, Little Big Horn and now Bastogne!

* Manteuffel: P3 Ethint 46
** Lüttwitz: MS no 1940, June 13, 1950.

Moreover, where there is a will, there is a way; and when you are firmly determined to reach an objective, luck often gives you a hand. In this instance, luck often came to the rescue of the Americans, never of the Germans.

Let us recapitulate a few of the fortunate instances:

General Bayerlein was directed onto the wrong road, made a mistake as to the strength of the American forces facing him and finally stopped before he got to Bastogne, even though the town was undefended at that point.

On his way to Werbomont, General McAuliffe suddenly decided to go and see what was happening in Bastogne. A short time later, Colonel Sherburne directed the division towards Bastogne. None of this was planned, and if the 101st had gone straight on – as they should have done – they would have reached Bastogne after Bayerlein's men and the other German divisions.

The sun reappeared at the exact moment that the artillery ran out of shells, thus enabling the Air Force to take over and to drop the necessary supplies.

On the 30th December, the American counter-offensive ran unexpectedly into the flank of the most powerful German attack to be directed at Bastogne.

There was the messenger, who arrived at the wrong place and informed the Americans of the offensive planned for the next day.

There does not seem to be a single instance of the Germans being lucky.

GOD WAS NOT WITH THEM ANY MORE!*

* The inscription on the Wehrmacht belt buckles was "Gott mit uns", God be with us.

THE BASTOGNE PHENOMENON

How can one explain the fame of Bastogne in the Battle of the Ardennes, which the town has come to symbolize?

A series of events coincided to make the locality world famous, to the detriment of many other important points which also saw murderous and destructive fighting:

It was first the presence of an elite paratroop division, the 101st, which was used in a defensive action against an attacking army which was employing substantial armoured elements. This was in contradiction to the doctrine of the airborne troops, which were to be used only in surprise attacks against predetermined areas to the enemy's rear. Despite the strangeness of this situation, the paratroops handled themselves brilliantly, heavily reinforced by armoured troops.

Then, there was the siege and especially McAuliffe's "NUTS". This stinging response to a demand to surrender was an unhoped -for gift to the world's press.

The proof of this is shown by the following anecdote: when General Bruce C. Clarke, commander of the CCB of the 7th Armored Division, which had fought so heroically at St. Vith, sent a staff officer to the press conference held at General Eisenhower's headquarters at Versailles, a short time after the battle, this Major Treece was interrupted as he explained the situation, maps in hand, by a journalist, who asked: "Did General Clarke say anything during the battle like NUTS?". "I don't believe he did", replied Treece. Whereupon the journalists declared that they had heard enough, and Treece was dismissed. He returned to his headquarters in disgust.

After "NUTS", Bastogne became the main, if not the exclusive centre of interest, which was increased by Patton's spectacular break-through.

The Germans themselves began to play this game. The rapid failure of their offensive made the taking of Bastogne absolutely necessary to wipe out this symbol of American resistance.

Hitler did not hesitate to sacrifice several divisions, including some taken from the 6th SS Panzer, to reinforce Manteuffel's 5th Army in their attempts to take the town.

It was an act of useless pride, because the taking of Bastogne was no more of any strategic interest.

Bastogne, symbol of the battle, became also the costly epilogue of the battle of the Bulge.

The town was to enter history with an importance which was the result of publicity as well as of military actions.

For the Americans, it is the symbol of a great battle.

It is worth remembering that the battle did not take place in the town of Bastogne. Many of the veterans who return on their pilgrimages did not set foot in the town itself before. Most fought outside the town, in the surrounding villages which bore the horror of the major fighting.

...in the surrounding villages which bore the horror of the major fighting.

THE CONSEQUENCES OF THE BATTLE OF THE ARDENNES

This account has purposely limited itself to the battle for Bastogne, but, after commenting on the real importance of Bastogne in the German offensive, it seems interesting to ask the following questions:

What were the consequences for Germany?

What were the consequences for the world?

Here is General von Manteuffel's opinion:

"At the end of January 1945, the German armies were back where they had started on the 16th December before the beginning of the Ardennes Offensive. The Germans' last operational reserve had been used, and the panzer troops were unable to recover from their losses. The Allied forces were on the banks of the Rhine, and the final defeat of Hitler's Germany was only a matter of time, because of the lack of reserves and fuel which might have permitted to continue the fighting to defend the Reich".

What the General did not write down, but which he told me during our meetings, was that the offensive played right into the Russians' hands. I have also recently had the opinion of General Bruce C. Clarke, whom von Manteuffel knew well as an adversary at St. Vith and as an acquaintance after the war:

"The Battle of the Ardennes was the greatest American battle of the Second World War. The American Army suffered 80,000 casualties. The German offensive stopped the American progress and took away their opportunity to reach Berlin before the Russians".

It is true that the Battle of the Ardennes was strictly an American affair. The Americans bore the brunt of the attack, and they restored the situation.

But is was a nasty business.

It resulted from bad leadership at the very top of the American command, which had permitted part of the front line to be weak, without tactical reserves, and who ignored the alarming reports and substantial information from their intelligence services. It is important to remember also that the Germans were able to launch their offensive because the Allies faced logistical problems and a certain disagreement among themselves from September 1944 on.

There had been a serious planning mistake by the Americans: not enough fuel, too much ammunition. They could have calculated their needs better and organized adequate means of supply.

The shortage of fuel had stopped Patton's victorious break-through, forcing him to wait for seven weeks close to the German frontier. It was during this period that the Germans organized their offensive. As Patton said, "You must never sit still doing nothing".

The generals at the Supreme Headquarters of the Allied Expeditionary Forces had total contempt for what the Germans had and what their capabilities still might be. That the incident did not turn to disaster is due to the fighting-men on the ground and not to the strategists at the rear.

The length of the battle, the time required to reform the reserves and replace material, added to the other problems, meant that it took the Allied forces much longer than it should have to reach the capital of the Reich.

The Yalta conference would have been different if the Allies and not the Russians had been at the gates of Berlin.

Stalin's first question to Roosevelt at Yalta was: "How are things going on the German Front?". It is reasonable to suppose that if the American President had been able to reply, "Fine, we're in Berlin", the conference would have been different, even if arrangements had been made previously.

The Russians arrived first, because the Allies wasted a lot of time, and because Berlin was not their objective.

In September 1944, Eisenhower declared that they should reach Berlin as quickly as possible. In April 1945, his opinion had changed somewhat: he now considered Berlin just as "a point on a map", and his main objective had become the destruction of the enemy forces.

He did have doubts later on!

I remember reading in a Belgian newspaper at the time of the 25th Anniversary of the Battle that the Russians claimed the credit for the Allied victory in the Battle of the Ardennes. This claim seems a little rich, when one remembers that their offensive started on the 12th January 1945 – when the battle was practically over.

The Russians may indeed have been the victors, but for other reasons, because it permitted the application of a theory that Stalin explained to Tito:

"Whoever occupies a territory, and as long as his army can advance, is able to impose his system".

If, launching his offensive of the winter of 1944-45, Hitler had hoped to force the Allies to negotiate an armistice and avoid war on his country's territory, he committed one of his greatest errors, fruitlessly destroying his last forces and weakening his eastern front.

But perhaps he was no longer thinking of the future.

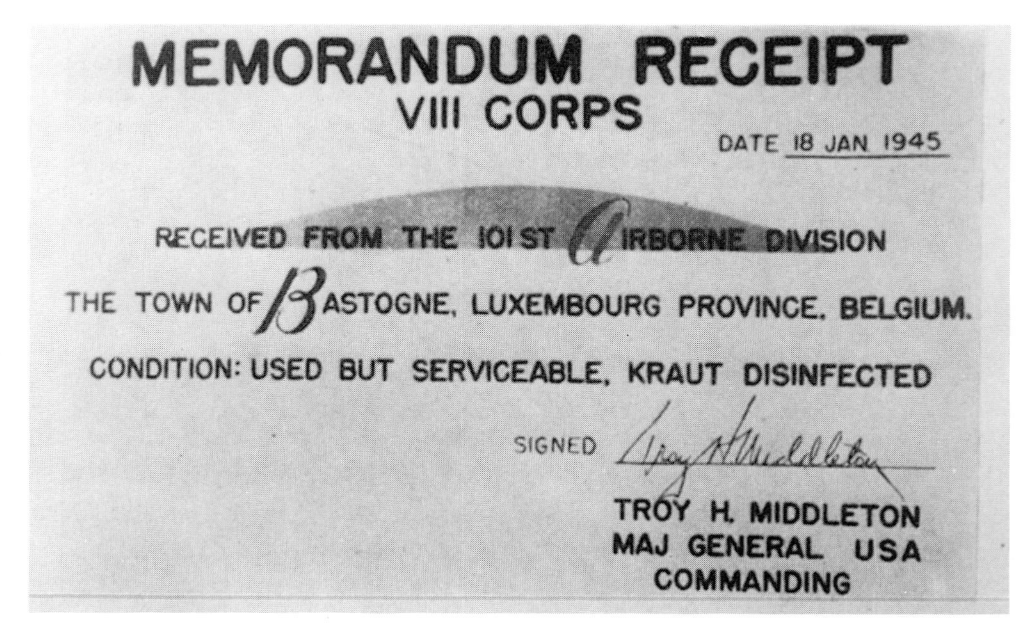
MEMORANDUM RECEIPT
VIII CORPS

DATE 18 JAN 1945

RECEIVED FROM THE 101 ST AIRBORNE DIVISION

THE TOWN OF BASTOGNE, LUXEMBOURG PROVINCE, BELGIUM.

CONDITION: USED BUT SERVICEABLE, KRAUT DISINFECTED

SIGNED Troy H Middleton

TROY H. MIDDLETON
MAJ GENERAL USA
COMMANDING

Memorandum receipt given by Major General Troy H. Middleton, Commanding General of the VIIIth Corps, to the 101st Airborne Division for holding Bastogne.

THE CIVILIANS

How did the troops and the civilians get along?

The military had imposed a curfew for the Bastogne citizens who might move about only between midday and two o'clock. This period was supposed to be used for finding food and other necessities, but the general presence of civilians in the streets was not permitted. Only those officially allowed by the mayor and wearing arm-bands could move about freely. Among them were the two doctors who had remained in the town, the young Doctor Govaerts and Doctor Heintz, trying to make up for the shortage of drugs by their devotion.

But the person who played the greatest role during the siege was undeniably Monsieur Léon Jacquemin who stood in for the Mayor who had left suddenly.

A true hero in all senses of the word, and considered by the American troops to be the real mayor, Jacquemin preserved the safety of his fellow citizens without regard for his own, obtaining from them a strict discipline. He organized a passive defence with all the able-bodied men who had remained in Bastogne, ensuring food supplies for the population and even the army, requisitioning, stocking and distributing food supplies. He set up a bakery in the Seminary and a centre of the distributing of meat from the animals killed during the fighting or found either wandering in the country or abandoned on farms, which helped the Bastogne population not to be hungry. He acted as liaison between the military, the population and his administration. In brief, he fulfilled a most important mission, both for the civilians and the military. He was helped notably by Monsieur Ernest Lambert, the Town Clerk of Works who spoke English, and by Monsieur Louis Lecomte, a town counselor.

Why did such a man never receive any distinction, decoration or official thanks, and why was he left in the shadows and ignored when his indispensable services were no longer needed?

The reason is well known.

It is because of a report which he wrote at the request of the then Prime Minister, Monsieur Pierlot, on what had happened during the battle in Bastogne.

In this report, and in the hope of obtaining compensation for their losses for his fellow citizens, either from the Belgian government or from the

Americans, Monsieur Léon Jacquemin listed, among other things, possessions and material belonging to the population which had been taken by the army for its use.

The report was presented by the acting Mayor to the Prime Minister in the presence of his secretary, the Minister of the Interior and his secretary, as well as two citizens of Bastogne, Judge Didier and his clerk, Monsieur Arthur Leboutte, representing the town of Bastogne.

THE NEXT DAY, the German radio announced from all its stations that the Mayor of Bastogne was accusing the Americans of having plundered the town. The news spread like wildfire, and Monsieur Léon Jacquemin was scorned almost immediately.

Who gave this distorted story to the Germans?

Is it possible to imagine what this admirable and unselfish man felt in the face of such injustice and ingratitude?

He had only done his duty, writing down what everyone else in Bastogne already knew and something which was probably justified by the circumstances, the Americans having taken mainly sheets to camouflage themselves with, to make bandages and blankets and other gear for their wounded, and to protect themselves from the cold.

Further, the gratitude and admiration of the population for the Americans was – and still is – unlimited.

This does not mean that there were not some minor problems sometimes between the military and the civilians hiding in their cellars, without electricity and generally lacking both heat and light as there was a great shortage of candles and other lighting material, as well as suffering from the problems of hygiene and of living in close proximity.

Some soldiers took pieces of furniture to make fires when there was a pile of wood ready at the back of the house. Some others searched the houses or their inhabitants to find things which were not indispensable. But most of the soldiers generously shared what they had with the civilians, and the "Civil Affairs" distributed food immediately after the first parachute drops, for which the people were very grateful.

What obsessed the civilians was to know whether the Germans were coming back. To what the Americans always replied:

"Germans here? No, never!".

An anecdote will close this chapter and illustrate the general state of feelings:

One day, Monsieur Massard, an English-speaking citizen of Bastogne, saw a young soldier, very drunk, leaving a house carrying a bottle which he had stolen from the cellar. The music teacher reproached him for taking what did not belong to him. The soldier reacted by chasing him and threatening him with the bottle, until they met an officer, to whom Monsieur Massard told what had happened.

The officer replied: "You are right, this man will be punished, but this wine is very little compared with the amount of blood we are spilling here!".

SYMBOLS USED IN MILITARY MAPS

Symbol	Meaning	Symbol	Meaning
●	SQUAD	▷	INFANTRY
● ●	COMBAT GROUP	▷	TANKS
▷ ● ● ●	SECTION	▷	PANZER GRENADIERS ARMOURED INFANTRY
▷ I	COMPANY		AIRCRAFT
▷ I I	BATTALION	▷	ARTILLERY
▷ I I I	REGIMENT		CAVALRY
▷ X	BRIGADE	▷	MECHANISED CAVALRY
▷ X X	DIVISION	E	SAPPERS
X X X	ARMY CORPS		ANTI-AIRCRAFT GUNS
X X X X	ARMY		MEDICAL CORPS
X X X X X	ARMY GROUP	S	SIGNAL CORPS
	MACHINE GUN	TD	TANK KILLERS
	ARTILLERY		TRANSPORT CORPS
	ARTILLERY BATTERY		VETERINARY CORPS
	MORTARS		AIRBORNE ARTILLERY
	TANKS	▷	AMERICAN AIRBORNE TROOPS
	SELF-PROPELLED GUNS	▷	GERMAN AIRBORNE TROOPS

EXAMPLE X B 10 COMMAND POST - BRIGADE B
10th ARMOURED DIVISION

▷ SYMBOLS USED IN MILITARY MAPS IN THIS BOOK

BATTLE ORDER OF THE GERMAN 5th PANZER ARMY, 16th DECEMBER 1944

Commander in Chief: General der Panzertruppen Baron Hasso Eccard von Manteuffel.
Chief of Staff: Generalmajor Carl Gustav Wagener.
1st Staff Officer: Oberstleutnant Neckelman.
2nd Staff Officer: Oberstleutnant Birk, Assistant Chief of Staff.
3rd Staff Officer: Oberstleutnant von Zastrow.
Commander of Artillery: Generalmajor Metz.
Commander of Engineers: Oberst Bujard.
Commander of Communications: Oberst Steiniger.

LXVIth Infantry Corps:
Commander: General der Artillerie Walter Lucht.
Chief of Staff: Oberst Siebert.

18th Volksgrenadier Division
Commander: Generalmajor Hoffmann-Schöhorn.

62nd Volksgrenadier Division
Commander: Generalmajor Frederic Kittel.

LVIIIth Armoured Corps:
Commander: Generaloberst Walter Krüger
Chief of Staff: Oberst Dingler

506th Volksgrenadier Division
Commander: Generalmajor Rudolf Lanhaüser

116th Armoured Division (Windhund)
Commander: Generalmajor Siegfried von Waldenburg.

XXXXVIIth Armoured Corps:
Commander: General der Panzertruppen Baron Heinrich von Lüttwitz
Chief of Staff: Oberst Bernstorff

2nd Armoured Division
Commander: Oberst Meinhard von Lauchert

"Panzer Lehr" Armoured Training Division
Commander: Generalmajor Fritz Bayerlein

26th Volksgrenadier Division
Commander: Generalmajor Heintz Kokott

"Führer-Begleit" – Führer Escort Brigade
Commander: Oberst Otto Remer.

What was the real strength of the German divisions engaged in the Bastogne sector during the time we are interested in?

The 2nd Panzer Division had had four weeks' rest in the rear. It had 80% of its material and men, leaving aside the repair and maintenance units. To save petrol, one battalion of panzer grenadiers had been equipped with bicycles. This was to prove a fatal mistake when the unit was confronted with the hills and winding roads of the Ardennes. Instead of fighting, this unit served as a reserve to fill the depleted ranks of the other divisions. The officers of the 2nd Panzer were very experienced, most of them having six years of war behind them.

The 26th Volksgrenadier Division were at full strength and had trained officers, though the men had no battle experience, their predecessors having been wiped out in earlier fighting. One regiment had to be kept in reserve at the disposition of the Corps, meaning that the 26th VGD began their attack without it.

The Panzer Lehr had come directly from the Saar fighting and had only 50% of its strength.

One of its panzer grenadier battalions had no arms.

The reinforcements which arrived later, the 9th Panzer Division, the 116th Panzer Division, the 3rd and 15th Panzer Grenadier division, the Führer Begleit Brigade Remer, the 167th Volksgrenadier Division, the Führer Grenadier Brigade, the 1st Panzer Division, the 12th SS Panzer Division "Hitlerjugend", were completely exhausted on their arrival and were at less than half strength. In the case of the Remer Brigade, it was less than 30%.

From General of Armoured Troops Baron Heinrich von Lüttwitz (MS n° A-940, 13-6-1950).

AMERICAN FORCES AT BASTOGNE

101st AIRBORNE DIVISION, attached to the VIIIth Corps on 18-2-1944.

Commanding General: Major General Maxwell D. Taylor, 43, absent during the first part of the battle.

Acting Commander of the Division during the first phase of the operations at Bastogne: Brigadier-General Anthony C. McAuliffe (officer commanding the 101st Artillery, 46, nicknamed "Old Crock").

Assistant Commander of the Division: Brigadier-General Gerald J. Higgins, 35.

The command was divided between McAuliffe and Roberts until the evening of 20-12-1944.

From midnight of the 21st, McAuliffe was the Commander-in-chief of the Bastogne forces.

G1: Lieutenant-Colonel Ned D. Moore
G2: Lieutenant-Colonel Paul A. Danahy
G3: Lieutenant-Colonel H.W.O. Kinnard
G4: Lieutenant-Colonel Carl W. Kohls
Surgeon: Lieutenant-Colonel David Gold
Civil Affairs Officer: Captain Robert S. Smith
Aide to the Commanding General: Lieutenant Frederic D. Starrett
Division Artillery Commander: Colonel Thomas L. Sherburne, Jr.

501st Parachute Infantry Regiment
Commanding Officer: Lieutenant-Colonel Julian J. Ewell, 29 years

502nd Parachute Infantry Regiment
Commanding Officer: Lieutenant-Colonel Steve A. Chappuis ("Silent Steve")

506th Parachute Infantry Regiment
Commanding Officer: Colonel Robert F. Sink ("Five-O-Sink")

327th Glider Infantry Regiment
Commanding Officer: Colonel Joseph H. Harper

321st Glider Field Artillery Battalion
Commanding Officer: Lieutenant-Colonel Edward L. Carmichaël

907th Glider Field Artillery Battalion (105 mm snub-nose)
Commanding Officer: Lieutenant-Colonel Clarence F. Nelson

377th Parachute Field Artillery Battalion
Commanding Officer: Lieutenant-Colonel Harry W. Elkins

463rd Parachute Field Artillery Battalion
Commanding Officer: Lieutenant-Colonel John T. Cooper

81st Airborne Anti-Aircraft Battalion
Commanding Officer: Lieutenant-Colonel X.B. Cox, Jr.

326th Airborne Engineer Battalion
Commanding Officer: Lieutenant-Colonel Hugh A. Mozley

101st Airborne Signal Company
Commanding Officer: Captain William J. Johnson

801st Airborne Ordnance Maintenance Company
Commanding Officer: Captain John L. Patterson

326th Airborne Medical Company
Commanding Officer: Major William E. Bartfield

426th Airborne Quartermaster Company
Commanding Officer: Captain George W. Horn

UNITS ATTACHED TO THE 101st AIRBORNE DIVISION

* **Combat Command B of the 10th Armored Division, 3rd Army**
  Commanding Officer: Colonel William L. Roberts
  Divided into 4 groups:
  Team O'Hara: 500 men and 30 tanks, installed a road-block on the Wardin road. Lieutenant-Colonel James O'Hara.
  Team Cherry: 500 men and 20 tanks, installed a road-block on the Longvilly road to support Combat Command R of the 9th Armoured Division. Lieutenant-Colonel Henry T. Cherry.
  Team Desobry: 500 men and 15 tanks, installed a road-block at Noville. Major William Desobry (replaced when wounded by Major Charles L. Hustead).
  A group of units consisting of:
  Headquarters and Headquarters Company
  Company C, 3rd Tank Battalion
  Companies A, B and D, 21st Tank Battalion
  Company C, 20th Armored Infantry Battalion
  Company A and C, 54th Armored Infantry Battalion
  Company C and Headquarters Company, 55th Armored Engineers Battalion
  Headquarters Company, 609th Tank Destroyer Battalion
  Battery B, 796th Anti-Aircraft Artillery Battalion
* **705th Tank Destroyer Battalion**
  Commanding Officer: Lieutenant-Colonel Clifford D. Templeton
* **755th Field Artillery Battalion** (155 mm Howitzers)
  Commanding Officer: Lieutenant-Colonel William F. Hartman
* **333rd Field Artillery Battalion** (manned by Blacks)
* **969th Field Artillery Battalion** (155 mm Howitzers, Blacks)
* **109th Field Artillery Battalion** (155 mm Howitzers)
* **771st Field Artillery Battalion**
* **687th Field Artillery Battalion**
* **158th Engineer Battalion**
  Commanding Officer: Lieutenant-Colonel Sam Tabets
* **420th Armored Artillery Battalion**
  Commander: Colonel Browne
* **73rd Armored Artillery Battalion**
* **9th Armored Engineer Battalion, Company C**
* **80th Armored Medical Battalion, section of Company B**
* **Group SNAFU: made up mainly of retreating soldiers of the 28th Infantry Division and of Combat Command R of the 9th Armored Division.**

Strength of the 101st Airborne Division at Bastogne on 23rd December 1944:
743 officers, 10,386 men.
Strength of units attached to the 101st at that time:
276 officers, 3,781 men.
Total American strenghth during the siege:
1,019 officers, 14,167 men.
101st Airborne Division casualties:
500 killed
2500 wounded
400 missing or captured.

Historical sources:

Official United States Third Army After Action Reports.
Official United States First Army After Action Reports.
(documents received in 1950 from the Historical Service of the 3rd American Army).
After Action Reports of the troops engaged in Bastogne.
(National Archives, Washington).
Bastogne, the first eight days by colonel S.L.A. Marshall.
The Men of Bastogne by Fred McKenzie.
Prisoner of War Interrogations of Generals von Manteuffel, von Lüttwitz, Bayerlein, Kokott, Wagener.
The Battle of the Ardennes by Hasso von Manteuffel.
General Patton's Diaries.
All the books written by General Bradley as well as the complete collection of works, magazines and articles written on the General and his fighting.
Conversations and correspondance with Generals Clarke, McAuliffe, Kinnard, Ewell, Harper and von Manteuffel.
Conversations and correspondance with numerous veterans.

Other sources:

Various books, articles and other material on the subject.

Readers wishing to comment on this book or add further information are invited to contact the author via the Bastogne Historical Center, Mardasson Hill, 6600 Bastogne, Belgium.

If you have photographs, documents or other material which is of interest in improving this book or the museum, would you please be kind enough to inform us. We will reply to all offers.

Thank you.

Layout cover: Guy Frans Arend - Design: Paul Rouard.

By the same author:
- Bastogne, "Célèbre par un mot NUTS".
- Bastogne, "Beroemd door één woord NUTS".
- Bastogne, "If you don't know what NUTS means".
- Bastogne, "Das Loch im Krapfen".
- Bastogne et la Bataille d'Ardenne.
- Bastogne and the Ardennes offensive.
- The Best Photographs of the Battle.
- Bastogne, "Avant, Pendant, Après".
- Patton et sa 3e Armée dans la Bataille d'Ardenne.
- Patton and the 3rd Army in the Bulge.
- Patton, George-le-Magnifique.
- Faits connus de l'étonnante histoire du château et du marquisat de Franchimont.
- Bastogne Historical Center, guide.
- Super Giant U.S.A.
- The Fabulous Collection of the Victory Memorial Museum

In the same series:
- Baron Panzer, les exploits militaires du Général von Manteuffel.

Any information concerning these books can be obtained at the
Bastogne Historical Center,
Colline du Mardasson,
B-6600 Bastogne – Belgium,
Phone 061/21.14.13, from abroad: 32 61 211413
Fax 061/21.73.73 32 61 217373
....where these books are on sale.

Edited for the
BASTOGNE HISTORICAL CENTER
by
SAGATO S.A.

D/1987/0019/5

Printed by Joh. Enschedé Belgium n.v./s.a.– Belgium